Markets in Developing Countries

THE INTERNATIONAL CENTER FOR ECONOMIC GROWTH is a nonprofit research institute founded in 1985 to stimulate international discussions on economic policy, economic growth, and human development. The Center sponsors research, publications, and conferences in cooperation with an international network of correspondent institutes, which distribute publications of both the Center and other network members to policy audiences around the world. The Center's research and publications program is organized around five series: Sector Studies, Country Studies, Studies in Human Development and Social Welfare, Occasional Papers, and Reprints.

The Center is affiliated with the Institute for Contemporary Studies, and has headquarters in Panama and a home office in San Francisco, California.

For further information, please contact the International Center for Economic Growth, 243 Kearny Street, San Francisco, California, 94108, USA. Telephone (415) 981-5353; Fax (415) 986-4878.

ICEG Board of Overseers

Markets in Developing Countries

Parallel, Fragmented, and Black

Edited by
Michael Roemer
and Christine Jones

A Copublication of the International Center for Economic Growth
and the Harvard Institute for International Development

ICS PRESS
San Francisco, California

© 1991 International Center for Economic Growth

Developed from a workshop sponsored by the Harvard Institute for International Development, Cambridge, Massachusetts, November 1988.

Inquiries, book orders, and catalog requests should be addressed to ICS Press, 243 Kearny Street, San Francisco, California 94108. USA. Telephone : (415) 981-5353; FAX: (415) 986-4878. To order call toll-free **(800) 326-0263** in the contiguous United States.

Distributed to the trade by National Book Network, Lanham, Maryland. Cover by Herman + Company. Index by Shirley Kessel.

——Library of Congress Cataloging-in-Publication Data——

Markets in developing countries: parallel, fragmented, and black / edited by Michael Roemer and Christine Jones.
    p.   cm.
    Based on a workshop sponsored by the Harvard Institute for International Development, Cambridge, Mass.
    "An International Center for Economic Growth publication."
    Includes bibliographical references and index.
    ISBN 1-55815-081-1. — ISBN 1-55815-082-X (pbk.)
    1. Informal sector (Economics)—Africa, Sub-Saharan. 2. Informal sector (Economics)—Philippines. 3. Informal sector (Economics)—Taiwan. 4. Black market—Africa, Sub-Saharan. 5. Black market—Philippines. 6. Black market—Taiwan. I. Roemer, Michael, 1937– . II. Jones, Christine Winton. III. Harvard Institute for International Development.
HD2346.A57M36   1991   90-24969
    381—dc20   CIP

92 - 3642

228812509

CONTENTS

             Markets
             David Bevan, Paul Collier, and Jan Willem Gunning

Chapter 6   Government Pay and Employment Policy: A   75
             Parallel Market in Labor
             David L. Lindauer

Chapter 7   The Parallel Labor Market for Illegal Aliens   89
             Trien T. Nguyen

Part 3   Fragmented Credit Markets

Chapter 8   Time and Money in the Western Sahel: A Clash of   113
             Cultures in Gambian Rural Finance
             Parker Shipton

Chapter 9   Transaction Costs and Quantity Rationing in the   141
             Informal Credit Markets: Philippine Agriculture
             Pan A. Yotopoulos and Sagrario L. Floro

Chapter 10   Heterogeneous Firms and Efficient Financial   167
             Intermediation in Taiwan
             Tyler S. Biggs

Part 4   The Black Economy

Chapter 11   Taxes, Corruption, and Bribes: A Model of Indian 201
             Public Finance
             Omkar Goswami, Amal Sanyal, and Ira N. Gang

Part 5   Conclusion

Chapter 12   What Have We Learned about Policy?   217
             Michael Roemer and Christine Jones

             Notes and References   223

             About the Contributors   255

             Index   261

LIST OF TABLES

LIST OF FIGURES

PREFACE

In developing countries, where government intervention is often used as a tool to achieve economic and political goals, parallel markets arise as producers and consumers seek to evade official regulations. By lessening the effectiveness of controls, parallel markets can also diminish the benefits realized when controls are removed. Understanding how these markets work is therefore necessary for predicting the outcome of deregulation. Only recently, however, have parallel markets become direct objects of research.

This volume is a copublication of the International Center for Economic Growth and the Harvard Institute for International Development. It is based on papers presented at a workshop sponsored by HIID to address issues relating to the dynamics of parallel markets. The authors investigate the realities of parallel markets—including fragmented and black markets—for consumer and producer goods, labor, currency, and credit in sub-Saharan Africa, the Philippines, and Taiwan. Several chapters delineate the economic and social contribution that parallel markets make in addressing needs not met by formal markets. Other subjects explored in the book include the interaction between government policy and the behavior of parallel markets, the influence of cultural preferences on parallel markets, and the capacity of parallel markets to increase economic efficiency and equity.

This book provides insights into an important area of economic behavior. Although little studied or understood, it is an important issue—one that must be considered in designing effective policy reforms in developing countries.

Nicolás Ardito-Barletta
General Director
International Center for Economic Growth

Panama City, Panama
April 1991

EDITORS' PREFACE

Government controls over prices and quantities, as well as taxes, are universally evaded by agents who deal in "parallel" or "black" markets. Development economists have been concerned for decades about the effects of government intervention on efficiency, equity, and growth. Indeed, liberalization or deregulation of developing economies was a dominant theme in the literature and an overriding concern of policy analysts during the 1970s and 1980s. Much less attention has been paid to the effects of parallel markets that spring up to evade controls. If parallel markets can counteract some of the impact of government interventions, their existence also qualifies the case for economic reform.

In November 1988, the Harvard Institute for International Development (HIID) sponsored a workshop in Cambridge, Massachusetts, on parallel markets. We had two aims. First, by gathering together some of the major contributors to the literature, we hoped to move toward a common understanding of the principles underlying the analysis of parallel markets. Second, we hoped to alert officials of developing countries and the major aid agencies to the implications of parallel markets for policy reform and implementation.

Twenty papers were submitted to the workshop. Nine of these were assembled into a special issue of *World Development* (volume 17, number 12 [December 1989]). The lessons of those investigations have been summarized in our paper "Modeling and Measuring Parallel Markets in Developing Countries," which has been revised and included in this volume as Chapter 2, "The Behavior of Parallel Markets in Developing Countries."

During the workshop, it became apparent that the concept of parallel markets, which arise as a consequence of government intervention, cannot explain all of the markets in developing countries that are divided into segments in which differing prices prevail for the same goods, services, or factors. At least one other market type, a *fragmented market*, is important. Fragmented markets are broken up, not (or not only) by government interventions, but by natural divisions that would prevent prices from being unified even if government did not intervene. Furthermore, terms such as *black market* and *informal sector* are widely used although less precisely defined.

The idea for this volume arose from attempts at the HIID workshop to sort out these terms and their meanings. Here we assemble papers dealing with three of these concepts. After an introductory essay on parallel, fragmented, and black markets, the next six chapters deal with parallel markets, including those for grain, currency, consumer goods, and labor.[1] A second set of three chapters covers the most important example of fragmented markets in developing countries: fragmented credit markets, both rural and urban. A final chapter describes how tax evasion—the major source of the black economy—works in India.

We had strong support in preparing both the HIID workshop and this volume. Dwight Perkins, director of HIID, encouraged us to undertake this project and was generous with financial support. Deena Khatkhate, then honorary managing editor of *World Development*, committed himself to a special issue early in our planning, an incentive both to the organizers and to potential workshop participants. Planning for this volume began at the same time: Nicolás Ardito-Barletta, general director of the International Center for Economic Growth, and Lawrence Chickering, associate director of the Center, promoted the concept of a second volume and agreed to fund travel expenses for workshop participants coming from outside the United States. Willing administrators and assistants at HIID made important contributions to the management of the workshop and compilation of the volumes,

---

1. Two of these chapters are based on papers that appeared in *World Development* 17, no. 12 (December 1989): Trien T. Nguyen, "The Parallel Market of Illegal Aliens: A Computational Approach"; and David Bevan, Paul Collier, and Jan Willem Gunning, "Black Markets: Illegality, Information, and Rents." The latter has been substantially revised for this volume. We are grateful for permission to use these articles.

especially Phyllis Glass, Alison McPhail, Laura Reichenbach, and Karen Seal. The authors of papers and other contributors to the HIID workshop guaranteed the success of this venture with their time, creativity, constructive discussions, and confidence in the outcome. We are grateful to all of them.

Michael Roemer
Christine Jones

Cambridge, Mass.
Washington, D.C.
April 1991

Part 1   Introduction

Christine Jones
David L. Lindauer
Michael Roemer

Chapter 1

Parallel, Fragmented, and Black: A Taxonomy

A broad consensus among economists favors the liberalization of markets as a strategy to achieve both greater efficiency and more rapid economic growth in developing countries. Policy makers in developing countries increasingly accept that prescription and are reforming their economies, particularly by deregulating markets.

Economists' recommendations for deregulation generally follow from an analysis resting on two assumptions. First, government controls over market prices or quantities are effective. Second, in the absence of controls, markets would approach the competitive ideal: all participants could buy or sell at identical prices. Economists have, however, identified many different markets in which one, or both, of these conditions is not met. Government controls are almost always evaded to some extent, and in the absence of controls many markets are not as unified as competitive models assume.

Policy makers in developing countries should be concerned about both these deviations from theory. If government interventions are not totally effective in controlling prices or quantities, liberalization of markets will yield some but not all of the benefits claimed for deregulation. It is even possible that liberalization will create net welfare losses if a market is not fully unified when controls are removed.[1]

The chapters in this volume illustrate these two kinds of deviations from the neoclassical ideal of a well-functioning market. This introduction presents a simple taxonomy of market structure as a means of organizing the material that follows.[2] Specifically, we identify *parallel markets* as arising to evade government controls; *fragmented markets* are not unified, even in the absence of controls, so that different participants face different prices for similar goods or services. We also consider *black markets*, a term that is sometimes a synonym for *parallel* but can also refer to different market situations, and the *informal sector*, a popular but more amorphous term.[3] Sorting out alternative types of market structure is important for economists who analyze market behavior. It is also important for government officials who plan and implement market reforms, because an effective policy prescription depends on an accurate specification of market conditions.

Parallel Markets

A parallel market is a structure generated in response to government interventions that create a situation of excess supply or demand in a particular product or factor market. Thus, if government attempts to subsidize urban consumers by controlling prices of basic commodities such as grain, farmers may bring less grain to the official market at the lower, control price, while consumers demand more grain than at the initial, market-clearing price. This excess demand will spill over into a parallel market, in which grain will be sold above the control price. Farmers or traders will sell at more rewarding prices, while consumers, unable to satisfy their demand at the official price, will pay more. In certain circumstances, such a market will clear. A similar process accompanies interventions such as import licensing or credit restrictions that directly control the quantities, rather than the prices, of goods and factors traded on official markets.

It is easy to think of a catalogue of market interventions that give rise to parallel markets in developing countries. Managed foreign exchange rates often cause overvaluation, hence excess demand for foreign currency spills over into a parallel and usually illegal market that clears at a depreciated rate. Import licensing, often a response to an overvalued currency, restricts the supply of imports and raises their domestic price, which in turn provides incentives for a parallel market in smuggled goods. Controls over interest rates reduce the flow of funds into banks but at the same time create excess demand for credit at official rates. The resulting disequilibrium in the official credit market may generate a curb market of moneylenders and borrowers who can realize a profit by responding to the excess demand in the official market.

Legislated minimum wages and employee benefits, which often raise labor costs above market-clearing levels, can also create parallel labor markets. Workers who cannot obtain jobs at legislated wages offer their services for lower wages to employers who are willing to evade labor regulations.

Government taxation policies may also generate parallel markets. When, for example, a sales or value-added tax is paid, supply and demand clear at the tax-paid price. Those willing to evade the tax can trade at a lower price in a parallel market. Excess demand exists at the pretax price, but it is illegal to offer goods at that price. If the risks of evading taxes are not prohibitive, supplies will meet that demand at a price that is less than the tax-paid price. For example, import and export duties give rise to smuggling, while payroll and income taxes give rise to unrecorded wage payments—all examples of parallel markets.

Parallel markets are not necessarily illegal, however. Some governments manage foreign exchange rates and control allocations of foreign exchange but permit currency transactions on open markets at uncontrolled rates. Curb markets in domestic credit have been encouraged in Taiwan and left alone in countries such as India and Korea.[4] Small-scale, informal sector employers may be allowed to pay subminimum wages in some countries, though in others they are harassed.

More commonly, governments attempting to control prices or quantities do try to enforce these interventions by establishing penalties for trading in parallel markets. Enforcement creates risks for parallel marketers and raises their costs of trading, thus affecting the quantities and prices of goods and services traded in official and parallel markets. To avoid paying higher parallel market prices, consumers compete for limited supplies of controlled commodities, dissipating some or all of their potential gains. The welfare implications for buyers and sellers, and hence the impact of market liberalization, depend on the nature of the risk function, the ways in which consumers get access to price-controlled goods, and the resource costs involved in buying and selling on the parallel market. These and related issues are discussed in Chapter 2, "The Behavior of Parallel Markets in Developing Countries," by Christine Jones and Michael Roemer, which summarizes the lessons on parallel markets from the HIID workshop.

Detlev Puetz and Joachim von Braun test some of these propositions about parallel markets in their study of groundnut and fertilizer markets in The Gambia. They also provide evidence on the distribution of rents from parallel market trading, a relatively neglected topic in the literature. Gambian farmers sell some of their groundnuts to the official market even though the purchase price in neighboring Senegal is higher. First, they face some risk as well as higher transport and information costs for cross-border sales. Second, farmers who sell legally to the official cooperative also benefit from subsidized fertilizer provided on credit. The income foregone by selling groundnuts to the cooperative may be offset by the gains from cheap fertilizer and credit. When budgetary stringency leads to a credit squeeze, it is the wealthier farmers who are able to take advantage of the parallel market, in which cash transactions predominate: only 17 percent of farmers in the poorest quartile sold in the cross-border parallel market, compared with 71 percent of farmers in the highest quartile. Puetz and von Braun point the way to some useful empirical work on the determinants of access to official and parallel markets.

Jean-Paul Azam identifies another parallel market in cross-border trade, this one between Nigeria and its neighbors Niger and Cameroon. Although the Nigerian naira is not convertible, the parallel market for the naira is unified by arbitrage with the submarkets for the CFA franc in the two neighboring countries. Because Niger is much smaller than Nigeria, changes in Nigeria's price level are transmitted to Niger through changes in the exchange rate in the parallel market. Thus, when Nigeria instituted restrictive demand policies, the price level dropped in Niger, exacerbating the recessionary impact of stabilization policies adopted by Niger's own government. Azam's work thus shows that macroeconomic policy prescriptions can turn on the existence and behavior of parallel markets.

Virtually all contributors to the literature assume that parallel markets clear. But this assumption is challenged by David Bevan, Paul Collier, and Jan Willem Gunning, who point out that if parallel markets are illegal, the risk of detection prevents normal market mechanisms from working. Sellers are restrained in advertising their goods, seeking buyers, or testing willingness to pay, because these activities increase their chances of being caught. Hence sales are made at prices that leave some consumers with unsatisfied demand. Illegality raises the cost of acquiring information, which prevents the market from clearing. Informational problems also give rise to fragmented markets, described in later chapters.

David L. Lindauer investigates the belief that government salary levels are responsible for high wages in the private, formal economy. To the extent that the private sector and the government compete for the same pool of talent, high government salaries could be said to determine wage levels in the private sector. If government decides, however, to pay a wage above the market-clearing level but, because of budget limitations, cannot afford to hire all those who would work at that wage, the private sector must absorb the excess supply of workers. Using a simple model of the linkage between parallel and official markets, Lindauer shows that the high government wage would have no impact on private sector wages. With no risk involved, the parallel market (in this case, the private sector) clears at the free market wage rate. In contrast, if government's policy is to increase employment by hiring more workers, the reduced supply of workers will drive up wages in the private (parallel) labor market.

One of the strongest lessons from the HIID workshop is the importance of examining parallel markets in a general equilibrium context. Outcomes that seem dramatic in partial equilibrium appear less so when the ramifications of effects on other markets are incorporated into the analysis. Conventional macroeconomic prescriptions can in fact be reversed in situations where parallel markets are important. A good example of the latter case is presented by Trien T. Nguyen. He uses an eight-sector model of the U.S. economy to examine the parallel market created by illegal immigrants who are willing to work for subminimum wages. Although illegal workers constitute only 1 percent of the work force, their presence, surprisingly, *raises* the income of legal workers by 5 percent and increases tax revenues by 11 percent. These effects are due to increased overall employment leading to higher private expenditure and to government enforcement efforts that also generate employment.

Fragmented Markets

Parallel markets arise to evade government controls. Even in the absence of controls, however, markets may be divided into segments in which participants face different prices of goods, services, or factors of production. The simplest and least interesting reason for price differences is high transportation costs. People farther from the source of supply pay more than those who live nearby. Although price differences occur, markets are well integrated: changes in market conditions in one area are reflected in price changes in other areas. The parallel markets described in the last section exemplify this form of market segmentation. Although there are price differences between the parallel and the official markets, the two are closely linked. Excess demand in the official market spills over into the parallel market and is reflected in the price at which the parallel market clears.

Certain characteristics of developing countries, however, may result in both price differences and a lack of market intermediation between different regions of production. The supply of grain in a region with an abundant harvest may not flow to a region with a poor harvest because transportation costs are prohibitive. Were costs lower, supply would flow from the excess region to the deficit region, equalizing prices between the two. Poorly developed channels of information can have the same result, as the cost to traders of obtaining information about conditions in distant markets exceeds the possible profits from trading in those markets. Thus, when market intermediation is impeded by high costs, prices in one region for goods or factors may move independently from prices in another region. We call these fragmented markets. Market fragmentation can be decreased by lowering transportation or information costs.

Credit markets in developing countries display characteristics of both parallelism and fragmentation. Parallelism arises from credit market regulations, especially interest rate ceilings, that prevent formal credit markets from clearing; such regulations drive both excess demand and a supply of funds into the informal or parallel market. This is financial "repression," as described by McKinnon (1973). If the informal credit market were strictly a parallel market, liberalization of interest rates would eliminate this channel of credit.

Informal credit institutions would exist, however, even in the absence of government-created financial repression. In markets in which lenders have imperfect information about borrowers, banks may choose not to raise interest rates high enough to balance the supply and demand for credit (Stiglitz and Weiss 1981). As interest rates are raised, borrowers have an incentive to adopt projects that yield higher returns but are also riskier, increasing the probability of default. As interest rates rise, low-risk borrowers may drop out of the market altogether.

Under these conditions, lenders will choose not to raise the interest rate to clear the market, but prefer to ration credit by selecting borrowers who are perceived as the best credit risks and who require the least supervision. Banks know the least about small, low-income borrowers, who in any case require substantially more supervision per dollar of credit, provide poor collateral, and may incur greater risk than larger borrowers. Smaller businesses, traders, and farmers, as well as poorer households, are rationed out of the formal credit market. Instead, local moneylenders, traders, and others who can acquire local knowledge at reasonable cost find it profitable to serve smaller, low-income borrowers at interest rates well above rates in the formal sector. The resulting credit markets are *fragmented* in the sense defined earlier in this section and popularized by McKinnon (1973).

The chapters in Part 3 of this volume describe the complex institutional arrangements through which individuals and small firms obtain credit, providing insights into the reasons for the fragmentation of credit markets. Parker Shipton describes the various types of credit market transactions in rural Gambia. The concept of a percentage interest rate based on the loan outstanding does not always apply to credit transactions; people often negotiate a fixed total amount of interest payments payable over a flexible period of time. Such a cap on interest payments may reflect considerations related to credit rationing. Although interest rates may be appropriate where people deposit their savings in bank accounts, in the rural areas studied by Shipton people did not rely on the banking system. This raises the interesting question of whether the terms of credit transactions become more regularized when the opportunities for would-be rural lenders to deposit their savings in interest-bearing accounts become more widespread. The credit market that Shipton describes appears to be highly fragmented with little intermediation between various transactors.

Pan A. Yotopoulos and Sagrario L. Floro analyze a rural credit market in the Philippines that appears substantially more developed than the array of transactions observed by Shipton. They describe a market fragmented into two sets of transactions: trader-lenders who lend to rich farmers and farmer-lenders who lend to poorer farmers. In the first kind of transaction, traders often lend to farmers who are linked to them through purchases of inputs or sales of output. In the second kind of transaction, land is typically pledged as collateral. The farmer-lender enjoys usage rights over the pledged land until the loan is repaid and acquires rights to the land in the event of default. Indeed, acquisition of such land by large farmers may be a prime motive for lending to small farmers. In both types of transaction, the loan is linked to the primary occupation of the lender, whether trader or farmer.

The businessmen of Taiwan have a preference for small, family-controlled firms, the kind that banks typically ration out of the formal credit market. These firms have, however, played a crucial role in Taiwan's development: medium-sized and small firms account for half of Taiwan's value added, much of it for export, and employ 62 percent of the work force. Tyler S. Biggs describes how these firms have been served by a sophisticated set of institutional arrangements through non-bank channels in the informal or curb market for credit in Taiwan. Among the most important of these institutions have been legally sanctioned, postdated checks, which are discounted in a secondary market. The evidence suggests that the development of the curb market improved the allocative efficiency of credit and was itself crucial to Taiwan's export success.

The papers on the Philippines and Taiwan both argue that if government removes interest rate and credit controls, formal financial institutions are not likely to replace or absorb the informal credit market. Yotopolous and Floro conclude that an expansion of credit through the formal sector may not increase the supply of credit to the categories of borrowers, mostly poor farmers, who present the greatest risk and are willing to pay the most for loans. It is likely that the traders who would receive much of the additional credit would rather lend more to rich farmers than to poor ones. If new credit is directed to poor farmers who pledge land as collateral, the rate of land consolidation is likely to increase.

In Taiwan, Biggs suggests, financial liberalization may reduce the total supply of credit and worsen allocative efficiency. Deregulation of interest rates would stimulate a transfer of funds from the informal to the formal financial market. The proclivity of banks to ration credit would lead them to expand loans to firms that they traditionally serve. Further, reserve requirements, which apply to banks but not to lenders in the curb market, would reduce total lending. These cases illustrate the ways in which fragmented credit markets, created by rationing and sorting rules, can lead to different outcomes than would be predicted by models of strictly parallel markets that clear through price changes.

Black Markets

For decades *black market* was the term of choice for parallel markets (Boulding 1937; Michaely 1954; Gönensay 1966) and remains in common usage for parallel foreign exchange and goods markets (Nowak 1985; Bevan, Collier, and Gunning 1989). But the term is not just a synonym for *parallel*. First, the term *black market* has a distinct implication of illegality; and, as noted earlier, not all parallel markets are illegal. Second, not all black markets are parallel: *black* can refer to the market for prohibited goods, such as cocaine or firearms, for which there is no legal market, hence no parallelism.

Third, *black money* is an expression used, especially in India, to denote income that has evaded taxes or been acquired illegally and held in liquid form (Acharya and Madhur 1983). Such funds are derived and then circulated in a *black economy*, a term that is somewhat analogous to the advanced economy notion of the *underground economy*. Efforts to avoid taxes may give rise to secondary parallel markets. If money earned from unrecorded transactions must be "laundered" to be useful, it will be offered at favorable terms on credit or foreign exchange markets, thus creating parallel financial markets. If, however, there is no risk in spending money earned from unrecorded transactions or income tax evasion, no laundering process develops, and the parallel markets are limited to tax-evading transactions such as the hiring of workers at wages below the minimum or not paying employment taxes. Thus, income tax evasion, to the extent that no laundering of undeclared income is necessary, does not give rise to a parallel market.

Omkar Goswami, Amal Sanyal, and Ira N. Gang go more deeply into the risk and enforcement functions assumed in other chapters to examine the impact of tax policy when individuals pay bribes to avoid declaring their income. Their model shows that an increase in tax rates, combined with an increase in the probability of an audit, will increase tax revenues at the same time that it optimizes net revenue to government. This finding is contrary to the conventional wisdom that a decrease in tax rates will increase tax revenues. Their model has important implications for efforts in developing countries to reduce fraud in income or customs taxes and highlights the importance of specifying the determinants of rent-seeking behavior in analyzing black markets.

Informal Sector

This book is not about the informal sector. Yet the concept has become so popular, and has been used to cover so many characteristics of developing countries, that its relationship to parallel, fragmented, and black markets should be discussed. Peattie (1987) has observed that the multiplicity of definitions of *informal sector* has led to complete confusion about the meaning of the term. Various definitions distinguish between the formal and informal sectors on the basis of ease of entry, scale of operations, regulated versus competitive markets, reliance on indigenous resources, family ownership, wage earning versus self employment, choice of technologies, or low labor productivity. This array of alternative definitions certainly complicates comparisons with other types of market structure.

One thread that weaves its way through much of the analysis of the informal sector is the relative marginality of informal activities. This is a product of the excess supply of labor characteristic of many developing countries; however, such surpluses are not analogous to the disequilibria that give rise to parallel markets. Structural features of the economy are the root cause of both the excess supply of labor and the existence of an informal sector. In this sense, informality is more akin to fragmentation than to parallelism. Government interventions such as minimum-wage and benefits regulations, high government wages, and taxation may, however, all contribute to parallel markets that have become part of the informal sector.

Conclusion

In describing market structure in developing economies, economists employ a number of terms not found in traditional discussions of industrial organization. The notions of parallel, fragmented, black, and informal markets all convey the existence and persistence of differences in prices and, hence, of multiple market settings for seemingly homogeneous goods and services. Although these terms are often employed interchangeably, they really describe different phenomena.

The notion of parallel markets proves especially valuable in assessing the consequences of market liberalization. The removal of government interventions can unify an otherwise parallel market. By contrast, market fragmentation suggests natural barriers to the unification of prices and implies that liberalizing policies will have far less impact on market outcomes.

Part 2   Parallel Markets

Chapter 2

Christine Jones
Michael Roemer

The Behavior of Parallel Markets
in Developing Countries

Parallel markets are created inadvertently by government controls. Attempts to control prices or quantities of goods, services, or factors of production engender excess supply or demand that spills over from official markets to unofficial, illegal, or parallel markets.[1] The concern of economists in analyzing parallel markets is thus motivated largely by an interest in government policy and its implications for economic welfare.

Economists on Parallel Markets

Among economists, interest in parallel or black markets is a comparatively recent phenomenon. The first article in the modern literature, by Boulding (1937), was followed a decade later by Bronfenbrenner (1947) and then by Michaely (1954) and by Gönensay (1966). These authors laid the geometric microeconomic foundations for studying parallel markets, but their concerns were not pursued until the 1970s, when a literature on parallel markets began in earnest.

Since then, the impetus for work on parallel markets has come from a number of sources. The earliest and arguably the most coherent body of work addresses the problem of smuggling, an outgrowth of the exploration by Bhagwati and others of the two-good general equilibrium trade model (for example, Bhagwati and Hansen 1973; Bhagwati and Srinivasan 1973; Sheikh 1976; Pitt 1981). This literature concluded that smuggling may increase or decrease welfare and made sellers' risk an explicit concern in determining outcomes under parallel markets. The adoption of price controls in the United States in 1971 and gasoline rationing in 1973 and 1979 prompted articles by Browning and Culbertson (1974) on the behavior of the firm under a regime of price controls and by Deacon and Sonstelie (1985) on consumer response to rationing.

By the 1980s, market intervention by governments in developing countries had become a dominant theme in the development literature. A small but growing number of economists began to look at the parallel markets that sprang up as producers, traders, and consumers tried to evade price and quantity controls. In India, pervasive price controls motivated research on the behavior of firms facing parallel markets (Mukherji, Pattanaik, and Sundrum 1980). Price controls are often placed on food grains in developing countries to stabilize prices and supplies, support the incomes of producers, or protect the purchasing power of low-income consumers. Consequently, parallel markets in grain are common. Studies of grain markets include some of the very few attempts to measure the prices and costs of goods traded in parallel markets (Chinn 1978; Alderman and von Braun 1984; Morris 1988).

The exploration of repressed financial markets by McKinnon (1973) and Shaw (1973) led eventually to work on parallel (curb) markets in credit (Acharya and Madhur 1983; Cole and Park 1983; van Wijnbergen 1983; Timberg and Aiyar 1984; Edwards 1988; Biggs 1988). Overvalued exchange rates accompanied by foreign exchange controls, characteristic of many developing countries, gave rise to a literature on parallel markets for foreign exchange, work that often addressed smuggling as well. Several articles have analyzed these markets using general equilibrium models that sometimes reach conclusions contradicting standard prescriptions for economies in disequilibrium (May 1985; Nowak 1985; Pinto 1988). Recently, Nguyen and Whalley (1986) have investigated interlinked parallel markets in computable general equilibrium models.

The Harvard Institute for International Development sponsored the Workshop on Parallel Markets in November 1988 to enhance this literature in two ways. First, by gathering together some of the major contributors to the literature, we hoped to move toward a common understanding of the principles underlying the analysis of parallel markets and to explore the implications of alternative models. Second, we hoped to alert officials of governments in developing countries and the major aid agencies to the implications of parallel markets for policy reform and implementation.

This article summarizes the lessons of that workshop.[2] It should come as no surprise that more questions were raised at the conference than were settled. At this stage of our understanding of parallel markets, however, even a catalogue of questions is a contribution. Five concerns seem particularly important for future work on markets under price and other controls: (1) the nature of the risks and costs of dealing in parallel markets, (2) how consumers gain access to price-controlled or otherwise rationed goods, (3) illegality and information in parallel markets, (4) linkages among different official and parallel markets, and (5) the impact of parallel markets on economic welfare. We discuss these issues in turn, then summarize the policy conclusions that emerge from this research and close with an agenda for future research on parallel markets.

Risks and Costs of Dealing in Parallel Markets

When controls such as price ceilings are imposed by government, producers (sellers) can earn higher profits by diverting some of their output from the official to the parallel market. Their ability to realize those profits depends on the costs they incur in selling outside official channels. These costs include the risk of being caught and punished for selling illegally, the cost of avoiding detection, the cost of bribes to avoid arrest, or of fines if caught, the higher unit costs (diseconomies) of trading in smaller quantities, and the costs of dealing in underdeveloped markets. If buyers also incur risks and costs in parallel markets, they will reduce their demand, thus driving down the premium available to sellers in the parallel market. Most studies assume that sellers face the greater risks and costs, so that parallel market prices are higher than equilibrium prices in the absence of controls.

In competitive markets, sellers earn no "pure" profits at the margin from selling illegally. Higher parallel market prices simply compensate for the higher costs of dealing in these markets.[3] Controls such as price ceilings reduce output of the regulated good. Given controls, parallel markets provide the opportunity for output to rise above the control-determined level.

The workshop papers raise questions about three aspects of sellers' costs and their impact on market outcomes: (1) the nature of the risks facing sellers in parallel markets, (2) the implications of economies of scale or scope, and (3) the role of risk aversion in determining market outcomes.

Much of the literature employs a risk function in which the probability of being caught and penalized depends only on the quantity sold in the parallel market. One implication of this formulation is that either (1) the total quantity offered will depend solely on the control price, with the parallel market price determining only the share going to the illegal market, or (2) all sales will go to the parallel market (Devarajan, Jones and Roemer 1989; hereafter DJR). The reason is simple: Producers will sell to the parallel market until the marginal cost of operating on the parallel market rises to equal the difference between the parallel price and the official price. At that point, there is no further advantage to selling on the parallel market. Producers will continue to sell on the official market until the marginal cost of production (exclusive of risk) rises to equal the official price.

The issue of the specification of risk was first raised in conjunction with models of smuggling. Pitt (1981) introduced the possibility that the risk of being caught might not only increase with illegal sales (smuggled goods, in his case), but could also decrease with legal sales. Selling through official channels provides legitimacy and may reduce suspicion by officials about sales in the parallel market. DJR apply this specification of risk to price control models and show that total output exceeds the amount that would be sold assuming the simpler (univariate) specification of risk. Legal sales increase revenues by reducing the risk of facing penalty costs, thus allowing the producer to increase output beyond the point at which the marginal cost of production equals the official price.

Pitt's analysis of the welfare effects of smuggling also applies to price controls. Under the simple specification of the risk function, output is the same with or without a parallel market. If transactions in the parallel market involve real resource costs, rather than fines or bribes, then the same goods could have been sold legally using fewer resources. Parallel market sales thus reduce welfare.[4] Under the bivariate specification of the risk function, however, output increases relative to the univariate case, reducing the distortions caused by price controls. The emergence of the parallel market may then increase welfare, depending on the extent of the real resource costs involved in illegal transactions.[5]

Direct evidence on the costs of operating in parallel markets is provided by Morris and Newman (1989), who studied the trade in rice and coarse grains in Senegal. Over half of the marketed surplus of rice is handled by parallel market traders. Morris and Newman show that these traders pay farmers more than the official farmgate price for rice and sell to consumers at or below the official sales price. Incorporated into these lower margins are the costs of bribing officials. Moreover, parallel market traders have to live with the uncertainty of knowing whether a capricious enforcement mechanism will find their operations illegal or not.

This somewhat surprising outcome can be explained if the high official marketing margin is viewed as an implicit tax to cover the costs of operating the notoriously inefficient government marketing board. If traders' costs—including risks, penalties, and bribes—are less than the marketing board's costs, traders can evade the marketing board's "tax" by buying from farmers at a higher price and selling to consumers at a lower price than does the board, thus increasing the total quantity traded.[6] If traders can reduce the risk of selling through the parallel channel by also selling at official prices, we would observe transactions at both the official and parallel market prices. The total quantity marketed would then exceed that sold by the marketing board in the absence of a parallel channel.

Farmers and consumers each benefit from the greater efficiency achieved by parallel market traders. (Although the private gain to farmers and consumers is partially offset if they also risk having to pay bribes or fines by trading unofficially, these are transfer payments, not real costs to society.) Traders, some of whom may be new entrants to the market, incur additional costs in diverting trade from the marketing board; some of these are likely to be real costs and some are transfers to officials (bribes or fines). If, as is likely, a large share of the marketing board's costs are fixed, its total expenditures on marketing activities would decline less than proportionally as traders move part of the grain supply into the unofficial market. The net impact of the parallel market on welfare is therefore indeterminate: The gains to farmers, consumers, and officials may be greater than, equal to, or less than the additional costs of trading in the parallel market.

The second cost-related question posed by the workshop is whether the risks or other costs of parallel market operations are characterized by economies of scale or scope, or learning by doing. Most analysts assume that the marginal costs of smuggling or illegal trading rise with the volume traded, that is, that there are diseconomies of scale. In principle, however, there is no reason to rule out economies of scale in bribing or in illegal marketing activities. It is an empirical question whether the reduced unit costs of trading at higher volumes outweigh the increased risks associated with more visible operations. There may even be economies of scale in bribery, as the total bribe rises less than the volume traded. Costs could also decline over time, as traders learn better how to evade controls and as parallel marketing institutions develop to reduce costs. Neither the literature nor the workshop papers systematically explore the differences that may result from these alternative specifications of average costs.

In their paper on Ghana, however, Azam and Besley (1989) use a cost function that posits economies of scope: Smuggling out exports reduces the costs of smuggling in imports. In Ghana, the official price for cocoa is set below the world price. Farmers sell part of their crop to traders who smuggle it to neighboring Togo or the Ivory Coast. Having established the transport facilities and paid the necessary bribes to smuggle out cocoa, traders incur lower unit costs if they use the same trucks to smuggle in consumer goods that are rationed domestically. Azam and Besley embed this cost function—which implicitly models risks and other costs as depending only on the level of smuggling—in a general equilibrium model with parallel markets in exports, imported consumer goods, and foreign exchange. They consider a number of comparative static results, including the impact of an increase in the official price of cocoa exports, which increases the domestic price level. The assumption of economies of scope exacerbates the inflationary impact, since a decrease in the amount of cocoa smuggled out results in a decrease in consumer goods smuggled in, hence a reduction in total goods available, holding other variables constant. This is one example of many unexpected policy outcomes that emerge when parallel markets are built into macroeconomic models.

The third cost-related question is the impact of risk aversion on outcomes in parallel markets. The literature generally assumes that producers and consumers are risk neutral, that is, that they treat the expected cost of being caught and fined just like any other cost. If, however, traders are averse to risk, they demand additional compensation to undertake risky activities. Sheikh (1989) employs Tobin's portfolio approach to analyze smuggling behavior in the presence of risk aversion. Using the simple univariate specification that risk depends only on the level of smuggling, he demonstrates that smugglers earn profits that just compensate them for the disutility of the risks they incur.

Consumer Access to Rationed Goods

When official prices are set below the market-clearing price, consumers have the choice of competing for limited supplies of the goods sold on official markets or seeking supplies in parallel markets at higher prices. In their workshop paper, Deacon and Sonstelie (1989) show that consumers seeking limited supplies at the control price incur additional costs: time spent searching and waiting, bribes to avoid these costs, and investments in storage facilities to permit hoarding when the controlled good is available. In the absence of a parallel market, these transaction costs are incurred up to the point at which the effective price clears the market. Thus, consumers dissipate the benefits (rents) resulting from price controls by spending time and money to obtain and store supplies.

Deacon and Sonstelie's framework can easily be extended to incorporate a parallel market. Nguyen and Whalley (1986) have shown that in a parallel market consumers will compete for the rationed good until transaction costs absorb all of the difference between the prices in the parallel and official markets. They label these costs "endogenous transactions costs."

Krueger (1974) noted the possibility that rent-seeking behavior may lead to activities whose costs exceed the rents created by price controls. Deacon and Sonstelie explored the implications of consumer rent seeking when the costs associated with gaining access are fixed. To reduce queuing costs, consumers attempt to purchase more of the rationed good with each transaction. Larger purchases may lead to additional outlays for storage, for example, investment in tanks or refrigerators. Deacon and Sonstelie showed that this competitive behavior of increasing storage capacity, which is rational for each consumer, results in costs that can exceed the rent generated by the price restriction. In that case, even those consumers who gain access to rationed goods would be better off had the price not been controlled.

Devarajan, Jones, and Roemer (1989) suggest another possibility: Governments may provide access to rationed quantities at no cost through ration shops, through coupons, or by virtue of some attribute such as location or occupation. They call this strategy "costless rationing." In this case, consumers do gain rents by purchasing rationed quantities at below-equilibrium prices. The assumption of costless rationing does not rule out the possibility that consumers will resell their rations on the parallel market; it merely enables them to capture the full rent inherent in their allocations.

DJR show that in partial equilibrium this situation opens the possibility that consumers may then demand, and producers supply, more of the controlled good than would have been available in the absence of controls. This is possible because consumers, their incomes increased by rents, demand more of all goods than they did without controls. However, DJR are unable to reproduce this counterintuitive outcome in a two- or three-sector general equilibrium model because consumer gains are offset by producer losses, which in turn dampen gains in consumer income.

Deacon and Sonstelie show that it is difficult to design costless rationing schemes. Even in coupon systems, competitive rent seeking is likely to occur among consumers. If government hands out more ration coupons than there are goods available, waiting costs will rise until enough consumers are induced to forgo use of their coupons to balance demand and supply. Thus, part of the rents will be dissipated by the increase in waiting time. Giving the additional coupons to the consumers with the lowest marginal valuation will minimize the waiting time, but increase the loss due to misallocation of coupons. Undersupplying coupons also leads to rent seeking. The excess supply of goods will go to the consumers with the highest marginal valuation—the same outcome as if the coupons had been oversupplied to these consumers. Waiting time is reduced, however, because competition focuses only on the surplus above coupon entitlements.

Deacon and Sonstelie also demonstrated that, when supplies are fixed, allowing coupons to be transferred does not necessarily increase welfare. When coupons have been oversupplied, for example, consumers' marginal valuations will be equalized, eliminating the misallocation losses. All the rent will be dissipated, however, as waiting times rise to clear the market. In contrast, under certain allocations in which transferability is not allowed, the welfare gain from the rent may exceed the loss resulting from misallocation. The striking differences in outcomes, depending on the nature of the rationing regime, suggest that more empirical research is needed to determine the distribution of benefits associated with access to price-controlled goods, its impact on parallel market prices, and the extent of rent-seeking behavior.

Illegality and Information

It seems obvious that parallel markets must clear because they are unfettered by government intervention. Until recently, no writer has questioned this tenet. In their article in this volume, however, Bevan, Collier, and Gunning (hereafter BCG) observe that in rural Tanzania most consumers reported being unable to purchase goods despite the presence of an active parallel market. This led BCG to hypothesize that the high cost of obtaining information might be at fault. If price or other controls are enforced by arresting or fining parallel marketers, sellers then run risks, not only in advertising their wares, but even in trying to strike bargains with potential purchasers. Any buyer might be an informant, the more so if the seller tries to discover the buyer's reservation price by asking prices well above the official level and thus offends would-be purchasers. In these circumstances, traders may reduce the probability of arrest and maximize their profits by offering goods at prices well below parallel market-clearing levels. Markets do not clear, because there are consumers prepared to pay higher prices who are not approached by the trader. By posing this possibility, BCG open up a new area of enquiry for the parallel markets literature.

Linkages among Markets

Price controls and parallel markets are rarely confined to one or two commodities. They generally proliferate across markets for factors, goods, and services. General equilibrium treatments are necessary to incorporate the linkages among these markets and to analyze the impacts of controls on markets not subject to intervention. General equilibrium models also allow one to investigate the impact of market liberalization. Nguyen and Whalley (1986) have led the way in using computable general equilibrium models to explore the welfare costs of controls in the face of parallel markets.

One of the workshop papers presented a particularly interesting application of the computable general equilibrium model that merits comment, even though it deals primarily with an industrial country. Nguyen (1989) formulates an eight-sector model of the U.S. economy that contains one parallel market, consisting of illegal aliens who are willing to work for subminimum wages. Illegal immigrants risk deportation, and resident employers risk fines if they employ illegal aliens. Employers' risks depend on the ratio of illegal-to-legal employees, so that employing more legal workers reduces the risk of being caught.

Illegal workers constitute only 1 percent of the work force. Yet in Nguyen's model, if there are no illegal workers, the income of legal workers is 5 percent lower and government tax revenues 11 percent lower than if illegal aliens are included. Thus, the parallel market in illegal workers can have an important and positive effect on macroeconomic outcomes, because (1) immigrants generate additional demand and expenditure, (2) the tax base and government expenditure both rise, and (3) government enforcement efforts provide additional legal employment. Nguyen's model provides another example of the counterintuitive policy results that emerge from models dealing explicitly with parallel markets.

Impact on Economic Welfare

The assumptions made about seller's risk and consumer's access have implications for the impact of parallel markets on economic welfare.[7] Assume that price controls are effective and that all transactions go through the official market. If a parallel market channel is then opened, how does it affect welfare?

The unofficial channel will decrease welfare if (1) there is no increase in output because seller's risk is a function of illegal sales only, and (2) the costs incurred by sellers in the parallel market are real costs, rather than transfers in the form of fines or bribes, or (3) parallel marketing costs are transfers, but these subsequently distort producer or consumer decisions.

The parallel market will increase welfare if (4) it leads to an increase in output because seller's risk is a function of sales in both markets,[8] and (5) the costs of selling illegally are nondistortionary transfers, and/or (6) use of the parallel market enables consumers to avoid real costs of rent seeking such as searching, queuing, or investment in storage equipment. A reasonable judgment is that parallel markets improve welfare by encouraging increases in output (point 4) and avoiding real costs of access for consumers (point 5). However, fines and bribes probably concentrate incomes that, if we permit interpersonal comparisons to enter the calculation, would presumably reduce welfare.

Policy Implications

An inevitable negativism seeps into any discussion of policies toward parallel markets. These illegal activities arise because government has intervened, sometimes with exemplary intentions, to prevent markets from taking their normal course. Such interventions, even when implemented efficiently and honestly, often fail to achieve their aims; and they are seldom so well implemented. There are almost always better ways to achieve government's economic goals than to control prices or quantities. In these circumstances, parallel markets generally ameliorate ill-advised policies and, as discussed earlier, are likely to improve welfare. Attempts by government to enforce controls by suppressing illegal trading not only make it more difficult for parallel marketers to serve their useful social function, but also add real costs of enforcement to society's burden (BCG 1989).

The best prescription for government would obviously be to give up its controls, deregulate the market, and seek other means to achieve the economic aims that unfettered markets are unable to serve. Such a policy would make parallel markets, as we have defined them, irrelevant. Failing that, and accepting the inevitability of some controls in most countries, the second-best prescription for government policy would be to relax enforcement of controls and let parallel markets work. Indeed, if parallel markets do improve welfare, government could even consider promoting the development of parallel market institutions. But this would be an extraordinarily cynical approach, with government embracing controls for legitimate policy purposes with the right hand while undercutting them with the left.[9]

If government is unwilling to give up certain controls and is reluctant to endorse a cynical attitude toward their enforcement, the research summarized here still offers scope for policies to reduce the welfare costs of controls. First, enforcement should be especially lenient on those parallel market traders who also offer substantial quantities at controlled prices on official markets. This would ensure that illegal traders reduce the risks of being caught and penalized if they also trade on legal markets. Not only would more goods be offered at official prices, but the total quantity supplied to both markets would also be greater than if enforcement was uniform for all illegal sellers (Pitt 1981; DJR 1989). The simplest form of this enforcement regime would be to allocate official market quotas to producers and to ignore (or even to encourage) unofficial market sales if the quotas have been fulfilled. Chinese communal farms have operated on such a system in recent years.

Second, when government agricultural marketing boards are charged with the task of establishing below-market prices for basic foods, there should be no quantitative restrictions on competitive marketing channels. Parallel marketers who can operate within the limits established by farmer and consumer prices should be permitted to obtain price-controlled produce, thus benefiting both farmers and consumers (Morris and Newman 1989). Indeed, enforcement would be unnecessary, because traders operating outside these limits would have to offer something else (convenience, quality, or credit) in compensation to induce farmers to sell to them or users to buy from them. Competition from parallel traders should help keep the costs of the marketing board under control. If this approach is to have a maximum impact on welfare, government will have to reduce the costs of the marketing board (and employment) as its volume of transactions decreases.

Third, the research suggests that consumer costs can be reduced if something approaching a costless rationing scheme could be devised (DJR 1989). One approach is the ration shop of south Asia, which can require a ration card for admittance or may limit its clientele to the poor by its location or the low quality of goods it offers. However, it is almost impossible to devise ration schemes that eliminate all consumer transactions costs. A practical alternative is to supply ration coupons with entitlements that do not fully exhaust supplies, then allow competition for the balance of supplies. This reduces search and queuing costs by limiting them to the surplus of supplies over coupon entitlements and ensures that consumers with the highest marginal valuations will obtain the surplus quantities (Deacon and Sonstelie 1989).

Fourth, just as the existence of parallel markets ameliorates the impacts of government market interventions, the benefits of removing controls are reduced by the operation of illegal markets. Until recently, analyses of market liberalization proceeded as if the official market told the entire story. That assumption makes a clear case for the positive net benefits of deregulation. But once we recognize that parallel markets are likely to increase welfare under controls, we must admit that the net benefit from liberalization is likely to be smaller. In the case of pure parallel markets, those engendered only by government intervention, there still remains some net benefit from deregulation because the parallel market cannot fully replace the unfettered market: There are likely to be some real costs to operating the parallel market, and the total quantity marketed through both markets will be less than under a single uncontrolled market.

When parallelism exists along with fragmentation, it is even possible that market controls improve welfare by driving resources from the formal market into the preexisting informal market, as happens with curb markets in repressed financial systems. In that case, liberalization will channel resources back into the formal market without fully incorporating the informal market (because fragmentation is the result of inherent characteristics of the market, and not of policy interventions). Those who purchase on the informal market will then be worse off, and they will tend to have lower incomes than the gainers, who purchase on the formal market. If we allow for interpersonal comparisons using welfare weights, liberalization can cause a net loss in welfare.

Fifth and finally, policy analysts and decision makers need to come to grips with the confounding effects of controls and parallel markets on economic policy. The few general equilibrium treatments of parallel markets are replete with counterintuitive and counterproductive results of policy reforms that make sense otherwise (May 1985; Nowak 1985; Pinto 1988; Azam and Besley 1989; Nguyen 1989). This is a matter for further research and refinement. It seems clear, however, that once parallel markets arise in response to price and quantity controls, the economy becomes more difficult to manage.

Research Agenda

The HIID workshop improved our understanding of several aspects of parallel markets and suggested a research agenda for future work on policy outcomes in the face of illegal markets. One avenue for further research is to relate the various alternative specifications—of the costs of parallel marketing, the nature of the risks facing illegal traders, the role of information, and the kinds of consumer access—to the institutions and behavior observed in real markets. Each of these specifications reflects certain assumptions about the way markets work, and the choices among alternative formulations are ultimately empirical issues. We need to observe institutions and behaviors in actual markets and then determine which functional forms are appropriate to use in analyzing them.

Some of this work has already been done. Pitt (1981), observing how some smuggling is accomplished by underinvoicing through official channels, suggested that the probability of being caught may decline as legal sales rise. Deacon and Sonstelie (1989) have observed and then modeled the costs to consumers of competing for rationed goods. Azam and Besley (1989) posit economies of scope from observing how two-way smuggling was carried on in Ghana. Bevan, Collier, and Gunning (1989) base their model of information costs on observations of markets in rural Tanzania. Empirical work has been undertaken to measure outcomes in parallel markets, including Alderman and von Braun (1984), Morris and Newman (1989), and Puetz and von Braun in this volume.

Not all of this work has been informed by the kinds of theoretical approaches we have just discussed or in the broader literature. The agenda for future field studies ought to be harnessed to the tasks of observing both (1) the market institutions that determine functional forms, and (2) the outcomes (prices, quantities, incomes) predicted by the models. Such disciplined field work should generate more of the interaction between observation and theory that marks the papers by Azam and Besley; Bevan, Collier, and Gunning; and Deacon and Sonstelie.

Field work on parallel markets has severe limitations, of course. Any enquiry into illegal activities is inherently difficult, even risky. In many situations, respondents will be reluctant to reveal crucial information such as the quantities they sold or bought in parallel markets, the prices they received or paid, the bribes paid, and the ways they reduce the risks of detection. The degree of difficulty in obtaining information may vary with the intensity of enforcement. Even if respondents are willing to reveal information, the very nature of parallel markets makes it difficult to assess the total quantities marketed, since many small traders are likely to be involved. Information on prices is probably easier to obtain, as the studies by Morris and Newman and by Puetz and von Braun show. Without data on all market variables, however, it will be difficult to evaluate the merits of competing models of parallel markets.

Another fruitful approach is to explore the various alternative microeconomic functional specifications in a common framework to test their implications for market outcomes. Reactions from those attending the workshop suggest that analysts need to become more sensitive to the variety of possibilities. A simple general equilibrium formulation, such as that in Devarajan, Jones, and Roemer or Azam and Besley, might be used to test alternative specifications for the risk function, cost functions, information barriers, risk aversion, consumer access, and so forth. Various suggestions for these functions have been made by different authors using their own models or analytical frameworks. If, instead, each specification were tested in the same model structure, it should be possible to demonstrate the relative effects of each of these choices on market outcomes in a systematic and consistent way.

The application of larger, more complex general equilibrium models can teach us much about the intricate linkages among all markets in an economy, some of which are marked by controls and parallel trading. The costs of controls to an economy, and the corresponding benefits from liberalization of markets, can only be assessed within a general equilibrium framework. There have been attempts to assess these costs, notably those of Nguyen and Whalley (1986). This line of enquiry holds vast possibilities for looking at different kinds of economies, an array of various market interventions, and the entire menu of alternative market institutions

Detlev Puetz
Joachim von Braun

Chapter 3

Parallel Markets and the Rural Poor
in a West African Setting

There is widespread dissatisfaction with the intervention of parastatal and public sector institutions in agricultural output procurement and input supply, especially in sub-Saharan Africa. The situation in The Gambia, West Africa—the case analyzed in this paper—is no exception.

Price and other market interventions in agricultural commodity markets frequently lead to situations in which official markets fail to meet demand for inputs at prevailing official prices. Taxed output prices, on the other hand, often discourage farmers from supplying official market outlets. Whenever governments impose such controls over quantities or prices, parallel markets arise to evade these controls (Jones and Roemer 1989). The costs of operating in parallel markets and the nature of the risks facing traders are important determinants of the quantities traded inside and outside the official system and the prices paid on the parallel market. Parallel commodity markets that appear as an illegal alternative to official, state-controlled markets often involve additional costs and risks for market participants. The Gambian groundnut market is a case in point. But some parallel markets may be officially tolerated or even approved of where governments perceive their complementary function or plan to initiate a transition toward market liberalization. The Gambian fertilizer market is an example. The government tolerated this market before liberalization; but after liberalization in 1986, the government approved of it.

Like many other countries, The Gambia has made efforts to develop and stimulate the private sector to take over functions in marketing agricultural goods and the inputs necessary to produce them. This usually takes time and creates frictions, at least in transitional periods when governments reduce their interventions only gradually and have substantial continuing influence on unofficial markets.

The evolution of private markets—or the legalization process of existing parallel markets—remains closely interrelated with activities on the official markets. In such situations, improved knowledge about interactions of official and parallel markets is critical for appropriate policy design, that is, the scheduling of the adjustment process and the definition of the role of the public sector in agriculture in countries at different stages of development.

In analyzing how official and parallel markets evolve and interact in this African setting, we empirically address three major questions:

1. Devarajan, Jones, and Roemer (1989) point out that wherever official and parallel markets coexist, participants shift their supply or demand from one market to the other until the expected marginal benefits in both market activities are the same. Behavior on these markets is determined by price differentials, penalties, and other transaction costs involved in getting access to the market. In such markets, equilibrium will be reached when these transaction costs equal the price differences of the commodity on the parallel market and the official (controlled) market. Basic relationships are traced empirically for the Gambian groundnut market. Differential producer prices in The Gambia and neighboring Senegal have led to an active parallel market involving the smuggling of groundnuts into Senegal. What determines the coexistence of official and parallel markets and the share of produce marketed to each of them?

2. Excess demand on a particular market may not necessarily be met by the parallel market, and a market disequilibrium may result. Bevan et al. (1989) observe that penalties and costs of collecting information can lead to parallel market prices below equilibrium. In the Gambian market for fertilizer, delivery failures and restrictive distribution and credit policies have rationed the supply of fertilizer. The excess demand is only partly met by the parallel market. What factors

may keep a parallel market—created by government interventions—from clearing in the short run?

3. Much of the research on parallel markets to date has focused
on the efficiency of market operations and related economic
costs. Very little, however, is known about the income distribution effects of parallel markets in different socioeconomic
settings. Because participation in the parallel market—and
therefore access to potential gains—by certain groups of
households may differ, we ask: What are the distributional
effects of parallel market activities, especially the impact for
the rural poor?

The empirical evidence presented in this paper is based on two
household surveys conducted by the authors between 1985 and 1988.[1]
The study area is located in the center of The Gambia, 270 kilometers
east of the country's capital, Banjul. The survey was not designed to
address the issue of parallel markets specifically, but the results contain
information useful for assessing the outcome of government interventions that create parallel markets and permit the analysis of the distributional effects of parallel markets in this setting.

An initial section examines market institutions in The Gambia and
reviews the policy decisions that led to the rise of parallel markets. In
the second part, empirical evidence is provided on market outcomes in
terms of prices and quantities traded on each market and the distributional impact of parallel market activities.

Market Features

More than 90 percent of the Gambian population lives in rural areas and
is highly dependent on agriculture. In this small English-speaking enclave within French-speaking Senegal, no place is farther than twenty-
five kilometers away from the Senegalese border, and there are close
ethnic linkages between the two nations. As in neighboring Senegal,
groundnuts— produced on smallholder farms—are the core of the agricultural economy, providing more than 80 percent of The Gambia's
(official) export earnings and nearly 80 percent of farmers' cash income,
and making groundnut marketing a major activity. The average annual
per capita income in the study area was about US$140 in 1986, ranging
from US$48 for the poorest income quartile to US$227 for the highest.

Mechanization levels in this land-abundant savannah agriculture
are low, and major production constraints include scarcity of farm implements, quality groundnut seeds, and fertilizer. In this environment,

efficient marketing systems, notably for inputs, assume a vital role for growth and equity.

Market institutions and operations. For more than a decade, agricultural input and output markets have been dominated by a parastatal marketing board and the Gambia Cooperatives Union (GCU), with both institutions subsidized through a variety of special project funds and access to interest-free loans. Only recently, in the course of a structural adjustment program, did the government adopt a policy of deregulation and privatization for input and cereal markets, but the groundnut market remained state controlled.

The state marketing board, a monopsony, licenses buyers and agents to purchase and collect groundnuts in the countryside to deliver them to the board's processing factory in the capital. In the last decade, GCU has emerged as the largest licensed buyer. Lower marketing allowances and multiple subsidies to GCU have driven private buyers out of the market: Their share declined from nearly 60 percent of the marketed groundnut volume in the 1974–1976 period to less than 20 percent today.

GCU's eighty-five primary cooperative societies and stores cover the whole country. In the study area, GCU is the only official groundnut buyer on the Gambian side of the border; it operates four stores along the main roads where farmers take their groundnuts for sale. These places happen to be as far as ten kilometers away from some of the most productive groundnut-producing villages in the survey. For many of these farmers, Senegalese cooperative buying points across the border are even closer.

Official prices for groundnuts are set annually by the government and are uniform across the country. The state marketing board, with its monopsony for purchasing and exporting groundnuts, guarantees these producer prices to each farmer. In making these price decisions, the government takes into consideration the world market prices and Senegalese procurement prices.

Fertilizer markets were completely liberalized in early 1986. Before that the state marketing board controlled all fertilizer imports into The Gambia (there is no fertilizer production in the country itself) and its national retailing through licensed sellers. Prices were fixed by the government. But even after deregulation there remains some important state influence on fertilizer trading: Because it had large carryover stocks and because it continued to handle fertilizer imports—which consist mainly of international donations—the government has remained the only importer of fertilizer. A system of an annual fertilizer auction run by the government and open to any interested party replaced former licensing procedures. But private traders at the national level so far have not shown any interest in retailing fertilizer. In 1987 this left GCU as the only bidder at the auction and the only national retailer of fertilizer in The Gambia.

The two markets analyzed in this chapter have one important feature with high impact on parallel market outcomes: Both groundnuts and fertilizer marketing are highly seasonal, confined to relatively short trading periods of about three months for groundnuts and less than two months for fertilizer. This means that agents need to make their market assessments during a very short time period, the more so since interventions vary from year to year and increase the uncertainty about market behavior in a given season.

Market assessments are also complicated by limited market transparence and high transactions costs in this rural setting, thereby increasing market imperfections. Although a wide variety of trading activities take place (trading of consumer goods, including cereals, and reexporting), the public policy of favoring GCU has left only a small number of private agents who could handle agricultural trade without major investments in transport, storage, and distribution/collection systems.

Fertilizer has a high marginal productivity in the study area, and farmers are aware of this fact (von Braun and Puetz 1987). Demand for fertilizer is restricted, however, by farmers' liquidity constraints at the time of need in the growing season. In addition, production risks— especially after the recent drought—may keep risk-averse farmers from using scarce cash resources for fertilizer purchases. Thus, especially for the poorest farmers, demand for fertilizer is closely tied to access to credit. Altogether in 1987, 41 percent of fertilizer for groundnuts and coarse grains was received as a loan and some 8 percent as a gift, while 51 percent was paid for in cash.

The creation of parallel markets for an output (groundnuts) and an input (fertilizer). A parallel market is a structure generated in response to those government interventions that create a situation of excess supply or demand in a particular product or factor market (Lindauer 1989).By imposing price and market controls and indirectly taxing the country's major agricultural export commodity, groundnuts, the Gambian government generated a surplus supply of groundnuts at the tax-exclusive price. On the fertilizer market, restrictions of the quantities traded through the official marketing system created a surplus demand at the subsidized price for this important production input. As a result, parallel markets arose for both groundnuts and fertilizer to avoid these controls and to equate supply and demand.

During the mid-1980s, both The Gambia and Senegal embarked on structural adjustment programs that included large price increases for groundnuts. The goal was to improve the terms of trade for the agricultural sector. But in both countries this policy raised domestic prices above the world market level (the nominal protection rates, that is, the ratio of domestic to world market prices was close to 2 in 1986–87). Subsidies were needed—and partly provided by international donors—to facilitate the export of groundnuts. Since 1984–85, the Gambian groundnut price has been between 73 and 84 percent of the Senegalese price (see Table 3.1). There has always been an outflow of groundnuts, especially from the villages close to the border, but very favorable price differentials in 1988 and institution of a purchase ceiling by the marketing board combined to stimulate the outflow. During the 1987–88 season, limited subsidy funds in The Gambia forced the government to decrease guaranteed prices, thereby increasing the price differential to Senegal. But even at a lower price level, the government was unable to guarantee the price for the country's total groundnut output and established a purchasing ceiling that covered only about two-thirds of the estimated marketing volume for the year. Because groundnuts sold to the parallel Senegalese market save The Gambia expenses on the export subsidy, the government did not attempt to prevent smuggling or to enforce sales to the cooperative.

The Gambia Cooperatives Union, on the other hand, has some vested interest in official market sales because its marketing allowance increases with the volume marketed. GCU also needs to recover input loans from farmers, which is easier when groundnuts are sold to the cooperative. Thus, GCU put pressure on farmers to market to the official channel.

A semilegal parallel market thus evolved, which tolerates parallel structures on the Gambian side and attempts to safeguard its procurement system on the Senegalese side. The Senegalese government in 1987–88 tried to discourage Gambian sales by ordering stores along the

TABLE 3.1   Groundnuts Price Ratio in The Gambia and Senegal and Fertilizer Subsidy and Use, 1981–82 to 1987–88

	Groundnuts price, Gambia/Senegal (%)	Fertilizer subsidy per unit (%)	Fertilizer consumption (tons)
1981–82	102	72	12,135
1982–83	108	77	8,357
1983–84	94[a]	63	9,582
1984–85	79[b]	31	12,066
1985–86	82	22	4,738
1986–87	84	26	4,080
1987–88	73	17	2,435

a. Down to 75% when the local currency was devalued during the trading season.
b. After price increases in The Gambia during the trading season.
SOURCE: Computed from various unpublished sources of the Gambian Ministry of Agriculture and Gambia Cooperatives Union.

border to close down, demanding Senegalese identification documents from groundnut sellers, and increasing its border controls. But the border is long, and during the course of the trading season most of these measures could not be fully enforced or were offset by bribes. Moreover, Senegalese groundnut-buying agents had an incentive to purchase Gambian nuts, since their allowances also depend on the volume of groundnuts purchased.

The parallel structures in the fertilizer market have different causes from those in the groundnut market. In the past five years, fertilizer use in The Gambia has declined by 75 percent. Although some of this decline can be attributed to lower demand in response to sharp price increases (such as the removal of subsidies; see Table 3.1), most of it is a result of delivery failures, the restrictive distribution policy of the official fertilizer retail system, and failure to involve private marketing at large.

In 1985 a national fertilizer crisis developed when a fertilizer grant was provided to the country by an international donor, and at the same time the institutional responsibility for the logistics of fertilizer marketing in The Gambia changed. This led to a disruption of supply, since fertilizer shipments arrived in the country too late for the 1985–86 cropping season. In the end, only carryover stocks from previous years were used during that season, resulting in substantial production losses for the country (von Braun and Puetz 1987). In this situation of limited short-term supply, farmers had to compete for scarce fertilizer on a parallel market. Although unauthorized fertilizer trading was officially illegal at that time, there was little enforcement to discourage trading of small quantities.

More disruptions and uncertainty followed when fertilizer markets were officially deregulated for the 1986–87 crop season. But the official marketing system was maintained, and the private traders who were invited to take over part of the retail trade have not embarked on fertilizer marketing. On the other hand, government and GCU policies restricted fertilizer supplies to the cooperative's primary societies despite ample supplies in government stores. As a matter of policy, annual allotments to each of GCU's eighty-five primary societies are based on its sales the year before and are adjusted downward for outstanding loan repayments from each society. Until 1985 GCU had provided loans under generous interest and repayment conditions. Individual loan defaulters did not lose access to new loans as long as their primary cooperative society maintained a certain collective repayment rate. With the structural adjustment program this policy changed in 1986, and individual loan defaulters have since been strictly excluded from further loans. The new credit policy also limited new input loans to the amount individual farmers had received the previous year, and only cooperative members who actually got credit the year before are eligible for new credit.

Tightening access to credit had an adverse effect on overall input use, since GCU did not put out special contingencies for cash sales. Thus, in 1987 GCU purchased only 3,000 tons of fertilizer in the public auction (Table 3.1). Fertilizer shortages and excess demand remained symptomatic for the fertilizer market. At the local level a parallel fertilizer market exists but is limited in size, because private traders—operating interregionally—have not gotten involved.

Market Outcomes at the Farm Level

Causes for coexistence of official and parallel markets. Farmers may participate in both official and parallel output and input markets.

The output market. During the 1987–88 season, 53 percent of all groundnuts marketed in the study area were sold outside the official Gambian market, either taken directly by farmers to Senegal or sold, illegally, to unlicensed middlemen in The Gambia. Average prices on the parallel market were 34 percent higher than on the official Gambian market. As these prices are exogenously fixed and guaranteed by the respective governments, demand for groundnuts is either completely elastic (as in Senegal) or elastic in the range of a rationed procurement quantity (as in The Gambia).

Why, in this situation, do official and parallel markets coexist, that is, why do farmers sell groundnuts at lower prices in The Gambia to official procurement stores? The answer to this question can be derived from a comparison of costs and profit on the parallel versus the official market.

Farmers receive higher prices for groundnuts on the parallel market in Senegal, but may incur higher marketing costs and risks on the parallel markets. Farmers will supply to the parallel market outlet as long as incremental transactions costs (*in addition* to those incurred on the official market) are lower than price differentials. Direct transaction costs include transport, costs for collecting marketing information, and bribes. But there are also indirect costs that farmers need to consider. The timing of marketing may turn into a crucial cost factor if farmers' time opportunity costs and/or capital interest rates are high. It is common that farmers must wait longer for their revenue when they market their produce in Senegal; Senegalese restrictions and controls tend to be toughest at the beginning of the trading season, and collecting market information (for example, finding a border trader or a safe passage across the border with one's own produce) takes time. Also, modes of payment are different: GCU traditionally pays cash at delivery, while the Senegalese often pay with coupons to be cashed several weeks later.

Indirect costs of marketing in Senegal also rise with a potential loss or reduction of business standing with the Gambian cooperative. Close contacts with the cooperative often reduce marketing time and other transaction costs (for example, so-called weighing losses at delivery) and facilitate access to future inputs and credit. In addition, farmers expect a premium to offset the risk of fines or even confiscation of produce, depending on their risk aversion.

Transaction costs and the risk premium vary from farmer to farmer—leading to individual differences in the expected rents to be gained by parallel marketing. Some farmers may not gain at all, since their additional costs can be higher than the additional revenue. These differences in transaction costs, risk aversion, and market imperfections lead to the coexistence of parallel and official markets.

Three different situations lead to different choices by farmers for supply to official, parallel, or both markets. First, those firms with marginal transaction costs less than the price differential will abandon the official market completely, and price controls will have no effect on them. Thirty-nine percent of farmers in the sample sell exclusively on the parallel market. Their risk of being caught on the parallel market does not decrease with the quantity traded on the official market, although not trading on the official market increases their indirect transaction costs on the parallel market because they may forgo some indirect benefits of official market participation (for example, better access to inputs). Moreover, as there seem to be no significant diseconomies of scale for trading on the parallel market, marginal revenue does not decrease with sales.

Second, those firms with marginal transactions costs above the price differential will sell exclusively to the official market. This group comprises 53 percent of surveyed farmers.

A third group of 8 percent of farmers split sales: Their indirect benefits from selling on the official market decrease with the quantity sold, because they will obtain these benefits once they sell a certain quantity. This simultaneously *decreases* their incremental indirect transaction costs for selling on the parallel market. Thus, they will sell on the official market until these costs are less than the price differential and then switch to the parallel market.

Most of The Gambia's parallel groundnut market consists of local trade; farmers themselves, or friends in the village, take groundnuts across the border and sell them directly to the Senegalese stores. Individual farmers often find it difficult to assess total transaction costs and risk and may face a variety of logistical constraints in taking their produce to Senegal. In this situation middlemen—private traders— running a parallel market inside The Gambia can reduce these costs and risks because of economies of scale and specialization. As a matter of fact, private local traders, mostly from Senegal, moved in on tractors and donkey carts and purchased groundnuts from farmers in Gambian villages, mainly those farther away from the border. This happened only relatively late in the trading season, however, and only 3 percent of the marketed produce was sold to these middlemen.

In a later section, we analyze the characteristics of those farmers who participate in the parallel market under these conditions.

The input market. At the local level, GCU provides fertilizer only to cooperative members, either for cash or on credit. Usually allocations depend on how much members received the year before and whether outstanding loans have been settled. In principle, the allocation system provides costless access to rationed quantities for those consumers who are qualified. In reality, however, costs may sometimes be incurred when supplies are scarce, and better information about the arrival of supplies at the local store or favors for officials can improve the chance of receiving a fertilizer allocation or increase the amount.

After receiving their allocations, many cooperative members with access to supplies then retail fertilizer to other farmers, often family members, friends, or neighbors who have no direct access to GCU allocations. The recipients may have chosen not to be GCU members (there is an annual membership fee) or may have defaulted on earlier loans. These relationships create part of the parallel market outside the official one. It should be noted that this retrading of procured quantities from the cooperative via relatives and friends is a personalized market in which sellers do not completely exploit scarcity rents because of family ties and obligations. The nonofficial market is also supplied by fertilizer that often is illegally leaked from cooperative or government stores or carried over from the last season's supplies. This is a less "personalized" section of the parallel market.

The parallel fertilizer market, which results from access limitations to the official fertilizer market, is limited in its scope because large amounts of its supplies are obtained through the cooperative, at least in the short term, and farmers with access to the cooperative consume much of their allotments themselves. The 1987 survey found that 33 percent of the fertilizer consumed in the end originated from sources outside the official cooperative system. On this parallel market 24 percent was provided by fellow household members, 45 percent by friends and neighbors, and 30 percent by local traders.

Market clearance in parallel market structures. Marginal returns to fertilizer are substantially above prices.[2] Farmers are aware of this, and many reported that they would have liked to purchase more at the prevailing price than they were able to find. Similar statements were made during the 1985 shortage. Thus, there are apparent market-clearing problems despite the existing parallel market.

Counterintuitively, during the 1987 season we did *not* see average parallel market prices rise above official cooperative prices—a situation similar to that in 1985.[3] This was the case for both cash and credit sales. Two factors explain this unexpected similarity of observed official and parallel market prices.

First, when farmers retail to family members, friends, and neighbors they can hardly charge more than they paid themselves. In this Muslim society, charges of usury are serious. Since part of the parallel market fertilizer comes from stocks acquired in past seasons, they may even charge only the original price, which may be lower than current official prices. It is, however, not uncommon to interlink cash sales with other transactions to circumvent customs, for example, tying them to labor or other obligations of the recipient. In this case, the effective price the buyer has to pay differs from the cash price measured in the survey. The instrument of interlinkage is also used to sell to persons with cash liquidity constraints. Such contracts of interlinkage and the complications arising from the assessments of actual prices in such situations have been described by Bardhan (1980) and Porath (1980).

Second, in the more "commercialized" part of the parallel market a risk element keeps prices down: The fertilizer market in the past has been characterized by official market interventions favoring the consumers. Such interventions often come suddenly in the middle of the trading season; for example, fertilizer is sold at dumping prices (as happened in 1986), or credit conditions change and constraints are relieved (as in 1985). Such experiences encourage consumers to adopt a "wait and see" attitude. The uncertainty about such interventions makes consumers reluctant to buy early in the season at a high price.

Traders with fertilizer in stock at the beginning of the season can only lose by these interventions, unless they carry their stocks over to the next year, which would entail high capital costs and uncertainty. Since these traders receive much of their supply from illegal channels— often far below current official prices—they still make a profit charging at or slightly below official prices. Traders' interest in selling early and consumers' interest in buying late lead to supply and demand imbalances during the season. Thus, partial markets at certain times within the season may well be in equilibrium. This is not the case, however, in retrospective view of the seasonal market and its average price and demand.

The groundnut market was also temporarily in disarray in the 1987–88 procurement season, but for very different reasons than the input market. After reaching the purchase ceiling set by the government, official Gambian procurement was interrupted for a while because of fiscal constraints. Thus, farmers temporarily had only the option of the parallel market across the border. This "pushed" into the parallel market farmers who otherwise—because of transactions costs, risk, and so on—would have marketed on the official channel in The Gambia. This situation—different from the fertilizer market case—cannot be interpreted as a basic market-clearance problem, since the parallel market obviously absorbed the excess supply. The temporary breakdown of the official channel induced additional costs that apparently—as shown in the next section—had unequal distributional effects. This is because the temporarily closed official channels are normally used by the poorer farmers to a greater extent than by more prosperous farmers.

In 1987 one obvious constraint on the parallel fertilizer market's ability to equate demand and supply efficiently was limited local supply, since private traders failed to participate in interregional fertilizer trading. Partial market liberalization has resulted in inefficiencies and a lack of private sector interest in fertilizer marketing for various reasons.

First, unstable pricing and market policies in the past and subsidies to the official marketing channel have increased uncertainties about the development of the market in the future. Second, continued interventions in the groundnut market spill over on the "liberalized" fertilizer market: Fertilizer trading requires substantial investments in transport, storage, and distribution networks. The same network could be used for marketing outputs *if* the groundnut market were simultaneously liberalized. Fertilizer trading costs would then be drastically reduced because of economies of scale. Given the importance of credit for input purchases, legal groundnut marketing would also facilitate private traders' recovery of loans, thereby limiting loan defaults and encouraging private loans. Third, opportunity costs of working capital for traders in The Gambia are high, and investments in reexport (smuggling to Senegal) or local retailing of other consumer goods may promise higher returns.

In a case described by Bevan, Collier, and Gunning (1989), the risk for traders involved in advertising their goods and finding out more about customers' reservation prices kept parallel markets from clearing. Traders' risk is also a driving factor in the Gambian fertilizer market: The erratic and unpredictable nature of government interventions in the fertilizer market itself and in other linked markets (groundnuts and credit) increases risks for private agents acting on the parallel market, which in the end leads to limited supplies on the parallel market and to prices below clearing prices.

In a similar way, the uncertainties about interventions and risk on the groundnut market—combined with the short trading period—prevented the prompt establishment of more effective parallel market institutions that could have considerably reduced the costs of parallel marketing. Thus, a lack of appropriate institutions—in the form of private traders—reduces the ability of the parallel market to effectively compensate consumers and producers for state market interventions.

The degree of market uncertainty makes the Gambian groundnut and fertilizer markets different from the Senegalese cereal market described by Morris and Newman (1989), with its active trading by intermediaries. The Senegalese cereal market provides ample local demand, basically throughout the year, especially since traders can provide cereals to consumers below official prices (as reported by Morris and Newman 1989). This reduces the marketing risk for intermediate cereal traders in Senegal. In The Gambia, on the other hand, high risks on the seasonal and intervention-prone groundnut and fertilizer markets keep the participation of intermediaries low.

Parallel market participation and equity effects. As hypothesized earlier, different categories of farmers face different costs and risk functions in participating on the parallel groundnut and fertilizer markets. Who, in the end, sold on the parallel market, and who could not make use of parallel market rents? A clear picture emerges for the groundnut market when sample households are arranged by income classes: Households in the poorest quartile participate in the parallel market to a much smaller extent (17 percent) than households in the richest quartile (71 percent) (Table 3.2). The story is not so clear-cut in the fertilizer market, although in this case also the richest households are more involved in the parallel market than are other households.

In the following regression analysis, we assess factors that determine the share of groundnuts that individual farmers sell on the parallel

TABLE 3.2   Participation in Parallel Markets, by Income Groups, 1987–88

		Income Quartile (%)			
	Share of total (%)	Lowest	Lower medium	Upper medium	Highest
Groundnuts					
Official	47	83	81	58	29
Parallel	53	17	19	42	71
Fertilizer					
Official	67	70	72	70	60
Parallel					
Own household members	8	4	5	8	7
Friends, relatives	15	16	9	10	17
Local traders	10	7	9	8	12

SOURCE: Joint surveys by the International Food Policy Research Institute (IFPRI) and the Planning, Programming, and Monitoring Unit of the Ministry of Agriculture, The Gambia (PPMU), 1987–88.

market (see Table 3.3). The results show that villagers close to the border sell a much larger share of their groundnuts on the parallel Senegalese market (64 percent more than in the nonborder villages). Their transaction costs are lower because of lower transportation costs. Another reason is that relatives in Senegalese villages are helpful in getting information about Senegalese market conditions and risks and may directly improve market access in this closely knit society. Farmers who received credit from the Gambian cooperative sell 11 percent more on the official market. This underlines the importance of maintaining a close business relationship with the cooperative. Many of these are farmers who actually split their sales on official and parallel markets.

The advantage of early selling is crucial for migrant farmers. These people often leave the area for their home villages after the sale of their crop. They will avoid the risk of losing their main source of annual income—the groundnut money—in an illegal transaction. The same applies to those farmers who had low cereal yields and urgently need money for food purchases. They cannot afford to embark on the more risky and time-consuming border trade. Thus, cash constraints and imperfect credit markets raise the supply to the official market. On the other hand, women farmers trade more in the parallel markets; women, especially from the Wolof community, are very active in village and intervillage food and commodity trading.

TABLE 3.3   Determinants of Groundnut Share Sold on the Parallel Market
(dependent variable = PARALLSH[a])

Independent variable	Parameter	
GNSOLDKG[b]	+1.174E–05	(0.70)
BORDER[c]	+0.635	(20.35)
FEMALE[d]	+0.064	(1.97)
MIGRANTW[e]	–0.175	(–3.66)
COOPCRED[f]	–0.109	(–2.43)
(Constant)	0.224	
R^2	0.409	
Degrees of freedom	712	
F-value	100.060	

NOTE: Numbers in parentheses represent t-statistic.
a. Share of groundnuts sold on the parallel market by individual farmer.
b. Total groundnuts sold, in kilograms.
c. Dummy = 1, for villages close to the border.
d. Male = 0; female = 1.
e. Dummy = 1, if groundnut seller is a migrant worker.
f. Dummy = 1, if farmer received any credit from the Gambian cooperative during the same cropping season.
SOURCE: Author.

When we correct for these factors, the analysis also shows that a farmer's volume of groundnut output does not play a significant role in participation on the parallel markets. This result suggests that there are no diseconomies of scale; marginal costs for marketing on the illegal market do not rise with volume.

When we trace the development of fertilizer use in upland crops from 1984 to 1987 (see Table 3.4), we find that, while overall fertilizer use

TABLE 3.4   Fertilizer Use in 1984, 1985, and 1987 for Identical Households in All Upland Crops, by Income Group

| | Consumption (kg) | Share by income quartiles (%) | | | |
		Lowest	Lower medium	Upper medium	Highest
1984	52,600	17	20	24	39
1985	21,835	15	20	24	41
1987	24,014	10	15	32	43

SOURCE: IFPRI-PPMU surveys, 1985–86, 1987–88.

went down by more than 50 percent during that period, the share of low-income groups in total fertilizer consumption fell continuously. In 1987 the two bottom-income groups still consumed 37 percent of all fertilizer, but for 1987 this figure fell to only 25 percent.

Much of this decline in the relative access of the poor to fertilizer is a consequence of limitations in access to credit. Fertilizer cash purchases are lowest in the poorest income groups: 44 percent for the poorest quartile versus 57 percent for the highest. For loans, however, farmers depend significantly on the official marketing system: While on average 41 percent of all fertilizer was sold on credit, the credit share varies from 60 percent for sales by the cooperative and 17 percent by families and friends to a mere 1.5 percent by local traders.

A variety of factors limits the supply of agricultural credit on local markets: Covariate production risks in agriculture (for details, see Binswanger and Rosenzweig 1986), problems related to charging interest in a Muslim society, and high opportunity costs for the alternative use of capital are among the most important.

Since poorer farmers need credit more than rich ones to buy fertilizer, the government's restrictive credit policy, introduced in 1986, had a higher impact on the poor. Even though the policy itself limited official credit access similarly for all income groups—because loan defaults did not differ much across groups—the upper income groups were better able to redirect their demand to the parallel market and to pay cash for fertilizer.

As a result, in the case of fertilizer, the negative equity effects of differential access to the parallel fertilizer market are mainly a result of liquidity constraints and restrictions on the credit and capital markets.

Conclusions

In The Gambia, as in Africa generally, with widespread state intervention (often of an erratically changing nature), limited market information and high transaction costs because of a lack of infrastructure, and complex public versus private sector interaction, parallel markets are the norm rather than the exception. This chapter explains three basic issues in the context of the complex reality of parallel market structures.

First, official and parallel markets coexist because of both price and nonprice factors. Even when price differences between official and parallel markets are large, the supply to the official market can be high because information costs, risk in the parallel market, liquidity considerations, and other transactions costs limit supplies to the parallel market. The Gambian groundnut market is a case in point.

Second, specific circumstances may, even in the context of prevailing parallel market structures, prevent efficient market clearing. Personalized markets—quite relevant for local trading in this African setting—on the one hand, and traders' risks in an environment of unpredictable official market operations, on the other, can be underlying causes of these indications of inefficient market clearance. The Gambian fertilizer market gives us an example of such a situation.

Third, parallel market structures have an impact on income distribution, which depends on proximity to trading points, endowment of market participants, liquidity of the participants, and—in an agricultural system in which production and marketing are influenced by gender differences in the division of labor and access to resources—also on gender. The location of farms close to the border becomes an advantage where exploitation of changing cross-border price differentials may be a continuous feature. The Gambia-Senegal border trading is in that sense not atypical in the African context. Finally, the poorest households clearly participate much less in parallel markets than do upper income groups.

The evolution of parallel market structures and their underlying imbalances suggests that long-term efficiency losses are the result of sequences of short-term disruptions—induced by instabilities in the official channels. This picture emerges especially for the fertilizer market. On the other hand, parallel markets can function as a savior for farmers, providing a fallback position or even enhanced incentives in an environment of unstable official procurement policies. This was the case with the Gambian groundnut market.

The policy mix of half-hearted market liberalization, with rapid dismantling of existing public marketing channels and changing strategies toward export orientation, has led to frequent supply and demand imbalances. Here parallel markets can only partly compensate for government interventions and are certainly second best compared with a more market-oriented policy. Most noteworthy in this regard is the spiral of declining fertilizer use in many African countries such as The Gambia. A detailed look at the development of the fertilizer market suggests that the causes of this decline are more often policy failures than market failures.

Chapter 4   Jean-Paul Azam

Cross-Border Trade between Niger and Nigeria, 1980–1987: The Parallel Market for the Naira

Niger belongs to the CFA franc zone, whereas Nigeria has an inconvertible currency, the naira; but this fact does not prevent these two countries from having a very active trade across their common border. Niger has rather artificial boundaries, which were determined at the beginning of this century after long bargaining between France and the United Kingdom. These boundaries divide the land of the Hausa people between Niger and Nigeria without deeply affecting their cultural and ethnic unity. Nigeria is by far the largest country in West Africa, with an estimated population of around 100 million people. This is more than the total number of people living in the countries belonging to the two CFA franc monetary unions—Union Monétaire Ouest-Africaine (UMOA) in West Africa and Banque des Etats de l'Afrique Centrale (BEAC) in Central Africa.

Many opportunities for trading exist in the area, despite the inconvertibility of the naira. The cities of Maradi and Zinder in Niger have prospered, mainly thanks to the cross-border trade with Nigeria (see Arnoult 1983, 1986; Grégoire 1986). These opportunities have been enhanced by various events in Nigeria's history that have prevented

47

normal trade between northern Nigeria and the world market. The civil war in the late 1960s was one of these events, resulting in the Kano area of Nigeria being linked to international trade only through Niger. Nigeria's restrictive commercial policies later became a major incentive for trade across this border. Imports of cigarettes, for example, have been banned in Nigeria, so that enormous profits have been made by traders in Niger smuggling Benson and Hedges cigarettes into Nigeria. It is said that the profits made in this transit trade (by exactly fourteen big traders!) have been at times as important as the profits made out of uranium exports (the main official export of Niger). This information is of course impossible to verify.

Hence, parallel trade has flourished across the Niger-Nigeria border, with legal exports on one side of the border becoming sometimes illegal imports on the other side. In addition to transit trade, much parallel trade involves agricultural products—for example, cowpeas produced in Niger and exported to Nigeria, or groundnuts crossing the border in one direction or the other, depending on the changing prices paid by the two national marketing agencies, which generally reflect different rates of tax or subsidy. When a drought threatens in Niger, exports of cattle may increase, being either sold in anticipation of depressed prices resulting from the drought, or being simply displaced by the herdsmen toward the more rainy south (see, for example, Frelastre 1986). Trade in the other direction involves some manufactured goods such as fertilizers, which are heavily subsidized in Nigeria, or Peugeot cars, which are assembled in Nigeria and are much cheaper than those imported from France. One reason for this cost difference is that parts for assembling the cars are imported and paid for at the official exchange rate, and hence are implicitly subsidized because of the overvaluation of the naira (see, for example, Azam and Besley 1989). There is as well some transit via Nigeria, such as batteries made in China, which cost one-twentieth the price of batteries produced in Niger by a protected firm. Many other goods cross this border because of different regulations and tax rates. Johnson (1987) has especially emphasized this cause of parallel trade. But comparative advantage still plays a part, and seems, for example, to explain the exports of cowpeas by Niger to Nigeria.

Because the naira is inconvertible, all this illegal or semilegal trade in goods involves the exchange of nairas and CFA francs on the parallel market. From the point of view of the traders in Niger, the main impact of the inconvertibility of the naira is that it cannot be bought from or sold to the central bank (the Banque Centrale des Etats de l'Afrique de l'Ouest, or BCEAO) or the other banks or businesses in the formal sector. The BCEAO deals in naira only at the official exchange rate and only in a restricted number of cases. The recent attempt made by Nigeria to liberalize its exchange regime by adopting a flexible exchange rate determined by auction (see Quirk et al. 1987; Pinto 1988) has not changed this fact. The business of the "exchange brokers" in Niger is not repressed, and one can meet them sitting in the shade beside the BCEAO buildings in Maradi or Zinder (see Grégoire 1986). Therefore, no central banks intervene on the parallel market for the naira, and the balance between demand and supply must be achieved by adjustment of the flexible exchange rate.

This chapter discusses some consequences of the working of the parallel market for the naira for the economy of Niger. It further provides an indicator of the balance of cross-border trade between Niger and Nigeria for the period 1980–1987. This indicator is based on a simple analysis of the market for the naira, using both theoretical insight and institutional knowledge. This new approach is based on the observation of various flows of banknotes purchased by central banks of the CFA franc zone.

The theoretical analysis (presented in the next section) uses a simplified model that assumes that the naira market clears at the regional level, and that it is unified by arbitrage. The indicator of the trade balance of unofficial transactions between Niger and Nigeria is provided in the third section, which exploits institutional data about the two monetary unions of West Africa and Central Africa. The section "Determinants of the Cross-Border Trade Balance" offers an explanation for the determination of this indicator and presents, as a by-product, an econometric equation showing how the consumer price index (CPI) in Niger is affected by this cross-border trade. A final section contains some concluding comments.

Equilibrium on the Market for the Naira

We analyze in this section a simple model of the naira market, assuming that it clears at the regional level by exchange rate adjustment and that it is unified by arbitrage. This analysis may seem oversimplified to some readers, but it helps explicate the meaning of the flow of banknotes issued in the BEAC monetary union, which are bought by the BCEAO in Niger.

The simplified model. It is reasonable to assume that the market for the naira is unified by arbitrage. All the available anecdotal evidence suggests that "exchange brokers" in this market are able to seize any opportunities for making profits (see, for example, Grégoire 1986). Arbitrage can be performed between neighboring places along the borders or may involve connections between more distant points. A nice anecdote illustrates the degree of sophistication of these brokers. In the early 1980s, the government of Nigeria decided to withdraw the banknotes of a given denomination from circulation and to replace them by newly printed ones. The new notes, which had been printed in England, were supposed to be issued in Lagos first. For some reason, however, these newly printed notes were available on the northern border several hours before their release in Lagos. Perhaps some containers of banknotes disappeared en route when the airplane stopped in Kano.

This assumption of arbitrage is confirmed by direct observation of the series of the parallel market exchange rate in Zinder, Niger, and Lomé, Togo. We computed the premium on the Lomé market using eighty-six monthly data points collected by the BCEAO between August 1980 and December 1987. The Lomé series was computed as monthly averages of weekly data.

There are a few outliers for the six months of 1984 following the closure of the border by the government of Nigeria in April. The price of the naira then dropped in Lomé, and the negative premium there reached 43.1 percent in August 1984. If we omit these outliers, we can observe a striking arbitrage performance. The mean premium is not significantly different from zero (–0.012 percent), and the standard deviation is 2.72 percent. Only seven data points show a premium higher than 5 percent positive or negative with a maximum of 7.3 percent in November 1984. The distribution seems to be slightly skewed, however, with a mode at –1 percent, and a median between 0 and –0.5 percent.

Hence, neglecting possible transitory differences between the price of the naira at various points on the borders of Nigeria, it seems safe to assume that this market is unified by arbitrage and that a unique exchange rate between the naira and the CFA franc prevails in all places.

To simplify the analysis drastically, assume that there are only two countries in the CFA franc zone, Niger and Cameroon. These two countries trade actively with a third country, which has an inconvertible currency and which represents Nigeria. This simple model will prove shortly to be fruitful, yielding some useful empirical predictions. In the real world, the naira market is more complex, because other countries like Benin and Chad have borders with Nigeria, and because the naira may be exchanged as well against other convertible currencies. We will discuss some of these complications later on. To simplify the analysis even further, we neglect the direct trade that may take place between the two countries in the CFA franc zone and focus on the trade between each of them and Nigeria.

We therefore analyze the market for the naira as a flexible price market, which determines the exchange rate of the naira in terms of CFA francs. This market comprises two submarkets, which are connected by the arbitrage operations performed by the exchange brokers. We neglect any transaction costs or transport costs, so that a unique exchange rate, expressed in CFA francs per naira, prevails in the two submarkets.

In each local submarket for the naira we assume for the time being that the (flow) supply of this currency is the counterpart of exports to Nigeria, and we denote it N^{sn} for Niger and N^{sc} for Cameroon. Similarly, N^{dn} and N^{dc} represent the demands for nairas for Niger and Cameroon, respectively, and we assume that they correspond to the value in nairas of the imports of the two franc-zone member countries. We will discuss later on the issue of the capital flows that may occur in this market. Behind the supplies and demands of nairas are, of course, demands and supplies, respectively, of CFA francs.

The first point that this simple analytical framework shows clearly is that any deficit occurring in one of the francophone countries must be offset by a surplus occurring in the other one, because the flexibility of the naira price keeps the whole market in equilibrium. In other words, Nigeria's balance of payments, in the parallel exchange market, is always in equilibrium because of the flexible exchange rate.

This point does not imply that the bilateral trades with the two CFA franc countries are balanced. In general, they are not, but their balances are equal with opposite signs. Figure 4.1 illustrates this reasoning, showing a case in which Niger runs a surplus with Nigeria, which is compensated by a deficit in trade with Cameroon. The first two panels of Figure 4.1 represent supplies of and demands for nairas on the border markets of Niger and Cameroon, respectively. The demand curves slope downward, and the supply curves slope upward, assuming that exports to the French-speaking countries from Nigeria rise as the value of the naira falls and that exports from the francophone countries to Nigeria rise when the naira is strong.

FIGURE 4.1   Naira Supply and Demand on Border Markets

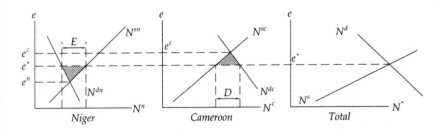

SOURCE: Author.

The third panel of Figure 4.1 shows the total demand and supply of nairas. To do this, one simply sums horizontally the local supply and demand curves:

$$N^s = N^{sn} + N^{sc} \tag{1}$$

$$N^d = N^{dn} + N^{dc} \tag{2}$$

Because of arbitrage by exchange brokers, the exchange rate cannot be different on the two local markets in equilibrium, and a unique price of the naira, denoted e^* on Figure 4.1, is determined by the equality of supply and demand on the global market for the naira. In Figure 4.1, equilibrium is achieved when Niger has a trade surplus, noted E on the diagram, compensated by a deficit of Cameroon, noted D. We have thus:

$$E = N^{sn} - N^{dn} \tag{3}$$

$$D = N^{dc} - N^{sc} \tag{4}$$

Then, as the global market is cleared by adjustment of e, one has

$$N^d = N^s \tag{5}$$

Now, using definitions (1) and (2) and the equilibrium condition (5), one simply finds

$$E = D \tag{6}$$

which proves the predicted result, namely, that in our simplified model Niger's trade surplus is exactly balanced by Cameroon's deficit as far as their cross-border trade with Nigeria is concerned.

The consequences of arbitrage. Two conclusions drawn from this analysis may shed some light on the role of arbitrage in the parallel market, from both a positive and a welfare viewpoint. First, as emphasized above, no central banks intervene on the local submarkets, so that their merger into a global market is exclusively the result of arbitrage. This is done by reducing the supply of a currency where the demand for it is low and increasing it where demand is high. Two mechanisms can be involved in this type of intervention. First, exchange brokers may hold large inventories of currencies, which they use for buffering excess demands and supplies, accumulating the currency that is in excess supply and dissipating the currency that is in excess demand. One may also view arbitrage as the purchase in one place of the currency that is in excess supply in order to sell it where it is in excess demand. In the case of Figure 4.1, in which Niger runs a surplus in its border trade with Nigeria while Cameroon runs a deficit of the same magnitude, arbitrage implies the purchase of nairas in Niger for sale in Cameroon. Obviously, the nairas bought in Niger would be paid for using the CFA francs bought in Cameroon, and vice versa. In the latter case, arbitrage would imply a physical movement of banknotes between the borders, with nairas flowing from the border of the surplus country to that of the deficit country, and CFA francs flowing in the opposite direction. (Banknotes are the dominant means of payment in this area.) Assuming that transportation costs are negligible, and that free entry prevails on this market so that pure profits are exhausted in equilibrium, we get a unified exchange market with a unique equilibrium exchange rate as a result of these money flows. In the following discussion, it will prove useful to assume that this second arbitrage mechanism is the dominant one in this area, an assumption that will enable interpretation of the observed flows of banknotes.

Before we turn to this application of the analysis, it is worth emphasizing a point on the welfare side of the problem. It is obvious that parallel exchange brokers have a useful role, enhancing efficiency by unifying the market. If the two submarkets were separated, we would observe a different price for the naira on the two border markets. In the case of Figure 4.1, the price of the naira would be low in Niger, and high in Cameroon, as shown by the intersections of the demand and supply curves in the first two panels. Hence arbitrage enhances efficiency by transferring the currencies from places where their price is low to places where it is high. The same point can be made in terms of the flows of goods instead of the flows of currencies. In the case of Figure 4.1, Niger would export less without arbitrage than when the market is unified, and Cameroon would export more. Arbitrage enables Niger to increase its exports, which are cheaper, and inhibits the flow of more expensive exports from Cameroon. Hence arbitrage enhances efficiency by unifying the price of goods imported in Nigeria.

An Indicator of the Balance of Cross-Border Trade between Niger and Nigeria

Despite its simplicity, the model presented in the previous section provides a useful empirical prediction regarding the flows of banknotes between the borders of Nigeria. In the case of Figure 4.1, a surplus of cross-border trade between Niger and Nigeria implies a flow of nairas from Niger to Cameroon, balanced by a flow of CFA francs in the opposite direction. The case of a deficit could be analyzed in the same way, mutatis mutandis. The institutions of the two monetary unions of the CFA franc zone make it possible to use this empirical prediction to provide an indicator of the balance of trade between Niger and Nigeria, apart from the transactions that use the official segments of the market for the naira.

The flow of BEAC banknotes into Niger. The francophone countries of West and Central Africa belong to two different monetary unions: the UMOA and the BEAC, with few exceptions. Although 1 CFA franc issued by the UMOA is worth 1 CFA franc issued by the BEAC, and although these two currencies can be exchanged for each other without restrictions or transaction costs, they are not perfect substitutes as a means of payment. Banknotes issued in the BEAC zone are not legal tender in the UMOA countries, and vice versa. BEAC- issued CFA francs are not generally accepted in the shops in Niger, for example.

This institutional factor enables one to observe the flow of CFA francs between countries belonging to the BEAC zone (such as Cameroon) and countries belonging to the UMOA zone (such as Niger). For example, in the case illustrated in Figure 4.1, one would expect an inflow of CFA franc banknotes from Cameroon into Niger. Exporters in Niger would then exchange their nairas into CFA francs from the BEAC zone. The only use they can make of these BEAC notes in Niger is to bring them to the BCEAO agency (the central bank of the UMOA), in order to buy BCEAO banknotes.

Hence, we can observe to some extent most of the inflow of BEAC banknotes into Niger, because these notes are purchased by the BCEAO, which maintains records of these purchases. As we know from the analysis performed earlier, this inflow is an indicator of the surplus in cross-border trade between Niger and Nigeria.

This indicator must be regarded as imprecise for several reasons, however. First, the level of the inflow of BEAC banknotes itself is not fully informative, because there is normally some flow of these notes into Niger through direct trade with Chad and Cameroon. One may expect such flows to be small, because the border between Niger and Chad is far from being as active a commercial zone as the Niger-Nigeria border, and because direct trade between Niger and Cameroon is also relatively unimportant. Nevertheless, this factor introduces an observation error, so that one should pay attention only to large changes in the inflow of BEAC notes.

Moreover, one must take into account that the market for the naira is not limited to Niger and Cameroon, and that a very active trade takes place across the border between Benin and Nigeria (see Igué 1983). A surplus in Niger could result in an inflow of notes issued in Benin or Togo, instead of Cameroon and the BEAC zone. In this case, one might expect to observe a much smaller share of the inflow of banknotes than is the case with the BEAC notes, because they are legal tender. Moreover, Niger and Benin have a common border along which trade is traditionally active, because Niger's regular trade passes through the ports of Lomé and Cotonou. Therefore, data on the purchases of banknotes from Benin and Togo by the BCEAO of Niger are much more difficult to interpret than the data on BEAC banknotes. Notice, however, that BCEAO notes issued in the different UMOA member countries can be distinguished from one another, because they are marked by a different letter (H for Niger, A for Côte d'Ivoire, and so on). Despite these distinguishing marks, traders have no reason to exchange them immediately at the local BCEAO agency.

Finally, the market for the naira involves not only the CFA franc but other convertible currencies as well. There must exist even a segment of the market where nairas are exchanged for cedis, and so on. These complications introduce additional observation errors, but we will overlook these difficulties to infer the balance of cross-border trade between Niger and Nigeria by looking mainly at the purchases of BEAC banknotes by the BCEAO in Niger. Other information will be used to refine the diagnosis.

The indicator: 1980–1987. Figure 4.2 shows the net quantities of BEAC banknotes (1982 = 100) and of UMOA banknotes from Benin and Togo purchased by the BCEAO in Niger between 1980 and 1987 (annual data). The series of BEAC notes bought in Niger has a very simple profile, with a downward drift before 1982, and after 1983, broken mainly by a sharp increase between 1982 and 1983. Hence, one can distinguish two periods: 1980–1982, with a small inflow; and 1983–1987, with a large, but decreasing, inflow.

FIGURE 4.2   Inflow of Banknotes, 1980–1987

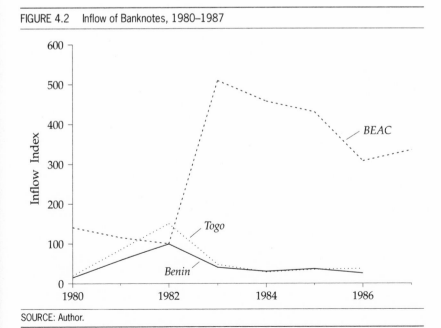

SOURCE: Author.

Figure 4.2 seems to show that the years 1983–1985 were surplus years because of the large inflow of BEAC banknotes. Similarly, it is likely that 1980 and perhaps 1981 were deficit years, despite the slight increase in the inflow of banknotes from Benin and Togo. Trade for 1982 is more difficult to characterize. The net inflow of BEAC banknotes was at its lowest point, but the net inflow of notes from Benin and Togo was at its peak. Nevertheless, we conclude that 1982 was a deficit year, using the next piece of evidence.

Figure 4.3 shows the series of "H" BCEAO banknotes (issued in Niger) bought in the BEAC zone between 1982 and 1986. The peak year for the inflow of banknotes from Niger into Central Africa was 1982, a fact that squares with the diagnosis of a deficit for Niger in that year. Figure 4.3 also helps confirm that 1984–1986 were probably years when Niger had a surplus in its cross-border trade. Although in Figure 4.3 the case of 1983 seems to be less clearcut than in Figure 4.2, it does seem to indicate an improvement in Niger's trade balance between 1982 and 1983.

The role of capital flows. Figure 4.3 also shows a series that provides some information about the role of capital flows. This helps to answer the question of whether it is legitimate to regard the balance of payments

FIGURE 4.3   Outflow of "H" Notes, 1982–1986

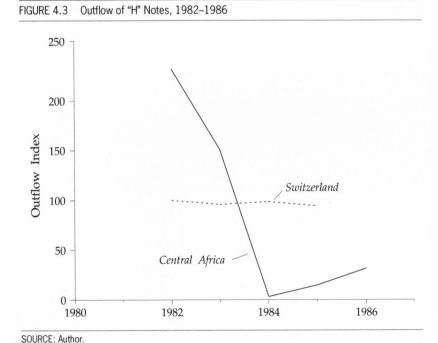

SOURCE: Author.

across the border as mainly determined by the trade balance, as we have done so far, or whether capital flows play an important part. Because of its convertibility, the CFA franc could serve as an intermediary for Nigerian investors wanting to move their funds abroad. A simple method would be to exchange one's capital from nairas into CFA francs, then to move the latter to Switzerland or elsewhere. Figure 4.3 indicates that the flow of "H" BCEAO notes bought in Switzerland remained normal when the balance of payments across the border seemed to change sign in 1982–1983.[1] Of course, this does not rule out capital flows taking place by other means, but it suggests nevertheless that the flows of banknotes described previously do mostly reflect the flow of trade, because Switzerland would be one of the main destinations for flows of capital.

One must note, however, that nonfinancial capital flows exist across this border. A standard practice among merchants in Kano is to lend a truckload of millet to an "Alhaji" in Maradi, who will later reimburse this credit by delivering a truckload of cowpeas of an equivalent value (see Grégoire 1986 and Arnoult 1983). It is reasonable to regard this operation as commercial credit, and to expect that the possible net balance of such a transaction will eventually be paid in cash, hence affecting our indicator of the balance of trade.

Despite some minor complications, then, we conclude that our indicator, imprecise as it is, probably correlates strongly with the trade balance between Niger and Nigeria. The next section analyzes the relationship of this indicator to the macroeconomy of Niger.

Determinants of the Cross-Border Trade Balance

This section presents arguments suggesting that the so-called elasticities approach to the balance of trade is not appropriate to explain the determination of our indicator. We should not conclude that the monetary approach should be applied in a simple form, however, despite some results close to the purchasing-power parity (PPP) theory. We present other explanatory factors in the following sections.

PPP with an exogenous exchange rate. The data suggest use of an analysis in which the balance of cross-border trade is determined as if Niger were a small country with an exogenous exchange rate. In particular, the consumer price index (CPI) in Niger is strongly influenced by the CPI in Nigeria, translated into CFA francs using the exchange rate in the parallel market. The following econometric exercise brings out this relationship quite clearly.

Let P denote the CPI in Niger. This is the price index for consumption by a representative African family in Niamey published by the

BCEAO. P^* denotes the rural price index in Nigeria, and e is the parallel market exchange rate in Zinder, Niger, collected by the BCEAO. We use quarterly data for 1980–1987.

The following equation shows that the price level in Nigerian markets has a significant impact on the CPI in Niamey:

$$\log P = 0.66 + 0.28 \log P(-1) + 0.36 \log P(-4) + 0.14 \log (eP^*) \quad (7)$$

$$(0.90)\ (2.00) \qquad\qquad (3.52) \qquad\qquad (3.79)$$

$$N = 28, R^2a = 0.68, FLM = 2.5$$

The figures in parentheses below the estimated coefficients are the usual t-ratios. $P(-1)$ and $P(-4)$ are the CPI in Niamey lagged 1 quarter and 4 quarters, respectively. N is the number of data points used for estimation. R^{2a} is the standard R^2 adjusted for degrees of freedom. FLM is the F-test version of the LM test of residuals autocorrelation, up to the second order. The latter is preferable to the more usual Durbin-Watson or Box-Pierce tests, which are biased toward accepting the assumption of serial independence when lagged values of the dependent variable are included in the equation. The F version of this test is preferable to its original Chi-square version in small samples, because it is adjusted for degrees of freedom. Here it must be read as an F (5, 19). Therefore, the assumption of serial independence of the residuals up to the second order is not rejected in this equation. The fit is reasonably good for quarterly price data.

Although a regression equation is no proof of causality, we can get an extra bit of information by testing whether nominal variables in Niger have an impact on the CPI in Niamey. To this end, we have added to equation (7) a variable representing the money supply, namely "currency in circulation," as published by the BCEAO and here denoted M. We have tried several current or lagged values of this variable, separately or jointly, and the coefficient closest to a significant impact is given in equation (8):

$$\log P = 1.15 + 0.28 \log P(-1) + 0.42 \log P(-4)$$

$$(1.47)\ (1.66) \qquad\qquad (3.93)$$

$$+ 0.14 \log (eP^*) - 0.14 \log M(-4) \qquad (8)$$

$$(3.83) \qquad\qquad (1.57)$$

$$N = 28, R^{2a} = 0.70, FLM = 1.33$$

Notice that M enters this equation with the wrong sign and with a nonsignificant coefficient. Moreover, the coefficient of $\log (eP^*)$ is unaffected by this variable addition, suggesting that the exchange rate e is not correlated with the money supply in Niger, and hence suggesting that Niger's economy is too small to have an important impact on the naira exchange rate on the parallel market. It therefore seems reasonable to think about the balance of cross-border trade between Niger and Nigeria as if the absolute version of PPP applied, that is, as if the CPI in Niamey were in fact determined outside Niger. This interpretation suggests that the trade balance is determined by the difference between supply and demand (absorption) in the relevant market.

Determinants of the trade balance. We did not have enough data to perform a satisfactory econometric analysis of the determinants of the trade balance of cross-border trade between Niger and Nigeria, as represented by our indicator. Hence, we shall be content with an impressionistic approach.

First, we show that the monetary approach to the balance of trade provides some explanation of the observed series, but cannot be regarded as the last word. We have quarterly data on the inflow of BEAC banknotes for 1984–1987 in Maradi and Zinder, the two main towns of the Hausa country north of the Nigerian border. This is an incomplete series because purchases made in Niamey are missing. Maradi and Zinder are, however, the major cities for cross-border trade with Nigeria, so that our data should be representative.

Using in addition the same CPI and the same monetary variable as in the previous section, we estimated the following equation for the period 1984.1–1987.4:

$$\log (I/P) = 0.59 - 0.66 \log (M/P) (-1) - 0.42\, DUM + \text{seasonals} \quad (9)$$

$$(0.63) \quad (2.01) \quad\quad\quad\quad (1.85)$$

$$N = 16,\ R^{2a} = 0.57,\ FLM = 0.15$$

I represents the net inflow of BEAC banknotes into Maradi and Zinder, and DUM is a dummy variable capturing the attempt by the government of Nigeria to close this border in April 1984. It turns out to be nearly significant, with the expected sign. The other symbols have the same meaning as in equations (1) through (8). Notice that the small number of observations (sixteen) did not allow a sophisticated dynamic analysis.

Nevertheless, this equation suggests that the real quantity of money has indeed a negative impact on this trade balance, as expected from standard macroeconomic theory. But the R^{2a} is rather low, although seasonal factors play a large part in the performance. In other words, the simple monetary approach is not enough to explain the behavior of our indicator.

We could not go any further with econometric analysis, but direct observation suggests other potential explanatory factors. First, Niger launched an economic adjustment program in 1983, which is supported by the International Monetary Fund and the World Bank. Budgetary policy has been quite drastic, with a cut in government expenditures of 20 percent in real terms in 1983. This is the year when our indicator crosses the line from deficit to surplus, and a causal link between these two events is plausible.

Another potential explanatory factor is the drought, which lasted from 1983 to 1985, peaking in 1984. Massive sales of cattle, on the export side, and massive cuts in purchasing power of the people of rural Niger, on the import side, might provide a link between the drought and the improvement in Niger's external balance. The year 1986 was very favorable for agriculture, while 1987 was quite dry, although less severely so than 1984. These two years display similar results despite the differences in weather, suggesting that one should not put much emphasis on the drought as an explanatory factor for the cross-border trade balance.

Conclusion

We have analyzed cross-border trade between Niger and Nigeria, focusing on the parallel market for the naira. This market owes its existence to two sets of restrictions on transactions. First, the naira is an inconvertible currency, so no banks or firms in the formal sector will buy it against a convertible currency, except under special circumstances. Second, Nigeria and Niger impose a series of restrictions on trade in goods across their common border; these restrictions create sufficient incentives for illegal trade. We have shown that it is safe to analyze the naira market assuming that it is unified by arbitrage. A simple theoretical model was then used to highlight the meaning of various flows of banknotes into and out of Niger. In particular, the inflow of BEAC banknotes seems to be a good indicator of the balance of trade across this border.

Some econometric evidence suggests that one should not explain the behavior of this indicator by applying the elasticities approach, because the CPI in Niger seems to be determined in Nigeria by PPP. The monetary approach seems to provide some explanation, but it is not definitive.

The interdependence thus created between the economies of Niger and Nigeria imposes some constraints on Niger's macroeconomic policy. The collapse of the naira on the parallel market, for example, has made structural adjustment difficult in Niger. The value of the naira fell by more than 75 percent between 1981 and 1987, leading to an imported deflation in Niger, with the CPI declining by more than 10 percent between 1984 and 1987. This deflation has probably affected the level of output negatively, especially so in the informal sector, which is more integrated with the Nigerian economy than is the formal sector. Because it has pursued a restrictive budgetary policy since 1983, with public expenditures cut by more than 20 percent in real terms in that year, Niger has suffered a depression, making adjustment more painful than analysts had anticipated.

David Bevan
Paul Collier
Jan Willem Gunning

Chapter 5

The Persistence of Shortages
in Rural Black Markets

In many developing countries, governments attempt to control the prices
of consumer goods. Shortages ensue, however, if they are successful in
holding all consumer prices below market-clearing levels. Such controls
can lead to a fall in agricultural production because peasants will not
bother to earn cash income that they cannot spend. They will therefore
react to shortages of consumer goods by reducing their marketed output.
This can have severe macroeconomic consequences. First, if the marketed output is an export, the resulting decline in foreign exchange earnings may reduce the availability of consumer goods in rural areas,
thereby intensifying the decline in agricultural output. Second, the supply response to changes in the price of crops is likely to be perverse: since
expenditure is constrained, peasants have no incentive to increase their
incomes so that a higher price is offset by a lower volume of sales. The
economic declines in Tanzania, Mozambique, and Madagascar have
been attributed to these processes (see Azam and Faucher 1987; Azam et
al. 1989; and Bevan et al. 1987a, 1987b, 1989a, 1990).

Price controls are often evaded, however, and transactions on black
markets coexist with transactions at lower official prices. It is often argued that rural shortages cannot persist in such circumstances, because

any excess demand at the official price will be eliminated by the black market. We will show that this argument neglects an essential characteristic of black markets, namely, their illegality. Because detection carries penalties, the ways in which the trader can disseminate information are restricted. Hence, illegality not only raises trading costs, it changes the way in which the trader seeks out potential customers. We will present evidence that peasants face shortages even in the presence of black markets, and then set out a theory explaining this phenomenon. In the final section we draw out the policy implications of the analysis.

Evidence of Rural Shortages in Tanzania

Our evidence of rural shortages comes from Tanzania. The Tanzanian Price Commission set the prices of some 2,000 consumer goods at levels that during the 1980s became increasingly lower than market-clearing levels. Even though these price controls applied nationwide, the shortages that they induced were more acute in rural than in urban areas (a phenomenon that is probably a common consequence of price controls). In Tanzania there were two reasons for this: the authorities found it easier to suppress black markets in rural areas, and disproportionately few supplies of goods reached rural areas. Sharpley (1983, 40) concurs on both points:

> The relative inefficiency of public transport has cut down on the flow of consumer items to rural areas, and some of these goods do not reach the villages since it is easier to sell on the parallel market in towns which are more accessible *and less closely controlled*. Even when villages do get their allocations these are often hopelessly small in relation to demand. (Italics added)

Our first evidence relates to the distribution of official supplies between rural and urban areas. Table 5.1 shows that as the national availability of a particular consumer good (radios) declined, supplies were systematically diverted to satisfy demand in Dar es Salaam and its environs. In response to a 65 percent fall in national supply of radios, the share allocated to Dar es Salaam doubled.

Further, much of the supply that was allocated to rural areas by the Board of Internal Trade was diverted onto black markets. As Sharpley notes, many of these diverted supplies were probably sold in urban areas. Table 5.2 provides evidence for the diversion of soap supplies from their dispatch from the factory gate to their arrival in the village. Three stages in soap distribution are identified: from factory to regional headquarters; from regional headquarters to district headquarters; and from district headquarters to villages. At each stage the quantity dis-

TABLE 5.1   Deliveries of Matsushita Radios by the Board of Internal Trade, 1977 and 1982

	1977	1982
Dar es Salaam and environs	37,290	22,579
All other regions	134,098	36,465
Total	171,388	59,044
SOURCE: Bevan et al. (1987b).		

TABLE 5.2   Penetration of Goods (Soap) from Factory Gate to Village Shops (percentage)

	Factory	Region		District		
Region	Distrib-uted to region	Received	Distrib-uted to district	Received	Distrib-uted to village	Received in village shops
Arusha	100.0	95.0	81.0	70.0	45.0	39.0
Mara	100.0	98.0	71.0	53.0	47.0	23.0
Mbeya	100.0	98.0	73.0	72.0	29.0	20.0
Morogoro	100.0	65.0	60.0	57.0	35.0	30.0
Mwanza	100.0	87.0	78.0	66.0	26.0	20.0
Tanga	100.0	60.0	53.0	48.0	39.0	21.0
Average	100.0	83.3	69.3	61.0	36.8	25.5
Diverted from offi-cial channels	16.7		8.3		11.3	36.3
SOURCE: Tanzanian Industrial Studies and Consulting Organisation (1985).						

patched substantially exceeds the quantity reported as being received. In total, these discrepancies amount to 36 percent of supply, and it must be supposed that these diverted supplies were sold on the black market. This black market soap may have been sold in either urban or rural areas. An indication of where it was sold is the stage at which it was diverted. Soap misappropriated during distribution from the district headquarters to the village is probably unlikely to have found its way back to the cities; soap misappropriated during distribution from the factory to the regional capital or between there and the district head-quarters is unlikely to have found its way to the villages. On this basis, only 30 percent of black market supplies of soap reached villages. Yet over 80 percent of the population of Tanzania lives in rural areas.

So far we have provided evidence that few supplies of consumer goods reached rural areas either by official channels or through the black market. These severely restricted supplies imply either very high prices or shortages. We now use survey data to show that shortages were in fact acute. Cooksey et al. (1987) asked peasants whether it was possible to buy seven basic consumer goods on either official or black markets. As Table 5.3 shows, the vast majority of households responded that these goods were not usually available.

This implies that the black market did not eliminate shortages. However, it does not distinguish between the intensity of shortages on black and official markets. Our final evidence explores this distinction. In Table 5.4 we show data on rural availability on both official and black markets for twenty-one basic goods. When households reported that in the past year they had sometimes wanted to buy one of these commodities but that it was not available, we report this as an access failure. For virtually all commodities the percentage of households for which we find access failures was above 50 percent and, more importantly, this is the case for both official and black markets.

Taken together, this evidence demonstrates that shortages of consumer goods were both pervasive and severe in rural Tanzania, and that there was no sign of their being eliminated by the operation of black markets. Although the evidence we have presented comes from Tanzania, it is clear that much the same has been true in a number of other African countries. We now turn to an explanation of this phenomenon.

A Theory of Nonclearing Black Markets

The conventional theory of black markets either ignores their illegality or introduces it only as an additional cost per transaction equal to the risk of detection times the penalty. Illegality not only raises costs, however, but also rules out normal ways of disseminating information. For example, advertising is clearly out of the question. The trader must instead approach potential customers individually and make an offer to sell. Illegality forces the trader to economize on his approaches, because each approach involves a risk. Although the risk of detection is obviously associated with the number of approaches, it is also associated with other aspects of trading such as the duration of bargaining and whether the trader comes to know his clients. To simplify, however, we abstract from these other aspects and concentrate on the first. To economize on approaches the trader needs to increase the chance that his offer will be accepted, which he can do by pitching his asking price low.

Consider the case in which a market—legal or illegal—is served by a single trader. We assume that the trader knows what price the market will bear. Formally, in economics this is referred to as the trader knowing the frequency distribution of the reservation prices of his potential customers, a reservation price being the highest price that a customer is willing to pay. The trader does not have complete information, however. In particular, he does not know the reservation price of each customer;

TABLE 5.3   Availability of Consumer Goods in Villages, 1986 (percentage)

	Available		
Good	Always	Sometimes or rarely	Never
Clothing	3	44	53
Sugar	0	68	32
Soap	5	68	27
Cooking oil	10	55	35
Kerosene	3	67	30
Salt	33	54	13
Matches	16	67	17
Average	10	60	30

SOURCE: Cooksey et al. (1987, table 1).

TABLE 5.4   Availability of Goods in the Four Regions, 1983 (percentage)

Good	Access failure in official market	Access failure in black market
Maize flour (kg)	52.4	47.9
Rice (kg)	75.2	72.4
Paraffin (bottle)	92.3	87.3
Cooking oil (bottle)	80.9	88.4
Soap (bar)	93.3	81.9
Sugar (kg)	93.5	96.1
Salt (cup)	78.4	74.1
Matches (box)	76.7	71.9
Cigarettes (packet)	61.1	80.9
Roofing sheet (number)	69.0	90.4
Bicycles (number)	60.3	82.9
Bicycle tubes (number)	57.7	98.0
Batteries (number)	77.3	88.2
Hoes/jembe (number)	61.8	63.5
Panga (number)	43.1	58.3
Rakes (number)	41.6	67.5
Axes (number)	48.1	62.4
Bags (number)	46.4	61.6
School uniforms	70.0	70.5
Khanga/vitenge (number)	91.7	90.9
Radios (number)	61.5	88.4

SOURCE: Bevan, Collier, and Gunning (1989a).

his knowledge is anonymous rather than personal. As long as the trader can advertise, this lack of personalized information does not matter.

The trader has access to goods at the official price, but his access is limited. If the market were legal the trader would act as a monopolist, and he would advertise his offer to sell at the profit-maximizing price. He would thereby inform the entire market, including the peasants willing to pay his asking price; they would then come forward to accept the offer.

When the market is illegal, the trader must take the risk of detection into account. This depends on his own behavior and on the enforcement process operated by the government. Faced with the task of enforcing its own price controls and hence suppressing a black market, a government will typically prosecute sellers, who are few, rather than buyers, who are many. A possible enforcement process involves agents provocateurs who inform on the trader when he attempts to sell to them. Under this process, it should be noted, risk is not attached to a transaction, but to the dissemination of the information that one is willing to sell.

The trader must now assume that each offer of sale he makes carries an equal risk of triggering detection. Instead of advertising, the trader makes individual approaches, the disadvantage of a higher cost per offer being offset by a lower expected number of offers per sale and therefore a lower risk. The trader chooses the price at which he offers goods for sale, and the customer he approaches either rejects this price or indicates how much he wants to buy. No other exchange of information takes place. There are now three possible outcomes: the trader is caught (and no further hawking can take place), his offer is refused, or the customer buys some quantity at the quoted price. Except in the first case, the trader can make new approaches until he has sold the maximum quantity to which he has access. Hence the process stops either when the trader is arrested or when the maximum amount has been sold at the quoted price.

In this situation, the black market does not clear. There will, in general, be unsatisfied demand—the demand of the customers who were not approached and who had reservation prices above the trader's asking price. This is so because unsatisfied customers cannot communicate their willingness to pay more to the trader. These potential customers may or may not be aware of his activities, but in either case the trader can accept bids only for a short period (because of the risk involved), so that some but not all customers with reservation prices above the asking price are aware of the opportunity to put in a bid. Excess demand cannot be eliminated through arbitrage, since potential arbitrageurs would face the same decision problem as the trader and would therefore not find it profitable to sell at a higher price. Hence the black market does not clear because its illegality induces the trader to make few approaches.

We now relax the assumption of a single trader, but for the present retain the assumption that the aggregate supply of goods to traders is exogenously constrained to a maximum of Q. If the quantity were to be auctioned, the market would clear at p_Q. We retain the assumption that the number of traders, n, is exogenous. Consider first the case of trade in a legal market. When there is only a single trader who does not discriminate (because his optimal selling technology takes the anonymous form of advertising), he may or may not choose to take up the whole allocation Q. His only cost is the cost of acquisition, and hence his marginal cost is the official price $\bar{p}$. If marginal revenue exceeds this at sales of Q, the trader takes up his full allocation, the constraint is binding, and he charges the auction price, p_Q. If marginal revenue does not exceed $\bar{p}$ at sales of Q, the trader will purchase a lower quantity of the good, Q^*, at which marginal revenue equals $\bar{p}$, and he will sell at a price above p_Q. In the former case, an increase in n, given Q, has no effect on the price, which remains at the auction price for the quantity Q, say p_Q. In the latter case, an increase in n will eventually lead to a fall in price to p_Q, but the detailed path of this fall will depend on the nature of the oligopolistic behavior of traders, and on the possibility of collusion. Eventually, as n becomes sufficiently large, the market converges to competitive behavior. In the illegal case, however, the increase in the number of traders does not tend to make the market competitive. This is because, as before, there can be no arbitrage.

In the case of a single trader in an illegal market, for a given distribution of reservation prices, $\bar{p}$, Q, risk of detection, and penalty, the asking price of the trader is uniquely determined. Suppose that $\bar{p}$ is very low so that the number of potential customers is large relative to Q. At the official price almost all agents would be buyers, but supplies on the black market are limited. If the penalty and the risk of detection are sufficiently large, the expected number of offers will be small relative to the number of potential customers. The trader will be constrained by Q, but even so, he will approach only a small proportion of potential customers. Suppose now that there are two traders, each with maximum supplies of $Q/2$, but both with the same $\bar{p}$, risk of detection, and penalty as the single trader. In this case, each trader can virtually ignore the possibility that potential customers to whom he makes offers may already have made a purchase from the other trader. In the extreme case, in which he completely ignores this possibility, each trader faces an unaltered distribution of reservation prices. The decision problem for each of the two traders is then identical to that of the single trader except for the tightening of the constraint upon Q, which has no effect on the chosen asking price. Now relax the assumption that the distribution of reservation prices is treated as unaltered. The presence in the market of other traders will then alter the distribution facing any single trader, because other traders may already have reached some potential customers. Thus, introducing more than one trader tends to lower the price.

To summarize the results so far, in the case of a single trader the price is lower if the market is illegal. If there are multiple traders, the price may fall or remain constant whether the market is legal or illegal. This may suggest that in the case of multiple traders the price might be lower or higher with illegality. However, in the legal case, competition can lower the price only to that which would be charged by the single trader were he to sell Q rather than restrict sales. But the single illegal trader selling Q sells at a lower price than this. Hence, the black market price must still be below the price that would prevail were the same quantity sold through a legal market.

Once we allow for differences between traders, we must expect price dispersion. In a legal market arbitrage eliminates price dispersion, but arbitrage is not possible in an illegal market. A uniform price will only prevail in the case of multiple traders if there is symmetry. That is, different traders will set the same price only if they face the same decision problem.

So far, n and Q have been treated as exogenous. As a result, there has been no tendency for rents to be eliminated. This may not, indeed, be inaccurate as a depiction of black markets, at least in their early phases. Some agents, generally the politically well placed, may have privileged access to particular quantities, there may be no market process for competition to dislodge them, and there are limits to the quantities that can be acquired.

Consider, however, the case in which the supplies available at $\bar{p}$ are endogenous. There are two possibilities: Supplies are endogenous for each trader individually, denoted by q, but Q remains exogenous; or Q is itself endogenous. Let Y be the quantity of the good which reaches consumers at the official price, and let Z be the exogenous total supply: that is, $Q + Y = Z$. First, take the case in which Q is endogenous. We first introduce a supply function for illegal traders: we assume that the supply of goods to an individual trader is larger the more he spends on bribes.

With free entry to black marketeering, the number of traders rises, and so does Q. As this process continues, the scale of the black market rises relative to the official market, and our assumption that black marketeers can ignore each other's activities ceases to be sustainable. In principle, it would be possible for the entire available quantity of the good to be traded through the black market, at a price below the market-clearing price. However, the rising number of black marketeers will drive down the traders' asking price, and there may be an equilibrium characterized by coexistence of legal and illegal markets in which the wholesalers have appropriated the black market rents.

In either case, the bribes, which endogenize supply to the black market, raise the question of competition for the role of wholesaler, the new recipient of the rents. This is because bribery is a form of rent seeking that transfers rather than dissipates the rents. It is, of course, possible to envisage processes of rent seeking that do the opposite: if traders fight each other outside the warehouse, the wholesaler does not benefit, but the traders incur costs. However, under any rent-transferring process the real black marketeer is the agent to whom the rents accrue. Other agents in the distribution chain through to the consumer can be eliminated should the black marketeer choose to run the distribution system himself, or they become in effect his employees. Since processes that fully dissipate rents seem somewhat contrived in the case of a black market, the rents accruing to black marketeers are likely to persist.

To conclude, black markets are liable to be characterized by persistent rents reflecting the political power of those who gain access to supplies. The existence of a black market does not result in a market-clearing solution. Many consumers remain rationed, since they cannot bid themselves into supplies. Even with many black marketeers, such a market is not competitive, because price dispersion reflects the absence of arbitrage.

So far we have made four assumptions about the trader's information set: He is perfectly informed about the distribution of prices; he has no knowledge about individual reservation prices; he has no knowledge about who is trustworthy (since he cannot identify the agents he deals with); and his information set is static (the trader does not learn). We now drop the last three assumptions.

Consider a market that is segmented in terms of information. The market consists of villages. A village has two characteristics. First, it has a social network. A trader may use this network to increase his information, but in doing so he obtains information only about the agents in the village. Since investment in information involves fixed costs, it is efficient for a trader to specialize, acquiring information about a single village. Second, traders are not aware of each other, except within a village; for example, a trader will know if a new entrant has appeared. Villages are identical in size and in the distribution of reservation prices. However, information involving the identity of agents (what an individual is willing to pay, or who may be an agent provocateur) is local. This information is obviously valuable. It can be acquired at a cost (but, we assume, without risk). We consider the implications of such investment for the black market in the case in which each village is served by a single trader and also the effects on entry barriers.

It is important to distinguish between two types of information: information about the trustworthiness of agents, and information about their individual reservation prices. We consider each type in turn.

Suppose it is possible to acquire information about who is to be trusted, but not about reservation prices. The trader can now partition the market into two sets of customers: A, those who can be trusted (that is, approaches are riskless for this set), and B. The more he invests in information the larger is set A. (In the limit set B consists only of agents provocateurs. Risk is then eliminated: The trader will only approach agents belonging to set A.) Since the trader has no information about individual reservation prices, he must assume that their distribution is the same for the two sets. For a given (incomplete) level of information the trader now must choose between two alternatives:

1. Approaching a member of set B. In this case his decision problem is the same as that considered above, except that the risk is now higher (since it previously applied to the whole population and now applies only to set B).

2. Dealing only with members of set A. In this case an individual approach is riskless. However, advertising is not a feasible strategy, as it is in the legal case. It is not possible to restrict advertising to members of set A. Illegality therefore continues to play a role; the trader will still have to make individual approaches.

The expected value (of making a single approach) is always higher for the second alternative. But at least initially, when little information has been acquired so that set A is very small, the A market will be cleared before Q units have been sold. It then may be optimal to sell the remaining units to customers in set B. Hence there are three possible outcomes:

1. The trader uses his access fully, selling Q in the A market: A risky market exists but no transactions in it take place.

2. The trader uses his access fully, selling Q_A in the A market and $[Q - Q_A]$ in the B market.

3. The trader sells less than Q in the A market and nothing in the B market.

The third possibility indicates that a corner solution is no longer necessary (as it was previously). The reason is that the partitioning of the market on the basis of trustworthiness introduces a discontinuity: the risk increases discontinuously when one moves from set A to set B.

As more information is acquired, set A expands at the expense of set B. In the limit everyone who is trustworthy belongs to set A, but this can be optimal only in extreme cases. In general, it will be optimal to stop investment in information before set A has reached its maximum size.

A new entrant would have to make the same investment in information before he could operate as profitably as the original trader. Without investment in information he runs a higher risk of detection per sale and would set a lower price. Whether or not he invests, a new entrant reduces the profitability of the original trader. Entry may not be profitable given the presence of a well-informed incumbent.

Now consider investment in the second type of information, about individual reservation prices. Again we may think of the trader who has invested in information as being able to partition the market into two sets. Set A now consists of customers whose reservation prices (for various quantities) the trader knows, and set B consists of all others. The trader can now act as a perfectly discriminating monopolist in market A. The one difference is that each sale to a different individual (irrespective of the quantity of the transaction) involves a risk of detection. Once the decision to ask a particular price has been taken, only one approach is necessary because the trader knows who is willing to buy at that price. As in the previous case, market A will be served first, not because the risks differ but because in market A the trader can discriminate between individuals. Only if it is profitable to enter market B will the previous considerations of curtailing approaches by a low offer price apply.

The entry characteristics of this model are similar to the previous case for market B. But in market A competition now works quite differently. A customer who knows that there is a new entrant may choose to reject an offer by the original trader at his previous reservation price, since he perceives some chance of a lower offer. The new entrant thus erodes the informational investment of the original trader: The previous reservation prices are no longer valid.

Clearly, in practice both types of information will be acquired by traders. Two conclusions follow from the villages story. First, competition is hampered by the fixed costs associated with investment in information. Second, even if this barrier is overcome by a new entrant, the market will not clear. Market B will not clear for the same reason as before. Whether market A clears depends on which type of information has been acquired. If the information is about reservation prices, the market will be cleared, because, as we have just seen, the trader will practice perfect price discrimination. If the information is about trustworthiness, market A will not clear. (In fact, it is possible that there is unsatisfied demand while at the same time the trader has not fully used his privileged access.) Except in the unlikely case that information acquisition is taken to its logical extreme, the market as a whole (sets A and B combined) will not clear. Hence our conclusion that a black market will not eliminate excess demand is unaffected by the introduction of investment in information and competition from new entrants.

Policy Implications

Shortages of consumer goods can have quite serious consequences in any economy, but particularly so in peasant economies because of the ability of the peasant household to withdraw partially or wholly into subsistence activity. That is, peasants have an atypically high capacity to respond to shortages of goods by withdrawing their labor from the production of marketed output. This is in sharp contrast to the situation in the centrally planned economies of Eastern Europe, where shortages of consumer goods have also been prevalent but the capacity of the labor force to withdraw from market activity is much more circumscribed. In many African economies the peasants are the principal earners of foreign exchange, on which the supply of consumer goods is heavily dependent. In consequence, a shortage of consumer goods may set off a cumulative decline in which the availability of consumer goods and the output marketed by peasants chase each other downward. Such has been the experience of several African countries.

Further, in an environment of shortages, despite the decline in crop sales it is not appropriate to raise crop prices without simultaneously increasing the availability of consumer goods. Hence it is not possible to overcome the problem by crop pricing reforms. Rather, the policy that controls the prices of consumer goods must itself be altered.

In this chapter we have presented evidence to show that black markets do not necessarily eliminate shortages and have provided a theoretical rationale to explain why we should not expect them to do so. The crucial reason for this failure lies in the intrinsic illegality of black market activity. The key determinant of whether price controls give rise to shortages is therefore not whether transactions that evade the controls take place, but whether these transactions are penalized. To eliminate shortages it is not necessary to abandon the practice of fixing a low official price provided that parallel market operations are not penalized. This is a policy choice: to eliminate shortages either price controls must be abandoned altogether, or they can be maintained (for example, for distributional reasons) while transactions at other prices are freely tolerated. The latter option is not only feasible in principle but has been adopted in practice. In Ghana, for example, low official prices did not give rise to shortages because transactions on parallel markets were not penalized in practice.

To conclude, it is possible for governments to favor target groups by fixing low prices without that strategy having extensive repercussions. The economy can be seriously damaged, however, if in addition to such policies markets are suppressed.

Chapter 6   David L. Lindauer

Government Pay and Employment Policy: A Parallel Market in Labor

The reasons for the existence of wage levels, especially for unskilled labor, which are too "high" are mainly institutional. In some countries, and at certain periods, trade unions play some role. But the major factor is government policy, and the ideological or political ideas which guide it. Government is a major influence on wage levels and structure in most LDCs, by its wage decisions with respect to government employees, and in its role as regulator through minimum wage policies, wage boards, Industrial Courts, etc.

—Elliot Berg

African wages are high compared with those of Asia. . . . Higher African wages reflect both government wage policy, which in many countries sets industrial wages above the level they would otherwise be, and better opportunities for agricultural employment.

—World Bank

Price adjustments and market deregulation can go only part of the way to correct the urban bias [in African economies]. Personnel policies in the public sector must also change: they influence urban earnings

because the government and public enterprises are the largest employers in most countries. Public sector hiring and wage policies have in-
flated wages and in many cases left them out of line with productivity
and labor costs in other developing countries.

—World Bank

The quoted passages above span sixteen years and repeat a basic theme
about impediments to economic development in the modern sector of
developing economies, especially in Africa. Government wage and employment practices are cited as a major source of wage distortion in the
formal economy, although little direct analysis, either theoretical or empirical, has been advanced to establish the mechanisms by which these
government policies contribute to economic inefficiencies.[1]

This chapter develops a simple, two-sector framework to analyze the
consequences of alternative government pay and employment policies.
Public sector compensation that either matches, exceeds, or falls below
the reservation wages of workers at the margin is considered. The use of
government wage fixing in the private wage-paying sector is illustrated
as well. The paper draws special attention to how government pay and
employment policies may spill over to influence private sector wages. In
addition, the influence of pay policies on government performance itself
is evaluated. The scenarios advanced here are applicable to many economies but seem especially relevant to Africa, where public employment is
often substantial relative to the rest of the wage-paying economy.[2]

An Analytical Framework

The literature on public sector pay determination in both developed and
developing nations has generally taken one of three directions: institutional descriptions of government wage-setting practices; econometric
estimation of public/private sector wage differences; or theoretical
models based on some type of politically responsive pay mechanism.[3]
This literature draws special attention to payment of "prevailing
wages" and, hence, to pay parity between private and public employers. The absence of such parity, especially when the wage advantage
rests with the government worker, forms the basis for much criticism of
government pay policies. Although pay comparisons are important in
evaluating government wage and employment decisions, most previous studies have lacked an explicit treatment of the interaction between
public and private sectors in determining wages and employment.

A two-sector treatment of public and private employers is developed as follows.[4] In order to evaluate pay differentials that are sector

specific, ceteris paribus, only homogenous categories of labor skills and job attributes are considered. Thus, we are abstracting from any compensating differentials between sectors caused by nonpecuniary job characteristics (for example, different degrees of job security) or productivity differences between different groups of workers. The private sector is assumed to be fully competitive with labor demand determined by standard value of marginal product criteria. To simplify the analysis, the public sector revenues required to compensate public workers are considered exogenous to private labor demand. In addition, intra–public sector distinctions, for example, between civil servants and public enterprise employees, are not addressed.

Private labor demand, D_L^v, is depicted on the left side of Figure 6.1 where wages, w, are a measure of total compensation, and N is a measure of hours worked. An objective function for government can be posited to derive a government labor demand relationship. Previous work has used vote maximization or the utility-maximizing behavior of bureaucrats as an objective function.[5] Given the difficulty of adequately portraying government behavior in an easily formulated objective function, this chapter employs a more limited technique. Instead of relying on a maximization procedure to generate a locus of optimum combinations of wages and employment, it analyzes the fiscal constraints facing government.

For any level of government employment, N^b, alternative budget constraints are depicted as iso-elastic expenditure functions with

FIGURE 6.1   Government Pay Matching Worker Reservation Wages

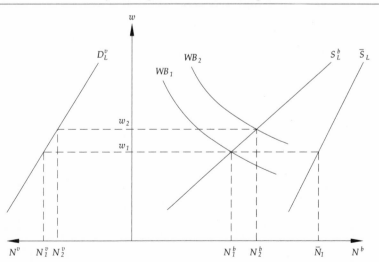

SOURCE: Author.

elasticities of employment to wages equal to one, that is, $N^b = \overline{WB}_i/w^b$, for $i = 1, \ldots, n$ levels of wage bill (WB) expenditures. Although not a labor demand schedule, the wage bill serves as a convenient analytical device for incorporating the fiscal limits on government hiring.

On the supply side of the labor market, $\overline{S}_L$ is available for employment in the entire wage sector. Since the private sector hires according to D_L^p, public sector labor supply, S_L^b, can be defined as $S_L^b = \overline{S}_L - D_L^p$. This does not mean that the government is a residual employer of labor, but it does suggest that the government faces some competition for workers from the private sector.[6] If in making pay and employment decisions the government ignores this constraint, some response, including vacancies or rapid job turnover, can be anticipated.

The two-sector analysis of Figure 6.1 is completed by recognizing that private sector labor supply depends on the public sector's employment decision; therefore, no unique labor supply schedule facing the private sector can be depicted. Instead, it is assumed that, given government employment levels, the private sector acts to maximize profits. Figure 6.1 shows that at every wage the horizontal distance between private labor demand, D_L^p, and the supply curve facing government, S_L^b, exhausts the total supply of available labor, $\overline{S}_L$.[7] With this two-sector framework in place, it is possible to evaluate some of the effects of alternative government wage policies on wage and employment outcomes within the formal economy.

Government Pay Matching Reservation Wages

Although decisions about government production, employment, and worker compensation are likely to be determined simultaneously, as a starting point for discussion consider a government's having elected to employ a given number of workers, N_1^b. This number might be the minimum required to produce a specific level of public output, or it might reflect a combination of government output and employment objectives. In Figure 6.1, if a government pay policy is chosen that minimizes costs—that is, one that matches the reservation wages of the final N_1^b worker, a wage of w_1 and a wage bill of WB_1 are required to secure the desired labor. Competition among remaining workers drives the private wage to w_1, with private employment settling at $N_1^p = (\overline{N}_1 - N_1^b)$, $\overline{N}_1$ equaling total labor supplied at w_1. Pay parity between sectors is achieved and no wage labor remains openly unemployed.

Note that this depiction of government pay and employment policy does not produce one of the high wage outcomes frequently alleged. There is no excess supply of labor confronting wage-paying employers.

There are, however, other possible interpretations of high wages. Consider an expansion of government output goals, now requiring N_2^b workers. Owing to the positively sloped labor supply curve facing government, the additional workers can be secured only at a wage of at least w_2. Such a wage increase draws labor into the public sector, and equilibrium is restored when pay parity between sectors is again achieved, but now at a higher wage, w_2, and lower private employment $N_2^p < N_1^p$. The expansion of public employment has led to a rise in private sector wages.

The comparative static result, requiring a transfer of labor from private to public employment, may be made more realistic in a dynamic context. A government sector growing more rapidly than the private sector, and facing a supply of labor that is both less than perfectly elastic and growing more slowly than total labor demand, will yield an analogous result. The relevance of this scenario to African countries may be found in the early post-Independence era when rapidly expanding government employment may have been partly responsible for raising private sector wages for specific labor skills. The notion of government "wage leadership" expressed in the literature may, in fact, date to the experiences of this period.

If the case depicted in Figure 6.1 or its more dynamic analogue portrays the mechanism behind the high government wages the authors quoted at the beginning of this chapter have been concerned with, attention should be drawn, not to government pay policy per se, but to government employment determination. Pay policy is at issue only insofar as it is a requirement for achieving desired government employment. Further, given government employment objectives, these high wages are the result of market forces, not restrictive wage-setting institutions imposed on the private sector. These cases of government employment "crowding out" private wage employment lead to a misallocation of labor resources if, at the margin, the private sector could make more productive use of scarce labor resources than could the government.

Government Pay Exceeding Reservation Wages

Given a level of desired public employment, government pay policy may or may not be cost minimizing, as in the previous example. Governments may choose levels of pay that either exceed or fall below the supply price of marginal workers, especially for specific groups or occupations.[8] Continuing to abstract from efficiency wage and productivity explanations for cross-employer wage differentials, we note that pay premiums for government workers may reflect political considerations. Because government officials determine their own salaries, for example, political or even personal objectives, as opposed to social ones, may account for benefits surpassing those received by comparable workers in the private sector.

In addition to acting on motives that are political or even corrupt, governments may select pay levels in an attempt to set reference wages elsewhere in the economy. The setting of compensation for unskilled government employees can reflect a government's concern to pay wages sufficient to meet some notion of basic needs. Such wages may exceed the prevailing urban wage floor, resulting in public pay greater than reservation wages. These policies may be outright attempts to redistribute income, or they may be intended as implicit guidelines for wage setting elsewhere in the modern sector.[9]

Whatever the motivation, government pay policies that mandate public sector pay premiums can generate a number of outcomes throughout the formal economy. In looking at Figure 6.2, assume that the government still wishes to hire N_1^b workers but now compensates them in excess of reservation wage requirements, $w_3 > w_1$. The situation becomes one, common to the analysis of parallel markets, in which administered pricing creates a disequilibrium in an "official" market. Where private wages and employment settle will depend on worker response to alternative pay offers.

FIGURE 6.2   Government Pay Exceeding Worker Reservation Wages

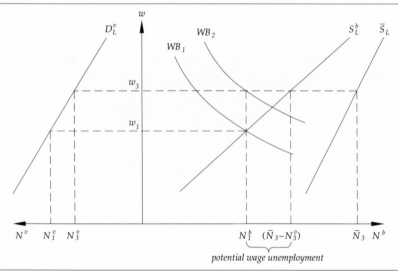

SOURCE: Author.

At a wage of w_3, $\overline{N}_3$ workers seek wage employment. Only N_3^v private sector jobs would be forthcoming at w_3, however, leaving $(\overline{N}_3 - (N_3^v + N_1^b))$ workers openly unemployed. Private employers, according to D_L^v, would be willing to hire more labor at a lower wage; however, workers might choose to remain unemployed while queuing for scarce high wage jobs. Such worker behavior is consistent with Harris-Todaro notions of urban unemployment and, generally, with job search models of unemployment (Harris and Todaro 1970). Under such behavior, pay parity between public and private sectors will be realized at w_3 while open unemployment characterizes the wage sector. A clear misallocation of labor resources results and can be traced to the combination of government pay policy and labor's response to prevailing pay offers.

Some workers, however, may not choose to behave in the manner just described. For some, the costs of voluntary unemployment are likely to be high, and they may choose to queue for government jobs while maintaining private sector employment. Such workers will bid private wages down to w_1. In this situation the private sector's wage and employment outcome has been unaffected by the government's generous pay offer. Private employment continues to settle at N_1^v at a wage of w_1, but, unlike the previous case, government pay exceeds private pay.

The economic costs of a government pay policy that grants economic rents to workers who obtain public jobs can now be evaluated. They include the forgone output of the workers who choose to queue for government jobs. Also included is the opportunity cost of government revenues in excess of those required to bring forth the desired number of workers. (In Figure 6.2, this excess equals $(WB_2 - WB_1)$.)

Some of the economic cost of government pay premiums may result from rent-seeking behavior. Workers, for example, may respond to existing pay differences by bidding for scarce well-paying government jobs. Since no market mechanism exists to erode government's pay premium and, hence, the excess supply of labor facing the government, there will be a return for individual workers to devote resources to securing government positions. At the same time, government will have to adopt rationing devices to allocate the desirable public jobs. As in other contexts, the inefficiencies stemming from rent-seeking behavior may be nontrivial.

In evaluating the case of high government pay illustrated in Figure 6.2 it is important to emphasize that, given government employment targets, there need not be spillover effects that distort private sector wage determination. Private wages need not follow any government wage "demonstration effect."

Government Pay Falling below Reservation Wages

Government pay offers that fall below reservation wages are illustrated in Figure 6.3. This case is likely to be more than hypothetical. Fiscal constraints throughout much of Africa have resulted in precipitously falling real earnings for public sector workers. In extreme cases, including Ghana, Sudan, and Uganda, starting salaries for government officials fell in real terms by as much as 70 percent to 90 percent from the mid-1970s to the early 1980s. For some labor skills, given government employment targets, the resulting wage offers probably fell below prevailing reservation wages.

In Figure 6.3, as in the previous cases, the government desires to employ N_1^b workers, but in this instance government offers public employees a wage w_4 lower than w_1, the reservation wage for the N_1^b worker. Such a policy can be explained in the following way. A sudden decrease in resources available to the government translates into lower wage bill allocations, $WB_3 < WB_1$. Prior to the decrease, N_1^b workers received w_1. Institutional rigidities may make it difficult to terminate public workers. If the government feels constrained to both maintain existing workers, N_1^b, and to expend fewer resources, WB_3, a wage offer of w_4 will be forthcoming.

Clearly there exists an inconsistency between the government's pay policy and its employment policy. As portrayed in Figure 6.3, a wage

FIGURE 6.3   Government Pay Falling below Worker Reservation Wages

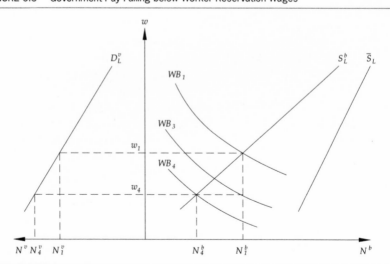

SOURCE: Author.

offer of w_4 would attract only N_4^b, not N_1^b, hours into the public sector. This situation of excess demand for government employees at a low wage, w_4, can be understood by considering how the inconsistency between government pay and employment policies is resolved.

One possibility is that competition between public and private employers leads to the *formal* withdrawal of $(N_1^b - N_4^b)$ hours of labor in the public sector. In this situation, which is nothing other than the "crowding-out" model working in reverse, initially higher private wages at w_1 would attract public sector workers. Private wages would be bid down, and private employment would expand until pay parity is achieved at a wage w_4, with the level of private employment indicated by N_4^v. Formal withdrawal implies that the government expends only WB_4, the cost-minimizing wage bill for N_4^b workers. Public savings of $(WB_3 - WB_4)$ are realized even though public employment and output targets are not. Government expenditures on labor are consistent with the hours of labor supplied.

Alternatively, government may expend WB_3 but realize less than N_1^b hours of labor time. This outcome requires further assumptions about the management of government workers, systems of worker compensation, and the nature of the labor supply facing government. If government continues to extend N_1^b job offers, even though pay has fallen to w_4, workers may maintain government employment but adjust their total hours worked (or effort supplied) commensurate with the now lower wage offer. Total labor supplied can fall as low as N_4^b. Some of the lost hours will be shifted to the private sector through increased absenteeism on government jobs or outright on-the-job moonlighting—that is, performing nongovernment work during normal government working hours. Other lost hours will be spent on non-wage sector activities. Although the real compensation per hour for government workers falls and so do hours worked, hours of paid compensation to all salaried employees in the government sector remain the same. The government, in essence, pays for more hours than it receives.

The model of on-the-job quantity adjustments not only appears as plausible but, based on impressionistic evidence, seems endemic to the Sub-Saharan region.[10] Although public sectors are often constrained by job tenure provisions and a general laxity in work rules, the problem of managing the public sector's work force is probably exacerbated when pay declines precipitously.

Lastly, the low government pay case portrays a situation in which government pay and employment policies appear costly in terms of their impact on the use of public resources and, hence, on public sector performance. In addition, this case helps to illustrate why pay parity between public and private sectors, by itself, is insufficient as an indicator of the appropriateness of a given government pay policy.

Wage Fixing in the Private Sector

In addition to pay and employment practices, government wage policy includes actions directed at influencing the private wage sector. Such actions can include minimum wage laws, dispute resolution by industrial courts, and statutes concerning firing practices, severance pay, and mandatory pensions. These policies have in common public imposition of specific wage costs on private firms. This section analyzes the impact of such policies on wages and employment in the private and public sectors.

Government wage policies directed at private employers can create a wage floor above that which would prevail under competitive conditions. Such wage fixing can be pursued independently of a government's own pay and employment practices. The general case of policies that fix private wages is depicted on the left side of Figure 6.4. A set of government wage policies constrains private wages to be no less than w_3.[11] If private employers maximize profits they will employ N_3^v workers.

Government use of such wage-fixing policies conditions the constraints facing government pay and employment policy decisions. The

FIGURE 6.4   Wage Fixing in the Private Sector

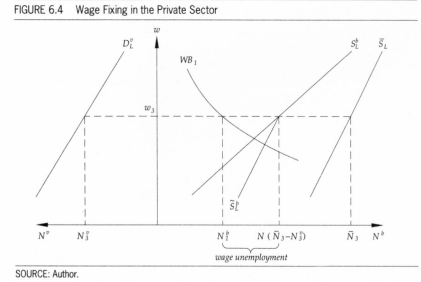

supply of labor to the public sector can no longer be portrayed as the total supply of labor less private labor demand at each wage. For wages greater than the fixed wage, w_3, S_L^p still holds. Below w_3, however, the supply of labor facing the government is the difference, $\tilde{S}_L^p$, between the total supply of labor at each wage minus the actual number of workers employed in the private sector, that is, $\tilde{S}_L^p = \bar{S}_L - N_{wi}^v$, where w_i is the private sector wage mandated by government policy. (In Figure 6.4, $w_i = w_3$.) Faced with this supply constraint, the government can choose among a number of pay and employment alternatives.

One possibility is for the government to encourage high wages throughout the modern sector. An example of such a policy is de facto wage parity between public and private wage sectors at a wage such as w_3 in Figure 6.4. This wage indicates both wage fixing in the private sector and pay above reservation wages in the public sector. If institutional arrangements constrain private wage setting to match government pay as in Figure 6.4, the absence of a public-private wage differential will not be a sign of an efficient pay policy. Maintaining the assumption of government employment objectives, N_1^p, such pay parity policies leave workers numbering $(\bar{N}_3 - (N_1^p + N_3^v))$ openly unemployed, or drive at least some of them to a lower paying uncovered or informal sector.[12]

The inefficiencies generated in Figure 6.4's model of public and private sector wage determination include a misallocation of total labor resources and lower public and private sector output. The private sector in particular can be expected to exhibit a capital-intensive bias in production. Problems associated with non-cost-minimizing government pay noted in a previous case will again appear, including those inefficiencies stemming from rent-seeking behavior by workers with regard to any modern sector job.

The economic costs of government wage policies appear especially severe in the scenario just described. Not only may government workers be overcompensated, but wage fixing in the nongovernment sector creates additional welfare losses. In fact, this scenario is probably the one that comes closest to the conventional wisdom, suggested by the quotations that introduce this chapter, on the distortionary influence of government wage policies in developing countries. When such a situation prevails, policy action may be required on two fronts. First, government pay should be brought into line with existing reservation wages. Second, the mechanisms that encourage or require private enterprises to follow government wages must be identified. If such mechanisms are the result of direct policy actions, or if they are amenable to government intervention, suitable initiatives could be pursued to break this tendency.

It is important to emphasize that the case of government pay in excess of reservation wages coupled with wage fixing in the private sector is a special case. More generally, wage fixing can occur concurrently with any choice of government pay and employment policy. Another alternative is for the government to offer more government employment in response to the open wage unemployment generated by the high wages imposed on the private sector. The government might choose to expend more on the wage bill, that is, provide more jobs at a wage less than or equal to w_3. This policy might even generate pay advantages accruing to private over public workers. Wage fixing in the private wage sector will continue to impose welfare costs on the economy. An added resource cost will be incurred if the government pursues employment creation in response to open wage unemployment.

Evaluating Government Wage and Employment Policies

This chapter illustrates some of the alternative ways in which a parallel market in labor can operate. If government actions, including public sector pay and employment policies and wage regulations governing private firms, create conditions of excess labor supply or demand, then the parallel market in labor will act to restore equilibrium.

Two areas of concern arise with regard to the impact of government wage and employment policies on labor market outcomes. First, what spill-over effects on wages and employment in the private sector can be anticipated from alternative government wage and employment policies? Second, what impact might such policies have on the performance of the public sector itself?

Concern over spill-over effects appears to be well established in the literature. The belief that government pay practices are responsible for high wages in the formal economy reflects this concern. This chapter suggests, however, that government pay policies by themselves need not have any direct effect on wage determination in a fully competitive private sector. In contrast, government employment certainly will affect private sector wages, since the level of public employment conditions the supply of labor facing the private sector. The spill-over effects of government pay policies are, therefore, important insofar as they permit government employment objectives to be realized. This is a different interpretation of the influence of government pay levels on private sector wages from one that views government compensation as setting wage standards that private employers feel constrained to follow.

By pursuing employment goals, government may increase the potential for public sector "crowding-out" of private sector employment. This may be especially apparent for specific labor skills. While such "crowding-out" may generate higher wages for these labor skills, attention, again, should not be focused on government pay policy alone but on government employment objectives. At issue is the appropriate division between public versus private employment.

High private wages may also be mistakenly attributed to government pay policy when governments actively engage in wage fixing in the private sector. Distortions in private wages may result from policies designed to fix private wages regardless of the level of government pay. Although governments may pay in excess of the reservation wages of marginal workers, any tendency for private wages to follow government pay should be traced to labor supply behavior or to the institutions that constrain private wage determination.

In addition to policy-induced wage and employment distortions in the private wage sector, attention needs to be focused on government pay and employment practices and their effect on the efficient use of public resources. Growing concern over public sector performance in Africa, coupled with empirical evidence of rapidly declining real pay for government workers, sharp compression in government pay structures, and continued growth in public employment even during periods of macroeconomic contraction, highlights the significance of these issues. The position that governments employ too many workers and overpay them all is not a useful starting point. The government's own wage and employment structures also require further examination. Pay adjustments may contribute to improvements in government performance in cases in which pay either exceeds or falls below the reservation wages of marginal workers.

The intra–public sector problems of government pay and employment determination do not appear to have received as much attention in the literature as have potential spill-over effects. Nevertheless, the economic losses associated with the misallocation of public wage expenditures may be of considerable quantitative significance. Informed policy advice on government pay and employment practices clearly requires a better understanding of the internal wage and employment structures in the public sector and of the relationship between pay and performance in government service. These should be fruitful areas for further research.

Chapter 7   Trien T. Nguyen

The Parallel Labor Market for Illegal Aliens

The passage of the Immigration Reform and Control Act of 1986 marked
the first time in the history of the United States that employers have
been forbidden by law knowingly to hire illegal aliens to work. Although exact counts are not available, it has been suggested that there
are usually between 6 million and 12 million illegal aliens in the United
States originating from nearby developing countries, with Mexico being
the largest single source by a wide margin. Immigration issues have
been the subject of lively, sometimes hotly contested, public debates
over the last decade (see, for example, Johnson and Williams 1981;
Morris and Mayio 1980, 1982; Greenwood and McDowell 1986; Pozo
1986; Ethier 1986a, 1986b; Rivera-Batiz 1986; Djajic 1987; Chiswick 1982,
1986, 1988a, 1988b; Reynolds and McCleery 1988).

The observation that motivates this paper is the notion of illegal
aliens as a parallel (or black) market that coexists with the regular market
of legal labor in the presence of both price controls on legal labor (minimum wage legislation) and quantity controls on illegal aliens (immigration laws). We develop an analytical general equilibrium structure that
links the market for legal labor under minimum wages with the parallel
market for illegal aliens, in which penalties are borne by employers. If
employers do not differentiate illegal aliens from legal workers, they face

the choice of either hiring legal workers at minimum wages or hiring illegal aliens at subminimum free-market wages but risking prosecution and fines. In equilibrium, risk-neutral employers hire illegal aliens up to the point at which minimum wages paid to legal workers equal expected costs of hiring illegal aliens. Unlike previous work on price controls and black markets, for example, Nguyen and Whalley (1989), the focus here is on factor markets rather than on goods markets.

Because of the clandestine nature of illegal immigration, our formulation also involves the migration decisions of foreign workers at the border and tax evasions by illegal aliens inside the United States. At the border, foreign workers face the choice of either remaining in their home countries or crossing the border illegally at the risk of apprehension by the border patrol. In equilibrium, risk-neutral foreign workers cross the border illegally up to the point at which their home country wages equal the expected wages of illegal aliens inside the United States. This is similar to the Harris and Todaro (1970) model of rural-urban migration, except that here the United States plays the role of urban areas while nearby developing countries play the role of rural areas. In addition, the uncertainty faced by migrant workers arises from active enforcement of immigration laws in the United States rather than from the usual characteristics of labor markets in developing countries such as urban unemployment and wage rigidity.

On the demand side, illegal aliens, once inside the United States, are indistinguishable from other workers. Income tax evasions are, however, unavoidable because of the illegal nature of their underground employment and immigration status. In the usual kinds of income tax evasion and underground economic activity (see, for example, Tanzi 1982; Alm 1985; Gaertner and Wenig 1985; Alessandrini and Dallago 1987; and Kesselman 1989), the government can collect back taxes from convicted tax evaders. In the case of illegal aliens, however, the government is not only unable to collect back taxes from those apprehended but also incurs the additional resource costs of deportation.

A feature of our approach is that the unemployment rate of legal workers, the number of illegal aliens as well as their free-market wages, and government enforcement costs are endogenously determined as a result of optimal decisions by employers, legal workers, illegal aliens, and government enforcement agencies. Consequently, given the differential wage structure between the United States and nearby developing countries, any policy attempting to reduce the number of illegal aliens in the United States must require joint efforts by all parties concerned.

The plan of the chapter is as follows. First I develop a general equilibrium structure in the presence of both minimum wages and illegal aliens, and show how such an equilibrium can be computed in a fashion similar to traditional general equilibrium tax models. The next section provides numerical calculations using U.S. data and presents simulation results of immigration policies to control the population of illegal aliens. A final section concludes the chapter with remarks on potential extensions and applications of the approach.

The Theoretical Framework

To explore the linkage between markets for legal labor and illegal aliens, I consider a multisector model of an economy with government market controls on both types of labor: price controls on legal labor by minimum wage legislation and quantity controls on illegal aliens by immigration laws.

Specifically, I assume binding minimum wages $\bar{w} > 0$ above market-clearing levels for all legal labor employed in the economy.[1] The analysis concentrates on unskilled labor, since most, if not all, illegal aliens work in unskilled jobs.[2] It is also assumed that employers do not differentiate legal workers (that is, citizens and legal aliens) from illegal aliens. If minimum wage legislation makes it too costly for employers to hire legal workers, they turn to illegal aliens as an alternative source of labor.

By law and because of lobbying pressures of labor special interest groups, the government is required to control illegal aliens through two enforcement agencies: the U.S. Border Patrol to prevent foreigners from illegally entering the country, and internal surveillance by the Immigration and Naturalization Service (INS) and other agencies to prevent illegal aliens already in the country from working. If illegal aliens are caught at work, they are removed from the labor market through deportation and their employers are fined. In equilibrium, risk-neutral employers, therefore, will hire illegal aliens up to the point at which minimum wages paid to legal workers equal the expected costs (including possible fines) of hiring illegal aliens. The fines collected are used to cover enforcement costs and to redistribute to legal workers as transfers.

On the demand side, illegal aliens, once inside the country, are indistinguishable from the rest of the population, since they can buy goods on free markets as anyone else. I assume that legal workers own both capital and labor endowments, and that illegal aliens own only labor endowment. Legal workers pay both sales and income taxes. Illegal aliens pay sales taxes but do not file income tax returns.

Employers. There are n sectors, indexed by $j = 1, \ldots, n$ characterized by constant returns to scale production functions

$$Y_j = F_j(K_j, E_j) \tag{1a}$$

$$E_j = L_j + A_j \tag{1b}$$

where Y_j, K_j, and E_j denote output supply, capital input, and labor input, respectively. Labor input E_j consists of legal labor L_j and illegal aliens A_j. In addition to rental price r on capital and minimum wage $\overline{w}$ on legal labor, which are paid to factor owners, employers are required to pay ad valorem factor taxes t_{Kj} on capital[3] and t_{Lj} on legal labor.[4] Since these taxes vary across sectors, employers face sector-specific gross-of-tax factor prices:

$$r_j \equiv r \, (1 + t_{Kj}) \tag{1c}$$

$$w_j \equiv \overline{w} \, (1 + t_{Lj}) \tag{1d}$$

Legal labor must be paid minimum wages (plus factor taxes) w_j, while illegal aliens are paid subminimum free-market wages w_A. There is a risk, however, that if illegal aliens are apprehended while at work, their employers will have to pay fines $\overline{f}_j$ per unit of labor by illegal aliens hired. Let π_j be the probability of apprehension and deportation of illegal aliens in sector j. If employers are risk neutral and do not differentiate illegal aliens from legal workers, then in equilibrium, the condition for coexistence of both legal workers and illegal aliens in sector j is that expected wages are the same across both types of labor, that is,

$$w_j = w_A + \overline{f}_j \pi_j \tag{2a}$$

The probability of apprehension of illegal aliens working in sector j and hence, the probability of employers being fined, is defined as

$$\pi_j \equiv \frac{A_j}{E_j} \pi_D \tag{2b}$$

where π_D is the economy-wide rate of apprehending illegal aliens enforced by the government. The ratio A_j / E_j denotes the proportion of illegal aliens hired in the firm's work force, and thus provides a proxy for the conditional probability of apprehending illegal aliens in the specific sector j, given the overall enforcement rate.

Using equations (1b) and (2b) we can evaluate the following signs of partial derivatives:

$$\frac{\partial \pi_j}{\partial A_j} = \frac{L_j}{E_j^2} \pi_D > 0 \tag{2c}$$

$$\frac{\partial \pi_j}{\partial L_j} = -\frac{A_j}{E_j^2} \pi_D < 0 \tag{2d}$$

The risk of getting caught thus depends *positively* on the number of illegal aliens hired and *negatively* on the number of legal workers hired.[5] In other words, the larger the size of illegal alien employment a specific sector has, the more attention it draws from the government, and hence *given the enforcement rate*, the higher the probability of getting caught in that specific sector.

Definition (2b) of the probability of getting caught π_j explicitly includes the enforcement rate π_D, which could realistically be well below unity. The formulation thus extends the literature on parallel markets, for example, Pitt (1981), Nguyen and Whalley (1989a), Jones and Roemer (1987), and Devarajan et al. (1989), where government enforcement is not explicitly modeled (that is, π_D is implicitly assumed to equal unity).

Given factor prices r_j, w_j, and w_A for capital, legal labor, and illegal aliens, respectively, and the equilibrium condition (2a) linking legal labor and illegal alien markets, a cost minimization yields factor demand functions per unit of output as follows:

$$k_j = \frac{K_j}{Y_j} = k_j(r_j, w_j) = k_j(r) \tag{3a}$$

$$e_j = \frac{E_j}{Y_j} = e_j(r_j, w_j) = e_j(r) \tag{3b}$$

In equilibrium, cost-covering prices are

$$p_j = r_j k_j + w_j e_j = p_j(r_j, w_j) = p_j(r) \tag{3c}$$

Equations (3a), (3b), and (3c) show that output prices p_j and factor intensities k_j, e_j are functions of sector-specific gross-of-tax factor prices r_j, w_j as in standard general equilibrium tax models of Shoven and Whalley (1984) tradition. Equations (1c) and (1d) in turn show that factor prices r_j, w_j are functions of minimum wages $\overline{w}$, market rental price r of capital, and ad valorem factor tax rates t_{Kj}, t_{Lj}. With minimum wages $\overline{w}$ being fixed by legislation and factor tax rates t_{Kj}, t_{Lj} exogenously given in the model, the market rental price r of capital is left as the only factor price to be influenced by market forces. In other words, equations (3a), (3b), and (3c) allow output prices p_j and factor intensities k_j, e_j to be expressed as functions of only one unknown, namely, the market rental price r of capital.

Legal workers. I characterize legal workers as one aggregate household holding initial factor endowments $\overline{K}$ of capital and $\overline{L}$ of labor.[6] Legal workers are subject to income taxes at ad valorem rates t_{KH} on capital income and t_{LH} on labor income, as well as sales taxes t_{Sj} ($j = 1, \ldots, n$) on goods purchased. The relevant prices for legal workers are

$$q_j \equiv p_j(1 + t_{Sj}) \tag{4a}$$

$$r_H \equiv r(1 - t_{KH}) \tag{4b}$$

$$w_H \equiv \overline{w}\,(1 - t_{LH}) \tag{4c}$$

for goods, capital, and labor, respectively.

Consumer incomes of legal workers consist of after-tax incomes from capital and labor employment plus lump sum transfers:

$$I_H \equiv r_H \overline{K} + w_H(1-u)\overline{L} + T = I_H(r, u, T) \tag{5a}$$

where u denotes the unemployment rate of legal workers as a result of minimum wage legislation, and T denotes the lump sum transfers received. Utility maximization is subject to the budget constraint

$$\sum_{j=1}^{n} q_j X_{Hj} = I_H(r, u, T) \tag{5b}$$

and yields the following consumer demand functions by legal workers:

$$X_{Hj} = X_{Hj}(q_1, \ldots, q_n, I_H) = X_{Hj}(r, u, T) \tag{5c}$$

Illegal aliens. Suppose that foreign workers from nearby developing countries make repeated attempts to cross the border illegally. If M denotes these would-be illegal aliens and π_B the rate of apprehension by the Border Patrol, then those who are caught at the border are

$$B = \pi_B \overline{M} \tag{6a}$$

and those who cross the border successfully to become illegal aliens inside the United States are

$$A = \overline{M} - B = (1 - \pi_B)\overline{M} \tag{6b}$$

The migration decisions of foreign workers are modeled along the lines suggested by Harris and Todaro (1970) in their formulation of rural-urban migration.[7] That is, they can either remain in their home countries and earn foreign wages $\hat{w}$ or cross the border illegally. If successful, they become illegal aliens inside the host country, and if they are not caught by internal surveillance, they earn the market wages for illegal aliens w_A. Therefore, risk-neutral foreign workers will illegally cross the border up to the point at which their home country wages equal the expected wages of successful illegal aliens inside the host country (less smuggling costs, which are assumed to be zero). That is,

$$\hat{w} = (1 - \pi_B)(1 - \pi_D)w_A \tag{7}$$

where $(1 - \pi_B)$ is the probability of not getting caught at the border and $(1 - \pi_D)$ the probability of not getting caught inside the country. The product $(1 - \pi_B)(1 - \pi_D)$ means that the events of being caught at the border are assumed to be statistically independent of the events of being caught inside the country.

On the demand side, illegal aliens, once inside the country, can buy goods freely just like legal workers, paying sales taxes on the goods purchased. Because of the illegal nature of their employment and immigration status, however, they neither file income tax returns nor receive government transfers. Income tax evasions by illegal aliens are thus explicitly modeled in the analysis.

Illegal aliens are characterized as one aggregate consumer having only labor income

$$I_A \equiv w_A \bar{h}(1 - \pi_D)A = I_A(w_A, A) \tag{8a}$$

where π_D is the deportation rate as in (2a), and $\bar{h}$ is a conversion factor that converts the head counts of illegal aliens into their labor services. The term $\bar{h}(1 - \pi_D)A$ thus represents the labor supply of those illegal aliens who escape deportation by the government. Utility maximization is subject to the budget constraint

$$\sum_{j=1}^{n} q_j X_{Aj} = I_A(w_A, A) \tag{8b}$$

and yields the following consumer demand functions by illegal aliens:

$$X_{Aj} = X_{Aj}(q_1, \ldots, q_n, I_A) = X_{Aj}(r, w_A, A) \tag{8c}$$

Enforcement agencies. Government enforcement plays an important role in the analysis as it directly affects the number of illegal aliens in the country. Enforcement is financed through revenues from taxes and fines, and hence, indirectly affects all other sectors of the economy. There are two levels of enforcement: border patrol to control the influx of foreign workers, and internal surveillance to apprehend and deport illegal aliens already inside the country.

These enforcement activities are explicitly modeled as productive sectors taking capital and legal labor as inputs to produce outputs as the numbers of foreign workers or illegal aliens apprehended. Formally, I characterize border patrol and internal surveillance as constant returns to scale production functions

$$B = B(K_B, L_B) \tag{9a}$$

$$D = D(K_D, L_D) \tag{9b}$$

where K_B and L_B are the capital and legal labor respectively required to apprehend B foreign workers at the border, and K_D and L_D are the capital and legal labor respectively required to apprehend and deport D illegal aliens inside the country.

The enforcement rates of these agencies (or the probabilities of getting caught for illegal aliens) are

$$\pi_B = \frac{B}{\overline{M}} \tag{9c}$$

$$\pi_D = \frac{D}{A} \tag{9d}$$

at the border and inside the country, respectively. These enforcement rates are policy objectives set by the government.

Given factor prices including factor taxes

$$r_B \equiv r \, (1 + t_{KB}) \tag{10a}$$

$$w_B \equiv \overline{w} \, (1 + t_{LB}) \tag{10b}$$

for the border patrol and

$$r_D \equiv r(1 + t_{KD}) \tag{10c}$$

$$w_D \equiv \overline{w}(1 + t_{LD}) \tag{10d}$$

for internal surveillance, cost minimization yields the following factor demand functions per unit of output:

$$k_B = \frac{K_B}{B} = k_B \, (r_B, w_B) = k_B(r) \tag{11a}$$

$$l_B = \frac{L_B}{B} = l_B(r_B, w_B) = l_B(r) \tag{11b}$$

for the border patrol and

$$k_D = \frac{K_D}{D} = k_D(r_D, w_D) = k_D(r) \tag{11c}$$

$$l_D = \frac{L_D}{D} = l_D(r_D, w_D) = l_D(r) \tag{11d}$$

for internal surveillance. In equilibrium, cost-covering prices for these enforcement activities are

$$p_B = r_B k_B + w_B l_B = p_B(r) \tag{11e}$$

$$p_D = r_D k_D + w_D l_D = p_D(r) \tag{11f}$$

General equilibrium. Given that equations (3c), (11e), and (11f) guarantee cost-covering prices for all producing sectors including enforcement agencies, equation (2a) links the wage rates of legal workers and illegal aliens, and equation (7) ensures equilibrium choices in the migration decisions of foreign workers, a general equilibrium with dual markets for legal labor and illegal aliens can be defined as the extended vector (r, u, T, w_A, A) such that the following sets of equilibrium conditions hold:

- Demand equals supplies for all goods.

$$X_{Hj} + X_{Aj} = Y_j \supset_j \qquad (12a)$$

- Demand equals supplies for all factors, namely, capital, legal workers, and illegal aliens.

$$\sum_{j=1}^{n} K_j + K_B + K_D = \overline{K} \qquad (12b)$$

$$\sum_{j=1}^{n} L_j + L_B + L_D = (1 - u)\overline{L} \qquad (12c)$$

$$\sum_{j=1}^{n} A_j = \overline{h}\,(1 - \pi_D)A \qquad (12d)$$

- Tax revenues and fines collected equal transfers redistributed to legal workers and costs of running enforcement agencies,

$$R + F = T + p_B B + p_D D \qquad (12e)$$

where R denotes the revenues collected from factor taxes on producers, income taxes on legal workers, and sales taxes on both legal workers and illegal aliens

$$R \equiv r\left(\sum_{j=1}^{n} t_{Kj}K_j + t_{KB}B + t_{KD}K_D\right) + \overline{w}\left(\sum_{j=1}^{n} t_{Lj}L_j + t_{LB}L_B t_{LD}L_D\right)$$

$$+ rt_{KH}\overline{K} + \overline{w}\,t_{LH}(1 - u)\overline{L} + \sum_{j=1}^{n} p_j t_{Sj}(X_{Hj} + X_{Aj}) \qquad (13a)$$

and F denotes expected fines

$$F \equiv \sum_{j=1}^{n} \pi_j \overline{f_j}\, A_j \qquad (13b)$$

Equations (12a–12d) are market-clearing conditions for all goods and factor markets taking into account the coexistence of both legal workers and illegal aliens, while equation (12e) ensures a balanced government budget in a fashion similar to general equilibrium tax models, for example, Shoven and Whalley (1984). By aggregating the budget constraints (5a) and (8a) of legal workers and illegal aliens, I obtain the following Walras's law:

$$
\sum_{j=1}^{n} p_j (X_{Hj} + X_{Aj} - Y_j) + r\left(\sum_{j=1}^{n} K_j + K_B + K_D - \overline{K}\right)
$$

$$
+ \overline{w}\left(\sum_{j=1}^{n} L_j + L_B + L_D - (1 - u)\overline{L}\right)
$$

$$
+ w_A\left(\sum_{j=1}^{n} A_j - \overline{h}(1 - \pi_D)A\right)
$$

$$
+ (R + F) - (T + p_B B + p_D D) = 0 \tag{14}
$$

That is, the sum of the values of market excess demands for all goods $(j = 1, \ldots, n)$ and factors (capital, legal labor, illegal aliens) plus government budget balances must *always* equal zero. Consequently, if market-clearing conditions hold for all but one last market, then that last market must also clear. In other words, one market-clearing equation in (12a–12e) can be eliminated in the general equilibrium solution of the model.

The formulation thus provides a highly interdependent general equilibrium structure in which, interestingly, the size of the labor market for both legal workers and illegal aliens can, among other things, be endogenously determined by the interactions of optimal decisions by employers, legal workers, illegal aliens, and the government.

Computational considerations. The necessary steps required to compute an equilibrium solution of interlinked markets are outlined as follows. First, using equation (7) for foreign workers' migration decisions and equation (2a) for employers' hiring decisions, we can calculate the wages for illegal aliens and the probability of getting caught in each specific sector:

$$
w_A = \frac{\hat{w}}{(1 - \pi_B)(1 - \pi_D)} \tag{15a}
$$

$$
\pi_j = \frac{w_j - w_A}{\overline{f_j}} \tag{15b}
$$

We can then determine the number of illegal aliens caught at the border, the number of illegal aliens inside the country, and the number of illegal aliens caught at work:

$$B = \pi_B \overline{M} \tag{16a}$$

$$A = \overline{M} - B \tag{16b}$$

$$D = \pi_D A \tag{16c}$$

Consumer incomes I_H and I_A and consumer demands X_{Hj} and X_{Aj} by legal workers and illegal aliens can be determined as in equations (5a), (5c), (8a), and (8c) respectively. Using the goods market-clearing equation (12a), we can determine total outputs

$$Y_j = X_{Hj}(r, u, T) + X_{Aj}(r) = Y_j(r, u, T) \tag{17}$$

and aggregate factor demands

$$K_j = k_j(r)Y_j(r, u, T) = K_j(r, u, T) \tag{18a}$$

$$E_j = e_j(r)Y_j(r, u, T) = E_j(r, u, T) \tag{18b}$$

Knowing the probabilities π_j of apprehension and aggregate labor demands E_j in each sector j, we can use equation (2b) to determine the employment of illegal aliens and legal workers in each sector:

$$A_j = \frac{\pi_j}{\pi_D}E_j \tag{19a}$$

$$L_j = E_j - A_j \tag{19b}$$

Now we can rewrite equilibrium conditions (12b), (12c), and (12e) of markets for capital and legal workers, and government budget balances as follows:

$$ZK(r, u, T) \equiv \sum_{j=1}^{n} K_j + k_B B + k_D D - \overline{K} = 0 \tag{20a}$$

$$ZL(r, u, T) \equiv \sum_{j=1}^{n} L_j + l_B B + l_D D - (1 - u)\overline{L} = 0 \tag{20b}$$

$$ZT(r, u, T) \equiv T + p_B B + p_D D - R - F = 0 \tag{20c}$$

Computing an equilibrium solution of interlinked markets can therefore be reduced to solving a system of nonlinear equations of factor excess demands and government budget imbalances in terms of three unknowns (r, u, T).[8] This equilibrium system is similar to that used in general equilibrium tax models, and hence can be solved with familiar techniques such as fixed-point algorithms or Newton-type iterative procedures; see, for example, Kimbell and Harrison (1986).

Illegal Aliens in the United States

My approach can be illustrated with some numerical calculations related to issues of illegal aliens in the United States. I concentrate on Mexican illegal aliens since they by far constitute the bulk of the illegal alien population in the United States because of favorable factors such as the geographical proximity of Mexico; the available pool of unemployed Mexicans, especially in Mexico City; and ample job opportunities for unskilled labor in border states such as California, Arizona, and Texas.

Eight sectors of the 1973 U.S. economy are considered:

- agriculture: agriculture, forestry and fisheries, food and tobacco

- textiles: textiles, apparel, and leather

- energy: mining, crude petroleum and gas, petroleum refining

- manufacturing: paper and printing; chemicals, rubber, and plastics; lumber, furniture, stone, clay, and glass; metal, machinery, instruments, and miscellaneous manufacturing; transportation equipment and ordnance; motor vehicles

- services: contract construction; transportation, communications, and utilities; trade; finance and insurance; real estate; services

- government enterprises

- border patrol

- immigration service

The first six sectors are extracted from the well-known nineteen-sector tax model—the general equilibrium model taxation analysis package, or GEMTAP—of the United States in 1973 documented in Ballard et al.

(1985). The last two sectors are added to model the endogenous enforcement feature of our approach. For simplicity, I abstract from GEMTAP features of interindustry structure, foreign trade, consumer goods, multilevel nesting, and dynamic sequencing.

On the production side, all sectors employ capital and legal labor as primary inputs, with the exception of agriculture and textiles, which also rely on illegal aliens for labor inputs. While data from GEMTAP refer to legal labor only, empirical estimates of illegal labor costs are almost nonexistent. We can therefore assume, for the central case, that agriculture and textiles employ illegal aliens as often as they do legal workers (that is, $A_j = L_j$ for $j = 1, 2$). Alternative shares for benchmark legal and illegal labor can be used in subsequent sensitivity analysis.

On the demand side, we can assume one aggregate legal consumer and one aggregate illegal alien. Illegal aliens pay the same sales tax rates as legal consumers, but do not pay income taxes. In addition, they receive neither transfer payments nor demand services from government. I use the RAS (row-and-sum) method to achieve a consistent consumer expenditure matrix.

Empirical estimates of the size of the population of illegal aliens are sketchy, although it is commonly believed that there are somewhere between 6 million and 12 million illegal aliens residing in the United States at any time. I use the conservative estimate of 6 million illegal aliens, $(A = 6)$ for the central case, with the understanding that alternative values can also be used for sensitivity analysis.

On the enforcement side, the U.S. Immigration and Naturalization Service reported about 1 million Mexican illegal aliens apprehended in each year during 1965–1978, that is, $B + D = 1$ (Johnson and Williams 1981, 89). North and Houstoun (1976, 18) further estimated that 81.3 percent of apprehensions were made by the border patrol and 18.7 percent by INS district offices. For the central case, I thus assume a ratio of 4 to 1 for border patrol apprehensions to INS district office apprehensions, which implies $B = 0.8$ and $D = 0.2$. This allows us to estimate the benchmark equilibrium number of potential illegal immigrants from Mexico as $\overline{M} = 6.8$,[9] benchmark equilibrium probabilities of apprehension $\pi_B = 0.1176$ at the border, $\pi_D = 0.0333$ inside the country, and the conversion factor $\overline{h} = 8.7559$ between head counts of illegal aliens and their labor services.

I choose physical units for goods and factors such that factor prices (capital rent and the minimum wage for legal labor) and goods prices all equal unity in the benchmark equilibrium. Empirical surveys, for example, Bailey (1985) and North and Houstoun (1976), confirm that illegal aliens are indeed paid subminimum wages. North and Houstoun (1976, 125) reported a ratio of $2.66/4.47 = 0.5951$ for the relative wages of illegal aliens and legal workers. For the central case, I assume that the

TABLE 7.1   Benchmark Data Set for the U.S. Economy in 1973 (billions of 1973 dollars)

Production costs

	Factor costs without taxes			Factor taxes and fines			
Sector	Capital costs	Legal labor costs	Illegal alien costs	Capital taxes	Labor taxes	Expected fines	Value added
1	32.5950	33.2210	19.9326	5.9860	3.0000	16.2884	111.0230
2	1.0860	17.4470	10.4682	1.5080	2.2680	9.2468	42.0240
3	12.7880	10.9670		3.1500	1.0110		27.9160
4	26.2760	172.6000		23.4880	17.7530		240.1170
5	101.4170	393.6390		61.7640	39.4080		596.2280
6	7.8110	15.1660			1.5570		24.5340
7	0.2547	0.4945			0.0508		0.8000
8	0.0634	0.1236			0.0127		0.2000
Total	182.2914	643.6582	30.4008	95.8960	65.0605	25.5352	1042.8420

Consumer expenditures

	Expenditures without taxes			Sales taxes			
Goods	Legal workers unemployed	Legal workers employed	Illegal aliens	Legal workers unemployed	Legal workers employed	Illegal aliens	Total
1	4.3147	103.5530	3.1553	0.0471	1.1312	0.0345	112.2358
2	1.6332	39.1965	1.1943	0.1104	2.6495	0.0807	44.8647
3	1.0849	26.0377	0.7934	0.0941	2.2595	0.0688	30.3385
4	9.3317	223.9611	6.8242	0.2855	6.8509	0.2088	247.4621
5	23.1713	556.1116	16.9451	1.4982	35.9568	1.0956	634.7786
6	0.9814	23.5526					24.5340
Total	40.5172	972.4124	28.9124	2.0353	48.8479	1.4884	1094.2136

Consumer incomes

Income sources	Legal worker unemployed	Legal worker employed	Illegal aliens	Total
Capital incomes	7.2917	174.9997		182.2914
Labor incomes		643.6582	30.4008	674.0590
Transfer incomes	36.3786	328.1027		364.4813
Less capital income taxes	−1.1178	−26.8275		−27.9453
Less labor income taxes		−98.6728		−98.6728
Total	42.5525	1021.2603	30.4008	1094.2136

NOTE: Blank cell = not applicable.
SOURCE: Computed from GEMTAP data.

free-market wages of illegal aliens are 60 percent of minimum wages of legal workers—that is, w_A = 0.6. Using equation (7), we then obtain Mexican wages $\hat{w}$ = 0.5118, which are consistent with the benchmark equilibrium values of the probabilities of apprehension and wages for illegal aliens in the United States.

Although GEMTAP is essentially a model with flexible prices and full employment, the present model introduces price rigidity through minimum wage legislation and the resulting unemployment of legal workers. I assume, for the central case, a 4 percent rate of unemployment of legal workers due to minimum wages (that is, u = 0.04). This means that the equilibrium level of labor employment in GEMTAP data corresponds to only 96 percent of the labor endowments of legal workers in our model. To obtain the labor endowments of legal workers in our benchmark data set, I thus have to scale up the benchmark labor employment in GEMTAP by the factor $1.0/0.96 = 1.04167$ to account for the benchmark unemployment of legal workers. As a result, endowments of legal workers are estimated at $\bar{L}$ = 670.4773, employment $(1 - u)\bar{L}$ = 643.6582, and unemployment $u\bar{L}$ = 26.8191.

The final result is a microconsistent benchmark data set (see Table 7.1) that satisfies all conditions (12a–12e) of a general equilibrium with dual markets for legal workers and illegal aliens. I use the same calibration procedure commonly used in the literature of computable general equilibrium modeling, for example, Mansur and Whalley (1984). Since I assume CES (constant elasticity of substitution) functional forms for production and utility functions, I need to specify their elasticities of substitution beforehand. For each of the production sectors, I use the average of elasticity values assumed for corresponding production sectors in GEMTAP. On the demand side, I assume Cobb-Douglas demand functions for both legal workers and illegal aliens. The parameter values calibrated by this procedure (see Table 7.2) should then replicate the benchmark data set as an equilibrium solution of the model.

After calibration, the model can be used to evaluate various counterfactual equilibrium situations. For example, columns 1 and 2 of Table 7.3 suggest that a standard general equilibrium tax model solution that did not take into account illegal aliens might produce results significantly different from our benchmark equilibrium solution. The gap in equilibrium national incomes with and without illegal aliens can be as high as $80 billion (1094.2136 – 1010.1330 = 84.0806) or 7.7 percent of benchmark national income. Benchmark national income consists of incomes of both legal workers (employed and unemployed) and illegal aliens (see Table 7.1).

Compared with my benchmark equilibrium solution, a standard tax solution without illegal aliens yields a higher unemployment rate of legal workers (4.34 percent rather than 4.0 percent) for two main

TABLE 7.2   Calibration of Model Parameters (Central Case)

| | CES production parameters | | | | Cobb-Douglas demand parameters | |
Sector	Constant term	Capital share	Labor share	Elasticity of substitution assumed	Legal consumer share parameters	Illegal alien share parameters
1	2.0884	0.2800	0.7200	0.6938	0.1025	0.1049
2	1.4424	0.0433	0.9567	0.9025	0.0410	0.0419
3	2.3312	0.5739	0.4261	0.9277	0.0277	0.0284
4	1.9758	0.1666	0.8334	0.8753	0.2260	0.2313
5	2.1954	0.2737	0.7263	1.0000	0.5797	0.5934
6	1.9982	0.3184	0.6816	1.0000	0.0231	
7	1.9982	0.3184	0.6816	1.0000		
8	1.9982	0.3184	0.6816	1.0000		

| | Ad valorem tax rates and per-unit fines | | | |
Sector	Capital tax by industry	Labor tax by industry	Per-unit fine by industry	Sales tax by consumer
1	0.1836	0.0903	29.4183	0.0109
2	1.3886	0.1300	31.7976	0.0676
3	0.2463	0.0922		0.0868
4	0.8939	0.1029		0.0306
5	0.6090	0.1001		0.0647
6		0.1027		
7		0.1027		
8		0.1027		

NOTE: Blank cell = not applicable.
SOURCE: Author.

reasons: (1) consumer demand by illegal aliens is ignored, implying lower production and hence, less labor demanded by producers; (2) enforcement sectors such as the border patrol and internal surveillance agencies are also ignored, implying less labor demanded by the government. In addition, without fines and sales taxes from illegal aliens, the standard tax solution results in a narrower tax base for government, which in turn implies lower lump sum transfers received by legal workers and hence their welfare losses of 2.78 percent of benchmark national income.[10] The preliminary results thus seem to suggest that a standard tax solution that does not account for the parallel market of illegal aliens can produce misleading welfare results.

Column 3 of Table 7.3 shows the effects of granting all illegal aliens legal status through a general amnesty (instead of ignoring them completely as in the standard tax solution), assuming that no additional

TABLE 7.3 Impacts of Amnesty for Illegal Aliens without Removing Minimum Wages (Central Case)

	Benchmark equilibrium (1)	Standard tax model (2)	General amnesty (3)	Selective amnesty (4)
Factor prices				
Capital rent	1.0000	0.9180	0.9957	1.0091
Legal minimum wage	1.0000	1.0000	1.0000	1.0000
Illegal alien wage	0.6000			0.6923
Legal workers				
Unemployment rate (%)	4.0	4.34	4.08	2.29
Unemployment	26.8191	29.1254	29.4154	15.4148
Employment	643.6582	641.3519	691.7299	658.1200
Total	670.4773	670.4773	721.1453	673.5348
Illegal aliens				
Caught at border	0.8000			1.5176
Caught inside country	0.2000			0.1644
Working	5.8000			4.7680
Total	6.8000			6.4500
Enforcement costs				
Border patrol	0.8000			1.5220
Internal surveillance	0.2000			0.1649
Total	1.0000			1.6869
Government revenues				
Capital taxes	95.8960	88.1738	95.5382	96.6363
Labor taxes	65.0605	64.9571	70.0650	66.5439
Expected fines	25.5352			17.1536
Income taxes	126.6181	123.9717	133.8678	129.0895
Sales taxes, legal workers	50.8832	48.3156	52.1850	51.3454
Sales taxes, illegal aliens	1.4884			1.4118
Total	365.4813	325.4181	351.6560	362.1805
Incomes				
Legal workers, unemployed	42.5525	43.8800	44.5029	24.5679
Legal workers, employed	1021.2603	966.2530	1046.5262	1048.9074
Illegal aliens	30.4008			28.8361
Total	1094.2136	1010.1330	1091.0291	1102.3114
Equivalent variations (% benchmark income)		-2.78	2.60	0.65

NOTE: Blank cell = not applicable.
SOURCE: Author.

illegal aliens enter the country. Compared with the benchmark equilibrium solution, this closed-border general amnesty program results in only a slightly higher unemployment rate for legal workers (4.08 percent up from 4.0 percent at benchmark) because (1) the consumer demand generated by illegal aliens is not lost but is now included with that of legal workers and (2) government enforcement agencies need not employ labor to apprehend illegal aliens.

On the revenue side, the inclusion of all illegal aliens in the income tax base results in an increase of $7 billion in additional income tax revenues (133.8678, up from 126.6181 at benchmark). This sheds some light on the extent of income tax evasions by illegal aliens—a subject of considerable controversy but of not much quantifiable analysis.

On the income side, with all illegal aliens now officially counted as legal workers, the consumer incomes of legal workers must increase (1091.0291, up from 1063.8128 = 42.5525 + 1021.2603 at benchmark) and hence their welfare gains of 2.6 percent of benchmark national income.

The last column of Table 7.3 simulates a scenario in the Immigration Reform Act of 1986 that provides selective amnesty to a maximum of 350,000 illegal aliens who can prove that they have been residents of the United States for at least three years.[11] In addition to this amnesty for illegal aliens already in the country, suppose that the government also tries to stem new illegal entries by increasing (for example, doubling) its border enforcement rate.

Compared with the benchmark equilibrium solution, this selective amnesty–increased enforcement policy results in a lower unemployment rate of legal workers (2.29 percent, down from 4.0 percent at benchmark) for several reasons. As the government increases its border enforcement efforts, the number of illegal aliens caught at the border increases and the number of illegal aliens who get inside the country decreases. This border interdiction, together with the amnesty program, will lower the supply of illegal aliens. As a result, wages for illegal aliens must go up (0.6923, up from 0.6 at benchmark), and employers must turn to legal workers to satisfy their demand for labor, implying more jobs for legal workers and a lower unemployment rate.

On the income side, the consumer incomes of legal workers go up (1073.4753 = 24.5679 + 1048.9074 up from 1063.8128 at benchmark), implying welfare gains of 0.65 percent of benchmark national income.[12]

Table 7.4 reports the results of increases in per-unit fines on employers. In general, an increase in per-unit fines will raise the cost of hiring illegal aliens relative to hiring legal workers. Consequently, employers will hire more legal workers instead of illegal aliens, implying a lower unemployment rate and higher welfare gains for legal workers. This effect is, however, not uniform across sectors: The agricultural sector, because of its bigger size in output and its traditionally greater reliance on illegal aliens, seems to be more sensitive to changes in per-unit fines than is the textile sector. A 5 percent increase, for example, in per-unit fines in the agricultural sector results in an unemployment rate of 0.46 percent for legal workers (down from 4.0 percent at benchmark), compared with 2.17 percent for the same increase in per-unit fines in the textile sector.[13] The corresponding welfare gains are therefore 2.52 percent of benchmark national income in the case of the agricultural sector and 1.31 percent in the textile sector.

In summary, an increase in per-unit fines will cause an allocational shift between the parallel labor markets for illegal aliens and legal

TABLE 7.4   Impacts of Increases in Per-Unit Fines without Removing Minimum Wages (Central Case)

	Benchmark equilibrium	5% increase in per-unit fines in agriculture	5% increase in per-unit fines in textiles
Factor prices			
Capital rent	1.0000	1.0368	1.0190
Legal minimum wage	1.0000	1.0000	1.0000
Illegal alien wage	0.6000	0.6000	0.6000
Legal workers			
Unemployment rate (%)	4.0	0.46	2.17
Unemployment	26.8191	3.1099	14.5285
Employment	643.6582	667.3674	655.9487
Total	670.4773	670.4773	670.4773
Illegal aliens			
Caught at border	0.8000	0.8000	0.8000
Caught inside country	0.2000	0.2000	0.2000
Working	5.8000	5.8000	5.8000
Total	6.8000	6.8000	6.8000
Value added			
Agriculture	111.0230	113.4486	112.2853
Textiles	42.0240	43.3893	42.7321
Per-unit fines			
Agriculture	29.4183	30.8892	29.4183
Textiles	31.7996	31.7996	33.3896
Expected fines			
Agriculture	16.2884	15.9908	16.5488
Textiles	9.2468	9.5665	8.9643
Total	25.5352	25.5573	25.5131
Equivalent variation (% benchmark income)		2.52	1.31

SOURCE: Author.

workers. It will not, however, affect the decision of foreign workers to cross the border; this decision is essentially based on the difference between the wage structure of the United States and those of nearby developing countries. Therefore, without eliminating the minimum wage, increases in fines, at least in my formulation, do not seem to be an effective way to control illegal aliens.

Conclusion

This chapter has outlined an approach that develops the notion of illegal aliens as a parallel market in coexistence with the regular market for legal labor in the presence of both price controls through minimum wage legislation and quantity controls through enforcement of immigration laws. In my formulation, employers hire illegal aliens up to the point at which the minimum wages paid to legal workers equal the expected costs of hiring illegal aliens, and foreign workers cross the border illegally up to the point at which their home country wages equal the expected wages of illegal aliens. In equilibrium, the unemployment rate of legal workers, the size of the population of illegal aliens, the free market wages of illegal aliens, and government enforcement efforts are all endogenously determined.

I have presented my theoretical framework as well as computational considerations and have reported numerical calculations based on U.S. data. The results, though preliminary and illustrative, suggest several conclusions:

- Use of a standard tax formulation without giving careful attention to the parallel market of illegal aliens is likely to produce misleading welfare results.

- An amnesty program could raise the unemployment rate of legal workers, while a strict border enforcement policy would lower it, as one might have intuitively expected. The effects of border enforcement, however, seem to be stronger and more direct than those of amnesty.

- Income tax evasion by illegal aliens can be as great as $7 billion in lost income tax revenues.

- Contrary to popular belief, increasing per-unit fines on employers without eliminating the minimum wage may not be an effective way to control illegal aliens.

In summary, illegal aliens, at least in my formulation, are both a black market phenomenon in response to price distortion in the legal labor market and a rural-urban migration phenomenon in response to wage differentials across international borders. This leads me to believe that any effective policy to control illegal immigration should require the cooperation, on both the domestic and international levels, of all countries involved.

There are several ways the model can be extended. The model is, for example, essentially a single-country model, taking nearby developing countries as exogenous variables. A more satisfactory formulation would be a general equilibrium world trade model that would explicitly account for labor market conditions in all countries and international migration.[14] The model also has a serious drawback in its static description of the migration process: Migrant workers cross the border illegally, are caught at the border or become illegal aliens inside the country, work, are caught and deported, *all at the same time.* A natural extension of the model in this direction is, therefore, to incorporate into the model an explicit intertemporal dynamic structure to describe the migration process fully—although including both migration and price controls within such a dynamic extension will not be a simple task.

Part 3   Fragmented Credit Markets

Chapter 8   Parker Shipton

Time and Money in the Western Sahel: A Clash of Cultures in Gambian Rural Finance

When Benjamin Franklin wrote, "Remember that time is money," in his "Advice to a Young Tradesman" in 1748, he revealed starkly a cultural assumption common to northern Europe and North America.[1] He continued, "Remember that credit is money . . . " and "Money can beget money," summing up a way of thinking that Max Weber, a century and a half later, would call a hallmark of the Protestant ethic. It is conventional in northern countries to conceive of interest charges on loans in terms of rates per unit of time, and to distinguish fair moneylending from usury in terms of such rates. So embedded is this way of thinking that savings banks advertise 6 percent interest, for instance, without needing to add that this is an annualized rate. Both borrower and lender take it for granted that the interest to be paid will depend on the time elapsed between loan and repayment, or between deposit and withdrawal. They assume, moreover, that the base interest rate is linear—6 percent after one year, 12 percent after two; nothing could be more natural. It is the rate, not the ratio of interest to principal, or just the amount finally paid, that determines whether the interest charge is fair.

Why might the young tradesman have forgotten that time is money? Does anyone think differently? Evidence from research in rural areas of The Gambia suggests that some West Africans do.[2] Among farmers and traders there, calculation of interest as "rates" per unit of time is only one of a range of conventional modes of thought about it, and certainly not the most common. Whether this mode or some other applies may depend on the borrowers' and lenders' identities, their relationship, their circumstances, and the forms the loan and repayment take, among other things.

The argument is not that rural Gambians cannot conceive of interest in terms of a linear rate, or that they never entertain such thoughts. Many can and do.[3] Nor, conversely, could one sensibly argue that American or English bank customers pay no attention to the absolute amounts they gain or lose as interest, or to the ratios between principal and interest when they finally withdraw their savings or repay their loans. The findings suggest, rather, that the *tendencies* and the *preferences* of time–money construction can differ between one culture and another. These are *not* differences of mental capability, but of idiom and convention. British-based national moneylending laws in force in The Gambia are based on assumptions that are fundamentally different from the rules of Islamic law and custom that pervade the countryside. The differences are far more complex than "interest versus no interest"; and the overlaps of European, Middle Eastern, and African cultural codes leave much room for local debate and uncertainty about what is correct behavior in rural finance. The personal and contextual dimension renders meaningless a conventional notion of "market interest rates." In The Gambia a financial market—the persons and transactions involved in borrowing and lending money or related commodities—is segmented or fragmented, and even the concept of a "market" fits rural Sahelian financial systems only up to a point.

Gambian Rural Society and Economy

The Gambia, a former British colony and officially English-speaking, is surrounded by Senegal (a former French colony and officially French-speaking) except for a short coastline on the western side. Essentially a narrow strip of land on both sides of the winding lower Gambia River, the country was affected by trade with Britain beginning in the late sixteenth century and by heavy slaving up to abolition in 1874. The country has a long and complex history of trade over long and short distances. The Gambia was hotly contested by European imperial powers during the early part of its British colonial rule (and intermittent company jurisdiction in the early years) from 1588 to its independence in 1965. Today, in a different way, a lively cross-border commerce of persons and things, legal and illegal, qualifies The Gambia's separate identity.

Ethnically, The Gambia has a rich mixture (in decreasing order of size) of Mandinko, Fula (or Peulh), Wolof, Jola, Serahuli (or Soninke), and other ethnic groups including Mauritanian Moorish and (now only urban) Lebanese trading minorities. Because several of these groups are also represented in Senegal and other neighboring countries, The Gambia shows in some ways a cross-section of a larger region of the western end of Africa. Within the country, ethnic group distributions do not correspond closely to national administrative units (which, largest to smallest, are divisions, districts, and villages). Rural Gambians live in nucleated villages with fields surrounding them. Many of the villages are multiethnic, though some have ethnically more homogeneous neighborhoods within them. Nearly all villages in the country are connected by some sort of road to The Gambia's two main highways. Each village has a headman and usually a woman who heads a women's or senior women's association. All or nearly all groups are strongly patrilineal, and villages tend to be endogamous. Broad age grades correspond to village associations and voluntary groups (*kafo* groups, in Mandinka). Most Gambian ethnic groups are also notable for endogamous castes (for example, *alkalo* or headman, *imam* or religious leader, metalworker, woodworker, leatherworker, and "slave"); but while these statuses structure marriage ties and some other social and economic relations, they do not necessarily correspond closely with individuals' actual occupations.

The country's roughly 751,000 people (1985), about 80 percent of them now rural at any time, live in an area of 4,361 square miles (somewhat smaller than Connecticut), at a density of about 172 per square mile overall. Rural land shortage is just now becoming a concern as farmers grow their coarse grains (millet, sorghum, maize), their groundnuts, sometimes their rice, and other crops with new tools including ox-ploughs; as livestock grazing challenges the country's sparse woodlands; and as soil quality, never high, deteriorates. The country relies on a single rainy season, usually from June to October, and on seasonal migrant laborers ("strange farmers") from Senegal, Mali, and Guinea.

By international development agencies' standards, including per capita gross national product (GNP), The Gambia is one of the poorest countries in Africa and one of the dozen poorest in the world.[4] It remains so despite a dramatic economic reform program in the 1980s, a liberalization and structural adjustment program designed and implemented by the Ministry of Finance, the International Monetary Fund (IMF), and the World Bank, that is generally considered to have stimulated trade and at least some kinds of investment.[5] The country remains heavily dependent on its main export crop, groundnuts, on fish, and on its formal and informal entrepôt trade for its foreign exchange; and it imports rice, some as foreign aid, to supplement its own production of that rural staple and of millet and maize and other crops.[6]

Formal Financial Institutions and their Relevance

Rural institutional finance in The Gambia revolves around the groundnut trade, reflecting the main foreign interests in Gambian farming.[7] Several large international and domestic trading firms operate in the capital Banjul, and (decreasingly in recent years) in the countryside.[8] Over the past two decades, state-controlled producer cooperatives for input supply and marketing, under the Banjul-based Gambia Cooperatives Union (GCU), have practically displaced them in the groundnut trade and related lending to farmers, becoming ubiquitous in the countryside with up to eighty-six primary-level societies ("seccos") in the late 1980s. These units cover areas not based on any indigenous social entities, being larger than villages but smaller than districts. Repayment rates are poor, by world standards, and the cooperatives have consistently run at a deficit at government expense.

The expansion of the cooperatives has been an issue hotly debated by foreign aid agents, many of whom now consider their workings corrupt and inefficient; the World Bank and IMF have recently been trying to "reliberalize" the country's groundnut trade by policy measures and stricter financial controls on the co-ops, resulting in the recent closure or merging of about a third of the primary societies. The cooperatives are instructed to charge an annual interest rate of 26 percent for farm input loans issued in cash or kind (1987–88). Their rates have sometimes been positive and sometimes negative in real terms, but never high enough to keep the cooperatives solvent.[9] The rates are lower than private traders normally offer, though few farmers know the official figure, and many doubt the honesty of the weighers and clerks (as with the private groundnut traders). Some men borrow from the cooperatives and relend to their wives or foreign migrant share tenants; and some add their own interest charges, even for their wives. Farmers are ambivalent about the cooperatives: although they mistrust them, they nonetheless feel dependent on them.

Banks are almost insignificant in rural areas. They include two commercial banks—the British-run Standard Bank and the government-owned Gambia Commercial and Development Bank (GCDB)—and the post office savings bank. All the institutions have interest policies based on annual rates, regulated by the Central Bank of The Gambia: in 1987, 22 percent to 29 percent for bank loans, 15 percent for commercial bank savings and 15 percent for post office savings.[10] Few farmers, and almost none of the women, know these rates. To most rural Gambians, these institutions remain rather exotic, and most, particularly the banks, are not fully trusted. Outside Banjul and nearby Serrekunda and Bakao, commercial bank branches are found in only two towns, Farafeni and Basse. Few farmers without major off-farm incomes use the formal banking system, as discussed later.[11]

Quickly entering the picture now, with a well-established local foundation of good will, are several foreign-based private voluntary organizations, including Action Aid, Catholic Relief Services, Freedom from Hunger Campaign, and Save the Children. All are trying to turn away from "relief" toward "development" efforts, especially promoting small enterprises. Most are experimenting with credit and, to a lesser extent, savings. The indigenously run but foreign-sponsored Gambia Women's Finance Company is trying to organize banking facilities for women, as are a few other small indigenous and foreign groups.

The expertise of the banks in money management and the public goodwill and trust of the private voluntary organizations have yet to be allied. Until they are, rural Gambians will prefer to organize their own systems of saving and credit. What are they?

How Rural Gambians Save

Gambians save most of their wealth in nonmonetary forms, a point foreigners are apt to misunderstand.[12] Much of it they keep in the form of livestock (large stock are particularly important for men), and gold earrings and other jewelry that smiths can expand with new metal (particularly important for women). These are forms of wealth the sexes use to safeguard it from each other's daily demands, among other things. Savings also take the form of stored crops, farm machinery, household furniture, radios, and other goods likely to be resold in rural villages. The main saving strategy of rural Gambians is to remove wealth from the form of liquid cash, and the game is to remove it from the constant claims of relatives and neighbors without appearing selfish. Gambians prefer to save in animals—cattle, donkeys, and horses for men, and sheep and goats for both men and women—partly because they breed.[13] Time is livestock, perhaps more than it is money; and the Qur'an (or Koran) does not forbid this kind of "interest."

Stored crops and seeds are an important form of saving, but not an ideal one, from the saver's perspective, since their divisibility makes them subject to demands for charity and loans from family granaries. Hence the locked crop stores in many villages, to which only one or two village leaders hold the keys. Farmers who sell food crops tend to do so just after harvest. They recognize that withholding crop sales until the scarce season, when prices rise, can yield them more cash. But few feel they can afford to wait, and needy relatives' demands make it hard to sell food in the scarce season rather than sharing it. A few of the best-off farmers serve as food pawnbrokers for other farmers, buying neighbors' crops and selling them back similar foods later in the season at higher prices.

To the extent that cash is saved, it is saved mainly by "informal" means within villages. These are many. Among the simplest is the wooden *kondem* ("condemned") box (or *kondaneh*, from the French *condamné*), which rural people will pay five or six dalasis (6.9 Gambian dalasis = US$1, 1987–1988) for a carpenter to construct, with a small slot. The box must be broken to be opened, rather like a western piggy bank. Some use locked suitcases or trunks.

Another widely used strategy is the money-keeper.[14] Some rural Gambians (about 34 percent in the twelve months preceding my 1987 survey) had given money to other villagers (7 percent), often trusted relatives or solvent shopkeepers, to hold for them. Sums deposited ranged from 25 to 2,000 dalasis; but over 80 percent of the deposits were below 500. Some 95 percent of the deposits were for periods of less than one year; most were for no longer than three months. Interest payments or service charges are unheard of in this money-keeping, and the saver often expects to receive back the same notes or coins left off.

A related way of saving, for wage earners, is to ask employers to withhold wages over short times to let them accumulate. Gambian share contractors, too, prefer arrangements in which they receive their main compensation seasonally rather than at shorter intervals (see Robertson 1987, 221).

Village women's and men's groups are being increasingly recognized, both by insiders and outsiders, as valuable for raising capital. Some women, in towns and increasingly in the rural villages, form rotating savings and credit associations (or ROSCAs, also known along the West African coast as *osusu* or *esusu* groups, from the Yoruba, or as *tontines*, from the French) to mobilize savings for personal or household purchases.[15] In each of a series of regularly scheduled meetings, all members contribute a fixed amount and one takes home the lot. Each member takes a turn until the cycle is completed; whereupon it may or may not start again. Among the many advantages of this system to members is that it allows them to save without appearing antisocial.[16] Another advantage is that the groups keep the money circulating in a community.

All these local savings mechanisms in The Gambia are interest free. Indeed, when inflation (12.5 percent in 1987–1988) is taken into account, nearly all represent *negative real interest*.[17] Gambians are thus willing to pay to remove their cash from their own individual hands—evidence of an *illiquidity preference*. Time erodes money, and it erodes it most quickly in one's own pocket.

Problems with banking. Obviously, the large majority of Gambians who save their cash at home or with money-keepers forgo the interest they might earn in banks or other financial institutions (lately 15 percent). A 1975–1976 survey of rural Gambian villages found that only 2 percent of 94 informants had bank savings (Dunsmore et al. 1976, 307). In my 1987 survey, 3 percent of 138 male and female informants stated they had deposits in commercial banks, and 3 percent more in post office savings. Only one of 69 women interviewed had either kind of account. Branch bank information confirmed that most farmer depositors held amounts below about 250 dalasis, that very few of them were women, and that almost no farmers borrowed from banks.[18]

When asked about their reasons for not using banks, farmers in the villages surveyed cited several: distance, inconvenient banking hours, minimum deposit rules, difficult paperwork, and distrust of clerks.[19] Some cited with bitterness their losses in the collapse of the Agricultural Development Bank in the early 1980s. A few, including Mauritanian shopkeepers, stated that they avoided banks because of Islamic prohibitions on charging interest, but since some of these merchants do charge interest in informal lending, this answer should probably not be taken at face value.

Though few use banks now, most farmers interviewed liked the idea that small branch banks should be established, or mobile banks tried or retried, in their areas.[20] A problem in The Gambia, as in some other countries dependent on rainfed agriculture, concerns the seasonal covariance of incomes. A savings bank has stronger financial incentives to stay open or make the rounds in the "trade season," when farmers have significant sums to deposit, than during the rest of the year, when farmers are more interested in withdrawals. Inaccessibility has clearly been a major barrier to institutional savings.

Here, "time is money" acquires another meaning. Whether in the "trade season," when farmers would be most likely to deposit, or in the hungry season that is also the busy weeding season, when they would be most likely to withdraw, time is valuable. The time required to obtain identification photos, to travel to the banks, to wait for them to open, to queue, and to wait for countersignatures all carries opportunity costs for rural people living far away from banks.

Sources of Informal Credit

Gambians do not share the European and American concept of "loan" as a single idea covering all types of exchanges for delayed compensation.[21]

In the Mandinka language, for instance, there is a sharp division between *furo*, to make a helping loan of, say, tools or clothes, to be returned in a few days; and *ndontoro*, to make a business loan, normally longer term and carrying an interest charge. Whether 20 percent, 40 percent, or 80 percent of the rural economy takes the form of "loans" depends on how one asks the questions, and in how many different ways.

The easiest loans: kin and friends. It is to relatives that farmers or small businesspeople turn first when they wish to borrow. Reasons for the preferences may variously include the lenders' proximity and per-suadability, the unlikelihood of interest charges, and the chances of le-niency in the event of nonrepayment. Kin are used for loans of all kinds of goods and services, including food, cash, labor, and farm inputs; and the smallest and biggest debts in life are likely to be incurred between relatives. Extended family members sometimes sell their livestock to lend large amounts of money—thousands of dalasis—to a promising young man to send him abroad for schooling, work, or both, as an investment in his future remittances and contacts.

Marriage entails some of the largest savings and debts that rural Gambians accumulate in their lives. Bridewealth payments from the groom's to the bride's family are commonly made on the "installment plan," often taking a decade or more to complete.[22] A bride's family is likely to have saved for many years for earrings and other jewelry to give her upon her marriage.

Loans between nonrelatives also involve an enormous variety of goods and services, on widely varying repayment schedules, but rural cash loans only seldom rise above a few hundred dalasis in value. Be-tween unrelated borrowers and lenders, small interest charges may be made—often about 5 to 10 percent over six months—though these ar-rangements too vary greatly.

Loan seekers lacking kin ties to invoke usually lean on village ties and other kinds of social commonality: age-grade and age-set (see Dunsmore et al. 1976, 278–79), caste, school ties, and ethnicity.[23] Among friends and neighbors, and among kin, no guarantees or collateral are used to secure loans— there is only the threat of refusing future loans— and debts may be canceled upon crop failures.

In The Gambia, land, labor, livestock, and farm implements are all directly exchangeable for each other at local levels by an infinity of ad hoc, unnamed, and individually tailored arrangements, many of which take the form of short-term loans and counterloans. Most often, these occur between close neighbors, who may also be close kin. But agricul-tural exchange partnerships also occur between seasonal migrants and their hosts: Land and lodging are given in exchange for labor, the details varying according to farmers' and migrants' circumstances.[24]

Harder bargains: local shopkeepers and other merchants. It is usually only in the absence of other kin, friends, or neighbors with disposable assets that a farmer or other rural person turns to an unrelated merchant (in Mandinka, *juloo*) for loans. The terms are stiffer. Interest charges are much more likely to be imposed and will probably be higher. The forms of the loan and repayment are likely to be more strictly specified, repayment periods may be shorter, and a defaulter may be prosecuted. But traders' possession of liquid capital makes them an important source of credit for rural people throughout the country.

While the major lending merchants in the villages and small towns are usually shopkeepers, many small-scale and seasonal traders, most of them at least part-time farmers, also lend from their houses without special shops. The Gambia does not have specialized rural money-lenders like those found in parts of southern Asia.[25]

In addition to money, shopkeepers and other merchants commonly lend household goods like rice, sugar, coarse grains, cooking oil, and some durables. They may lend groundnut or other seeds, but almost never fertilizers or farm implements. Merchant loans vary in duration from a few hours to a year, or occasionally longer. The largest loans these lenders offer are expected to be repaid at the time of the main harvest of groundnuts around December.

In choosing a merchant for a loan, the farmer will usually rely, again, on depth of acquaintance and ties of ethnicity, village coresidence, age-set, and similar ties. The roughly 1,000 Mauritanians and the eastern Gambian Serahuli and increasingly the Fula speakers have established reputations as rural merchants.[26] But shopkeepers appear at least as often to come from the majority groups of their villages or towns as from minorities (see Weil 1977, 14). Many Gambians have clear preferences on the ethnic groups from whose members they might borrow.

Relations between members of a local majority and minority traders are ambivalent and complex. Farmers depend heavily on the latter for capital and goods in times of need, but at the same time they resent the traders' wealth and insularity. The common Mandinka term for a small-scale trader or for a loan, *juloo*, also means rope, and Gambians speak of having debts tied around their necks with well-understood connotations of slavery. Particularly resented are Mauritanian traders, who repatriate profits from their sales and loans and return periodically to their home country, and who do not normally intermarry with Gambians.[27] Gambian institutions do not normally give Mauritanian traders financial or other assistance. The hostility behind the violent 1989 popular expulsions of Arabic-speaking Mauritanian traders from Senegal (and the reported temporary emigrations of some from The Gambia) reveal the ethnic and class tensions underlying daily trade relations in the villages. The Mauritanian migrants' families rely on their remittances for a part of their livelihood in their more desolate Saharan country.

It appears to be poorer villagers who must borrow most commonly from local or immigrant shopkeepers, and lending is liveliest after poor harvests. Richer farmers rely more on their own means, on kin or neighborly lenders, or on institutions to which they have privileged access. Of course, merchants' high interest charges can impoverish their borrowers in a vicious circle.[28] Merchants lend their clients not only staples, but also fancier consumer goods.

Village and town merchants lend to farmers only on the basis of personal acquaintance, on request of a trusted go-between, or on the strength of kinship and friendship ties that will be invokable for recovery, as ties sometimes are between residents of neighboring villages. Loans may be issued without written agreements, though literate merchants do keep records of the loans they have issued. To lend relatively large amounts to near-strangers, lenders may insist on witnesses or written agreements. Collateral or loan guarantees are not normally taken. Instead, lenders rely heavily on informal social sanctions; they can dishonor their borrowers and damage their informal local "credit rating" by pursuing them visibly. In cases of obvious hardship, as when the borrower's pledged crop fails, merchants and other local lenders normally defer collection until the following harvest season, with or without charging further accrued interest.

When personal and social pressures fail, merchant creditors frequently resort to local legal authorities to back up their claims. Debt cases are among the most common kinds of cases arising in civil law, and the courts usually favor creditors, but they do not knowingly uphold substantial interest charges. Lenders who charge interest and who wish to sue defaulters in court must weigh the risk of being exposed and stigmatized as usurers.

Default rates on merchants' loans are always hard to gauge, but some lenders suggest that about 10 percent of their loans are ultimately unrecoverable. In local lending, whether between merchants and villagers, or between friends or kin, loans not repaid after two or three years are normally left as dead. This is, incidentally, what the Qur'an instructs lenders to do—a point that may bear also on institutional lenders.[29]

Private groundnut traders as lenders. Private groundnut traders compete with the state-controlled cooperatives in lending to farmers and marketing their groundnuts. The largest are based in Banjul and deal through agents in market towns. The private traders' share of the groundnut market has fallen from 84 percent in 1962–63 to 19 percent in 1985–86, and most of the largest have abandoned the commodity because of the expansion of the cooperatives, though international funders and the government have lately tried to reverse the trend by cutting special allowances and discounts favoring the cooperatives.[30] A balanced system of public and private lenders in competition with each other has so far remained elusive.

Seasonal migrant share-tenants from neighboring countries finance groundnut inputs by borrowing indirectly, through their land patrons, from the cooperatives or private traders as they can; and the patrons pass on interest charges, perhaps at times adding their own.

Small business credit. Merchants lend cash and merchandise to other merchants, sometimes on very short terms, and this kind of credit, often following kinship ties, is how most small rural businesses in The Gambia appear to get started. On a larger scale, wholesalers and retailers in the provincial towns also borrow rice, sugar, and other merchandise from large Banjul wholesalers, sometimes indirectly through these large merchants' rural agents. Confidence built on long-term acquaintance and customer loyalty, if not also on kinship, is essential in these arrangements. The interest charges that urban wholesalers demand from provincial traders, often about 5 percent to 10 percent over six months, are much lower than those the latter charge their rural borrowers in turn, perhaps because the risks of default are smaller.[31]

Institutional credit has been far less important than informal credit in the establishment of small businesses. The government does have an agency to help arrange bank loans for small businesses, however, and private voluntary organizations are now entering the enterprise development field in The Gambia, as elsewhere.[32]

Interest charges in informal credit. To foreign observers, the rates of interest that private rural lenders in West Africa charge often appear extortionate, and those found in The Gambia are no exception. Gambian merchants and other rural lenders commonly charge interest of 50 to 150 percent over six to eight months, but rates vary enormously outside this range.[33] The wide variation may result in part from the secrecy surrounding interest charges. Not only is it common for researchers to receive inaccurate reports, but there are also uncertainties and disagreements in the rural population itself as to what rates are conventional.

Before judging the appropriateness or fairness of these seemingly high charges, many factors must be taken into account:

- Inflation rates. A loan at 5 percent interest in a year of 10 percent inflation is a loan with a negative real rate of interest.

- The likelihood of default. A lender who lends at 20 percent to borrowers whose probability of default is 10 percent can count on only an 8 percent nominal profit. High interest may be considered in part a risk premium.

* The opportunity costs of capital. Are there more profitable uses, like shop restocking, to which the lender might alternatively put the resources?

* Administration costs and overhead. How much time and money will the lender spend pursuing borrowers in arrears, or checking produce received as repayments?

* Seasonality. A sack of groundnuts lent as seed during planting time or as food during the hungry season is worth more in the rural community, in terms of either use value or exchange value, than a sack of equal weight in January just after harvest.

The seasonal dimension is particularly important in The Gambia, where most rural economic activity involving money revolves around the one annual groundnut harvest, and where, six months later, both food and money to buy it are everywhere short. To borrow in the scarce season and repay the same amount at harvest time is not considered an equitable deal. It is rather as if an American desert traveler said to a companion, "Lend me a glass of water now, and I'll pay it back when we get to Niagara Falls." In the western Sahel, poverty, wealth, and fair lending are all seasonally defined.

Not just a financial system. This discussion of rural lenders has suggested that their lending terms depend on the social distance between them and their borrowers, and on a variety of other circumstantial factors. The secretive nature of informal borrowing and lending in The Gambia, and the variability of the terms on which it occurs—in interest charges, repayment schedules, and other terms—mean that rural credit cannot easily be described as a "market" in the conventional sense of the word, with free information and readily identifiable prices based on supply and demand. Nor can the terms of lending, even at rates over 100 percent per annum, be summarily labeled fair or unfair.

In the following sections we examine some international influences on informal rural credit, considering first the role of Islamic law and then the role of colonially imposed British law. The relation of time and money in interest charges appears in these pages as a focal point of cultural clashes and misunderstandings.

Some of the differences stem from literacy. Gambian and many other local African traditions have historically differed from some of the great traditions of Islam, on the one hand, and from European financial custom on the other, in that loan contracts have been oral, not written. Their enforcement has often depended on multiple witnesses, and thus on continued good community relations and citizenship, since a borrower or lender who misbehaves may find that his or her witnesses have evaporated, or have permuted their stories over time. The renegotiability of oral contracts allows some flexibility to accommodate changing personal or family circumstances. Written contracts change the rules. Witnesses become less necessary, and so do the good behavior and favors or payments once needed to keep or gain their support.[34]

Rules are still invoked and manipulated, however, and after several centuries of Islamic and colonial influence, borrowers or lenders have several sets of rules by which to operate. The codes of behavior differ most profoundly in the underlying ideas about interest—especially with regard to the varying distinctions between fair lending and usury.

Islam and Rural Financial Custom

Islam in Gambian economic life. Some 85 to 95 percent of Gambians now participate at least nominally in Islam, which, since its appearance in the country in the fourteenth or fifteenth century, has waxed and waned in influence, affecting not just religious belief but culture and the economy more broadly.[35] The Qadiri and Tijani sects of Islam found locally also touch large parts of several neighboring countries, including Senegal. Most Gambians and seasonal immigrants combine Islamic with local religious and social practice and belief.[36] But Muslims in The Gambia, as elsewhere, like to conceive of their religion as influencing all aspects of life, rather than as being confined to particular times, places, or activities. Scriptural and oral Islamic teaching has something to say about trading, saving, spending, sharing, borrowing, lending, and investing; and many aspects of these activities are encoded in the *shari'a*, the sacred Law of Islam embodying ethical rules. Law, economics, and religion are so deeply intertwined in Islamic life that they cannot be understood separately: The sacred and secular merge.

Every Gambian village has one or more Muslim *imam*s (mosque and prayer leaders), who may serve at times as moral counselors on practical matters and as redistributive nodes of tithes and charities. Some also have *marabout*s (roughly, mystic holy men, counterparts in some ways to Sufis in the Middle East) who may variously combine Islamic and local religious traditions.[37] Some *marabout*s are major players in local economic affairs, though the Gambian ones tend not to be organized into politically powerful brotherhoods like some Senegalese ones. Gambians tend to practice alms giving (*zakāt* in Arabic, *jako* in

Mandinka), fasting, and feasting and ceremony as prescribed by the Qur'an and scriptural exegesis, sometimes with their own modifications. Arab countries have financed aid projects providing many Gambian villages with wells, mosques, and other constructions. Local branches of Pan-African and Pan-Arab educational and social institutions provide scholarships for study abroad and help organize pilgrimages to Mecca. Islam influences local financial matters profoundly across the country. So does the Arabic language, taught along with Islam in local Qur'an schools. Probably more rural Gambians can read and write Arabic than English or their own tongues. Written records of loan transactions, where they exist, are as likely to be kept in Arabic as in English. It is in Arabic that some of the most important concepts in financial life are expressed.

Interest and usury in Islamic law. Some Gambian practices and concepts concerning interest charges differ radically from those familiar to many foreign financiers, and the failure of outsiders to take into account these differences is a frequent source of misunderstanding. Rural credit and savings in The Gambia cannot be understood without noting a few basic tenets of Islamic law and custom. As noted above, the vast majority of Gambians are at least nominally Muslims, and Qur'anic interpretations have profoundly influenced both financial systems and the legal systems that enforce them.

The Qur'an explicitly forbids usury, repeatedly promising damnation for those who practice it (though it condones profitable trade).[38] Like other Muslims from West Africa to Indonesia, Gambians refer to usury by the Arabic term *ribā*, meaning unjustified enrichment, or consumption at the expense of others for no good reason.[39] Many consider *ribā* a sin second only to murder.[40] "Dirty money" from *ribā* (in Mandinka, *kodi jawo*, "bad money," or *haaramoo*, "forbidden" or "ill-gotten gains") may not be used for pilgrimages to Mecca, for charities or religious feasts, for funerals, or for other holy expenditures.[41] Nor does *ribā* refer only to money; interest-bearing loans in kind are also sinful. These rewards are dangerous.[42]

To many Gambian Muslims who interpret holy scripture strictly, the prohibition refers to *any* charges that could be considered interest. To others, usury simply means any interest charges they deem unfairly high. The key term that recurs in the scriptures is "doubling." There is much debate in The Gambia about whether the prohibition is absolute or leaves scope for lesser charges. Many Gambians will say that even 1 percent profit earned by loan interest is more sinful than 100 percent earned by trade.[43] For many others, however, the ideal and actual practice seem to differ; lending at interest goes on all the time.

Interest rates and ratios: when time is money and when not. What interest charges are accepted? A crucial point is that the Qur'an discusses usury in terms of the relation between the amount lent and the amount repaid, but not in terms of the amount of time elapsing between the loan and repayment.[44] This means that even if a low rate of interest is charged per month or year, it can eventually add up to an absolute amount that is considered usurious. What matters to rural Gambians is not so much the *rate* of interest per unit of time as the *ratio* of interest to principal. As a district chief explained it, his court might find a loan at 10 percent interest over a year acceptable, but it would never consider a loan at 10 percent annual interest over ten years acceptable, because that would be doubling. Moreover, he said, even a loan at 2 percent annual interest over fifty years would be unacceptable, for this too would be doubling.[45]

From this principle follow several others fundamental to Gambian financial custom. One is that the duration of loans is usually kept as short as possible, for the lender's sake if not also for the borrower's.[46] Local loans of cash, seeds, food, or other consumer goods are rarely if ever issued for periods exceeding one year, and most are for no longer than seven months. For small household goods, as noted previously, loans of only a few days are common.

Preferences for short-term lending seem to militate against local credit sales of large, nondivisible goods, including animal-drawn and engine-driven farm machinery. These goods simply are not available to farmers to purchase by installment or other credit arrangements, except occasionally from the cooperatives. Farmers certainly perceive this as a gap to be filled. Development planners may see it this way, too, but they should also realize that medium-term or long-term loans accruing high absolute interest will cause resentments that might lead to deliberate nonrepayment.

In informal lending in rural Gambia, interest is not necessarily assumed to accrue at a constant rate, month by month, as it does in a European bank account. Instead, charges are geared to the agricultural cycle. A lender who lends one sack of rice to an impoverished farmer early in June, at the start of the hungry season, demanding two in return at the December harvest time (in defiance of Qur'anic law), will also lend one sack for two to another borrower who needs a sack in September, even though the two borrowers are expected to repay at the same time. When asked about such cases, farmers insist that the lender is following the same policy for both. A three-month loan thus often carries the same actual interest charge as the six-month loan (one sack, or 100 percent interest). If time is money, it sometimes comes only in large denominations.

Gambian farmers, then, do not always think of interest in terms of annualized rates. They repay seasonal loans at harvest time if they are willing and able to do so; otherwise, they wait until the subsequent harvest. They are thus more accustomed to thinking of loan durations in terms of six- or eighteen-month periods than in terms of twelve-month periods. After the end of a harvest season, interest on an unrepaid loan may be expected to jump to its double on the expectation that it will not be repaid until the following year's harvest. It accrues stepwise, jumping year by year.

At least as often, however, *no* further interest will be charged after the first year. The lender simply agrees to defer collecting the principal and the initial interest until the following harvest, then collects the same sum. The interest-time function turns flatly horizontal. Rural groundnut seed lenders charging 100 percent on six-month loans sometimes demand further accrued interest after the harvest season; others do not. Shopkeepers sometimes sell items like cigarettes on credit for 100 percent interest within the month (as for buyers who may have monthly salaries or remittances). But these loans do not simply keep piling up interest if unpaid. It makes little sense to think of them in terms of a 1,200 percent annual rate, and no one does.

As these various patterns suggest, linear time is not taken for granted in loan arrangements. Rather, there are at least several modes or idioms, temporal or atemporal, linear or nonlinear, for constructing agreements. Which will be chosen is negotiable, if not at the time of the deal, then in renegotiation later. In rural Gambia, time is an optative element.

This variable conception makes sense in communities where many have no major sources of cash besides annual rainfed agriculture, but where some farmers or families do have remittances, salaries, and trading incomes throughout the year. Time seems in some way to be a bracketable or detachable part of rural Gambian interest calculations, included for rates or excluded for ratios, and negotiated into or out of contracts. Flexibility is the essence of the system, and interest and usury are context-specific.

Is the time dimension becoming more deeply entrenched or more prominent in local thought about usury? This is hard to determine. Statutory law and cooperative society practice have been based heavily on the linear-time principle, and in the past two decades farmers in nearly every Gambian village have dealt with the cooperatives. Evidence from other parts of West and East Africa suggests that "informal" land-pledging agreements have newly begun to incorporate time deadlines, becoming foreclosable mortgages, in crowded rural areas where competition for land has grown severe. In The Gambia, too, secular changes may be occurring in financial thinking, so that deals are being more closely linked to linear notions of time. Snapshotlike field investigation cannot track such changes well, and more longitudinal study is needed.[47]

How lenders conceal interest charges: the commodity switch and other strategies. Another practice that results from the Qur'anic prohibition of usury is that in lending for any but the shortest periods, lenders seek ways of making profits from lending without appearing to charge interest. To their borrowers and to outsiders, they may seem to be concealing or disguising interest charges. Several conventionalized dodges are found in The Gambia. These are known by the Arabic term *ḥila* (pl. *ḥiyal*), meaning "legal devices" or "evasions."[48] One way, used when written records of loans are kept, is a method one might call "double-entry bookkeeping" with a new meaning: to record a loan agreement by entering only the doubled amount to be repaid, but not the amount actually lent. Lenders' books, and local court records examined on debt cases, do not mention interest charges, though of course these are standard practice in reality. Some of the strategies involve semantics: A fee for a loan is more acceptable when it is considered a gift or a service charge.

Other elaborations involve reclassifying loans as sales and resales. A wishes to lend B money, and B wishes to borrow it. A "sells" B a sack of sugar with delayed payment, and repurchases the sack of sugar immediately, for cash, at half price. Thus B receives cash immediately, and returns its double later. The loan is disguised as two sales, and the sack of sugar need never move from the lender's shelf.

A common way of concealing loan profits is by insisting that a loan in one form be repaid in another. Loans issued in cash in June are frequently collected in groundnuts upon the December harvest, even if the borrower could easily have sold the groundnuts elsewhere for cash first to repay in cash, and even if the lender will only then sell the groundnuts to a third party for cash.[49] Even though both borrower and lender usually know well the cash values of the things borrowed and lent, the switch in the form of payments makes accusations of usury less likely. The changes in values of the two items over the course of the loan, and the fact that these changes are not fully predictable at the time the agreement is made, further obfuscate the lender's profit. All are aware that the lender is making a profit, but no one can be sure how much.

The switching practice in turn leads to interesting patterns of interest charging or profit taking in credit. In loans in which the forms of payment are switched, interest rates are usually much higher than in loans in which they are not. Thus, while a 300 percent interest charge in a seasonal cash loan repaid in cash is virtually unheard of, it is common practice for shopkeepers to lend in cash 25 percent of the expected value of a bag of groundnuts, demanding the payment of a full bag upon harvest. In monetary terms, this would of course be calculated as a charge of principal plus 300 percent interest. Interest charges in cash-for-cash loans or groundnut-for-groundnut loans seldom rise above 100 percent, and in many cases are much lower. Borrowers usually know all this, of course, and they perceive that it is in their interest to make agreements to repay in the same form as they borrow. But since most credit is demand-led, lenders can generally dictate the terms and succeed in effecting a switch.

Two general conclusions follow from these observations. One is that credit analysts working in The Gambia should not assume that the same interest rates acceptable in short-term loans will also be acceptable in long-term loans. As time elapses, interest accruing at a constant *rate* may rise to an unacceptable *ratio* (of interest to principal). Accordingly, rates of interest applied to smaller scale loans may be locally considered unreasonable in larger scale loans. The second conclusion is that financiers in The Gambia should not simply record, generalize about, or set interest rates without considering both the forms in which loans are issued and the forms in which they are collected. In this area, conventional European or American modes of economic analysis may not be applicable.

Loan forgiveness customs: a safety net for borrowers. Although rural Gambians do not always calculate interest as though time were linear and inexorable, rules and conventions about loan forgiveness in fact prevent interest from accumulating ad infinitum as time passes. If two or three years elapse without a repayment on a seasonal loan, the lender is usually expected to forgive the loan. (He or she will of course be wary of lending to the same borrower again.) As Gambians know, the Qur'an counsels lenders to give needy debtors extra time, or better, to forgive their debts.[50] Villagers expect the same of governmental and other institutional lenders.[51]

Further differentials. Some rural Gambians state that loans issued in cash should carry higher interest than loans issued in kind, other things being equal.[52] Why cash loans should be more expensive is not clear. One reason might be the opportunity cost of capital for lenders: They can use money in more ways than seednuts, for instance, and seednuts take time to sell for cash. Another reason might be that the value of cash is easier to assess than the value of groundnuts, which can vary in size or quality; and therefore a cash loan is more likely to be judged usurious. Might it also be that a kind of "spiritual risk premium" is being added to the interest charge in cash loans?

The size of loan may make a difference, as well. Whether coming from kin or neighbors, relatives, or merchants, the smallest loans are often expected to be given free of interest or profit. As the quantities or values of loans rise, so may the rates of interest charged. One group of

farmers indicated hypothetically that while they might expect a seasonal loan of D10 to be issued interest free, they would expect D100 to
be issued at 5 percent interest, D1,000 (a rare loan) at 10 percent and
D10,000 (rarer still) at 20 percent—between the same borrower and
lender, over the same period. But since the persons engaging in small
and large transactions are likely to be different, these distinctions may
not hold in the aggregate, and there are signs that the reverse may in fact
be the case when different lenders' and borrowers' transactions are
compared.[53]

The differences between the lending and borrowing habits of indigenous Gambian ethnic groups have not been thoroughly studied—this
is a field ripe for further research—but there is evidence of substantial
variation. Puetz and von Braun (1988, 18) have found that Wolofs
charged an average of 58 percent higher interest on loans than other
Gambian ethnic groups. Others have observed that village or town
lenders appear to give more generous terms to wealthier borrowers and
those who have salable property (livestock, machinery) than to poorer
borrowers or those who do not.[54]

Summary of Gambian interest practices. Informal interest charges in
The Gambia depend on many things, in addition to strictly economic
determinants. These include the presence and closeness of kinship and
friendship ties and the ethnic identities of the borrower and lender.
They also include the duration, amount, and time of year of the loan, the
solvency of the borrower, the nature of the commodity borrowed, and
its relation to the one returned. Time and money are not necessarily
understood as linked in linear function, and the notion of "rates" per
unit of time appears artificial and alien to Gambians in many contexts.
The complex calculations and negotiations involved in Gambian interest charges are not all easily amenable to conventional western economic analysis.

Some implications for financial institutions. Gambian farmers have
seen everything, from free handouts and loans with negative real interest to interest charges of several hundred percent. In this sense, at least,
there is some latitude for policy experimentation. These farmers' understandings of interest charges are so complex, however, and so deeply
embedded in religion and culture that institutional lenders are advised
to design and redesign their policies sensitively, carefully watching pilot
projects and listening with open minds.

Does institutional finance need to conform to all Islamic proscrip-
tions of usury? Some Gambians say not if the institutions are public, as
in a cooperative, since the public supposedly benefits from the interest
charged its members. Others reason, too, that the law of the land

governs banking and financial institutions, that the public has a sacred duty to abide by the law of the land, and that this duty can be just as important as other sacred duties. But a privately held enterprise is thought guilty of *ribā* in charging interest for someone's personal profit when that profit will not be shared with family or community. Some Gambian rural traders claim that they do not save in banks because doing so would be charging interest. This claim should not always be taken at face value—they often have other reasons—but the idea is always present in decisions and debate.

Although the Qur'an explicitly forbids charging high interest, it does not explicitly forbid paying it. Rural Gambians debate whether such borrowers are also sinners. A Mandinko *marabout* in Lower River Division explained that borrowing at interest to feed one's family is not sinful, but borrowing for strictly personal or unnecessary purposes is. Although an institution charging high interest may be resented and perhaps thought sinful, religious beliefs may not necessarily diminish the demand for its credit. No evidence is available on this point.

Of course, Islamic banks in other parts of the Muslim world have their own *hiyal* or legal devices for evading Qur'anic prohibitions on interest. These cannot be examined in detail here, but they usually label such payments "profit" or "profit sharing" instead of interest; this is more convincing if they declare them at the end of a year or a lending term rather than at the beginning. Provisions for risk sharing between borrowers and lenders may be incorporated to avoid Qur'anic prohibitions of unilateral risk.

We noted earlier that Gambians expect loan forgiveness, from institutional as from informal lenders, in cases of need and delayed repayment. Here the issues are not just religious or economic. Institutional credit is political. Just as dispensing loans can win voters or supporters, forgiving loans maintains loyalties. It is to the advantage of politicians that loan forgiveness by institutions not be too routinized— that is, that there be leeway for discretion about clemency because of drought, or the amount of time elapsed and interest accrued. Politicians try to arrange that announcements of new loan programs or forgivenesses be associated with their own names (and that they occur in election years). Patronage systems reinforce the Islamic-inspired safety net of forgiveness for borrowers, but they may desynchronize the timing of forgiveness from periods of peak need.

We turn now away from the subject of Islamic law to the other major international legal influence on Gambian financial customs: the legacy of the British Empire, from which the Gambian nation gained independence a quarter-century ago.

National Moneylending Law: The Imperial Legacy and the "Per Annum" Rule

Gambian statutory law prohibits usury under specific terms, copied with little modification from British law. The relevant law is written with reference only to money: It is the Moneylenders Act. The wording of the act refers to money loans but nowhere specifies whether the act applies to loans in kind, or to cash loans collected in other commodities.[55] The law is thus technically irrelevant, or only ambiguously relevant, to much rural lending in The Gambia.

The Moneylenders Act, with its deeply embedded assumptions about what constitutes interest and usury, has a centuries-long pedigree exotic to Africa.[56] Its immediate basis was the Money-Lenders Act of 1900 in the United Kingdom, redrafted and amended in 1927 to the effect that transactions would normally be considered unfairly harsh at interest rates above 48 percent per year. The figure was copied straight into Gambian law. It developed in the form of the Moneylenders Ordinance of 1934, which required the registration of moneylenders, and the Moneylenders Act of 1955 (Cap. 126), revised under the Revised Edition of the Laws Act of 1965. This was the law still in force and being distributed in pamphlet form by the Government Printer in Banjul in 1988.[57]

The law defines a moneylender as "any person who lends money at interest or who lends a sum of money in consideration of a larger sum being repaid" (Cap. 126, sec. 4), and it requires him or her to be licensed. It does not acknowledge that most of the moneylending in The Gambia is done by nonspecialist moneylenders.

The law refers to "interest" as permissible under certain circumstances. In this respect, it differs sharply from Qur'anic teaching, which never explicitly condones interest but instead prohibits "usury" (*ribā*), variously interpretable to allow some charges resembling interest. The law makes it clear that interest is to be calculated as an annual *rate* per unit of time, rather than simply as a ratio of principal to interest. Implicit is the assumption of linearity in the relation of time to money.

The Moneylenders Act of The Gambia states (Cap. 126, sec. 13, para. 1):

> The interest which may be charged on loans, whether by a moneylender or by any person other than a moneylender shall not exceed the respective rates specified hereunder—
>
> (a) On loans secured by a charge on any freehold property [or government bonds or other specified forms of collateral] simple interest not exceeding the rate of fifteen per centum per annum for the first five

hundred pounds or part thereof and not exceeding the rate of twelve-and-a-half per centum per annum on any amount in excess of five hundred pounds;

(b) on loans secured by a second charge . . . [2.5 percent higher than in (a)];

(c) on unsecured loans simple interest not exceeding the rate of forty-eight per centum per annum.

The "per centum per annum" clauses force lenders to record interest, and courts to assess fairness, in terms of time elapsed. Later sections make doubly sure (Cap. 126, sec. 16, para. 2, as follows; see also sect. 21):

Where the interest charged on a loan of money is not expressed in terms of a rate per centum per annum the rate of interest per centum per annum charged on the loan shall be calculated according to schedule A [which shows how to divide years into months, weeks, and days] . . . or schedule B to this Act [which gives the algebraic formula for calculating interest, by months elapsed].[58]

Significantly, the British-based laws still in force in The Gambia include nothing like a statute of limitations: They mention no period of time after which the amount of the accrued interest becomes unfair, and no period after which a loan or any of its interest must be forgiven.[59] Nothing in the law limits the ratio of interest to principal. According to the letter of the law, then, an unrepaid loan may legally continue accruing interest indefinitely. What the Qur'an condemns as "doubling and quadrupling" is quite legal under the British-based system, provided the rate is gradual enough and enough time elapses. This is a key difference between British law and local conventions based on Islamic and indigenous law and custom.

By the 48 percent per annum rule, many of the seasonal loans that Gambian farmers contract with each other and with shopkeepers are illegal. A six-month loan at 100 percent interest—about the most common arrangement—carries more than four times the legally allowable interest if calculated on an annualized basis.[60] Interest charges on many of the shorter term loans, for instance larger traders' loans to smaller traders for stocking up, appear ridiculously high when annualized: They may come to well over 1,000 percent. Annualization, and laws based upon this kind of calculation, thus become meaningless. Of course, since loans not issued in cash may not be deemed subject to the Moneylenders Act, the law is only of limited relevance.

Other areas of fit and misfit in the Moneylenders Act. The Moneylenders Act's breakdown of interest rates, in terms of security offered, tacitly takes into account lenders' needs to pass on the risks of unsecured lending to borrowers as an interest premium. Seen in a more critical way, it allows them to extract higher rates of profit from poorer borrowers, who are unlikely to have collateral to offer. Fair or unfair, the direction of the difference fits Gambian local practice.

There are, however, significant areas of misfit. Allowable formats for repayment schedules are also set out in English, but not in the Arabic that many Gambians learn to write in Qur'an school or in any other local language. Strangely, although the Moneylenders Act specifies allowable interest in terms of rates, thus accommodating loans of any amount (with only one minor differential for amounts above or below £500),[61] it specifies the fines in terms of a fixed (presumably maximum) amount:

> Any person who loans money at a rate of interest higher than that authorized by this Act shall be guilty of an offence and shall be liable, on summary conviction, to a fine of *fifty pounds* in respect of each such loan (Cap. 126, sec. 14, para. 1, emphasis added).

The law discriminates against smaller lenders. A loan of £10 or £1,000 could incur the same £50 fine. The lender who lent £1,000 in £10 amounts would risk 100 times the fines of the lender who lent a single £1,000 loan. Lenders are of course likely to try to pass such risks or costs on to the lenders as premiums on interest. This section of the law thus disfavors not just small lenders, but also small borrowers. Gambian law includes provisions whose enforcement would block some ḥiyal (legal evasions), but not others. The law prohibits direct or indirect payment of interest in advance by deduction from the principal sum borrowed or otherwise (Cap. 126, sec. 15, para. 1). It prohibits "negotiation fees" (sec. 17) and bonuses, fines, and expenses that might be levied as surrogate interest charges (sec. 13, para. 3). But, as noted earlier, the act does not address the commodity-switch device—for instance, cash loans repaid in groundnuts, one of the most important devices in local lending practice.

Loans with pledged property are subject to the Pawnbrokers Act of 1905, revised 1965 (Cap. 136) and still being issued from Banjul in 1988.[62] This law also lists maximum profits on loans or debts allowable, in terms of rates, calculated by monthly and fortnightly intervals, for instance: "On a loan of above forty shillings—For every month or part of a month for every sum of two shillings and sixpence or fraction of a sum of two shillings and sixpence . . . one halfpenny" (Cap. 136, sec. 12, item B.). Here again, profits may legally continue to rise indefinitely, as long as they rise slowly enough. What matters according to this act, like the Moneylenders Act, is not the amount of interest finally paid, nor its ratio to principal, but only the relation between time and money.

Implications for Policies and Projects

The differences in assumptions underlying Islam-based rules about interest and usury and more secular European rules are not just philosophical or religious. They also influence real behavior and thus resource flows. Project and program designers interested in issuing or recovering loans in the western Sahel, or in mobilizing savings there, should pay attention to both these sets of rules, as well as to local customs on which they are superimposed. The following is a summary of some practical implications about local and international finance in The Gambia.

- There is much latitude for experimentation in project design. Rural Gambians have seen most everything, including interest charges ranging from negative figures to several hundred percent (or several thousand if annualized). They have also seen other Gambians devise complex ways of dodging rules and laws, including sacred laws.

- Official attempts to regulate interest charges made by local lenders are likely to fail. Government policy can, however, influence the kinds and numbers of urban-based merchants who trade in particular commodities in the countryside, and who lend in connection with them.

- More emphasis should be placed on savings, to balance the heavy emphasis on credit, in policies and projects. Although they save mainly in nonmonetary forms, rural Gambians would like more, and more convenient, ways of saving cash. The *kondem* boxes, the money-keepers, the requests for delayed wage payments, and the rotating savings and credit associations all suggest an illiquidity preference and a possible demand for accessible saving deposit channels. If institutional interest rates on loans are to be raised, as is happening now, interest rates on savings should be raised as well.

- Institutions are publicly considered subject to Islamic rules concerning interest, but those rules are more tolerant of some kinds of financial institutions than others, and the public has ways of rationalizing counterventions.

- Rural Gambians often conceive of interest in terms of ratios rather than rates. The idiom of annualized rates, so familiar in the West as to be taken for granted, is not second nature, or even necessarily acceptable, to Gambians. They do not necessarily conceive of time as linear. It is detachable, optative, and not taken for granted in interest calculations. Time is, however, taken into account in debt forgiveness.

- One should not assume that the same interest rates acceptable for short-term loans will be acceptable for longer term loans. It is easier to collect shorter term than longer term credit. This is probably even more true in Muslim countries like The Gambia than in other poor countries. Institutional lenders may be able to charge higher interest than they are accustomed to charging if they keep their loans short enough.

- Cultural pressures favor smaller loans. Gaps are therefore left in large-scale, long-term lending. Large-scale investments like milling or threshing machines are likely to be impracticable to finance with credit, and unlikely to be replaced by local initiative except by unusually solvent traders or businesspeople. Such gaps may be hard to fill with institutional credit at anything like market rates and may instead require hire-purchase arrangements, grants, subsidies, or other arrangements.

- Financiers should not simply record, generalize about, or set interest rates without considering both the forms in which loans are issued and the forms in which they are collected. Conventional European or American modes of economic analysis may not neatly apply.

- Some institutional lenders to farmers may want to experiment with options of interest scheduling other than linear rates. Interest charges that accrue stepwise each year in the trade season might more closely reflect the realities of rainfed farming cash flows for some purposes.

- Lenders should be prepared to forgive loans that go more than two or three years without repayment. Letting interest accrue ad infinitum is not considered ethical in the Gambia. This is a further reason for caution when considering large-scale loans—for instance, for heavy machinery.

- Depreciation funds for replacing goods like farm machinery by regular deposits are likely to be considered unnatural.

They are based on a conception of a linear time-money relationship that is not second nature to rural Gambians. Moreover, they conflict with local assumptions about the transferability of profits from one sector of economic activity into others.

Conclusion: Financial Customs across Cultures

Indigenous and superimposed foreign understandings of time, money, and the relationship between them have left rural Gambians with a range of practices to choose among, to manipulate, and to debate. If these financial systems are to be understood as markets, they are certainly not unified or discrete ones. Kinship, friendship, neighborhood, and ethnicity are intimately concerned, and tangible and intangible reciprocities mix with profiteering as strategies of individual and group livelihood. Religion is also inseparable from economy, to the point of influencing whether repaying a loan in the same commodity or a different one changes the interest charge, and to the point of ensuring some secrecy in local financial dealings. Interest charges not only fluctuate but also vary simultaneously. The concept of markets is only half appropriate to describe a many-sided and partly covert financial life like this. Nor can one assume a universally shared understanding of how to distinguish fair from unfair lending once a market is identified. The distinction between interest rates and interest ratios is fundamental. Both tools—one overused by foreign financiers in West Africa, the other underused—are needed to understand financial thought in rural Gambia.

National moneylending laws, based on the concept of interest rates, are not widely heeded in the countryside. There is no reason why they should be. Their stipulations appear tailored to a different culture and have been arbitrarily applied to this West African setting. More appealing to locals by far is the sacred Qur'anic law, one far more widely known, even though its meaning may be debated. That local court records do not show interest payments that have obviously been made shows how much more attention is paid to the Arab-based than the European-based code: Not just high interest but *all* interest is concealed from the government in informal lending. But Gambian financial custom is equally remote from the letter of Qur'anic law in that, as elsewhere in the Muslim world, interest *is* charged and only thinly veiled between borrowers and lenders.

The Gambia has two legal codes, then, based more on exogenous ideals than on actual practice. Hence the wide latitude for borrowers and lenders to arrange their own deals on their own terms. This rural and peripheral area of West Africa, accustomed to centuries of competing alien powers and philosophies, is in a sense ironically cosmopolitan in its outlook and its tolerance.

Probably similar cultural clashes and overlays concerning time and money, and focusing on interest and usury, are widespread in Africa— as widespread as the Qur'an in the northern half of the continent, and the Bible in the southern half; as widespread as the legacy of colonial rule and the widening reach of international institutional finance. Would an African sage advise a young tradesman not to forget that time is money? Probably not without knowing whom that novice will be dealing with. That is the difference.

Pan A. Yotopoulos
Chapter 9   Sagrario L. Floro

Transaction Costs and Quantity Rationing in the Informal Credit Markets: Philippine Agriculture

The study of credit markets has rightfully become an integral part of the study of economic development.[1] Financial intermediation helps alleviate one of the two structural gaps in the development process, the disparity between savings endowments and investment opportunities—as well as helping meet consumption needs. The main focus, however, of the literature on development finance has until recently been formal financial intermediation.

Credit in developing countries is transacted in fragmented markets. Informal financial intermediation (IFI) becomes the institutional vehicle of extending the market environment beyond the easy reach of the formal financial intermediation (FFI), since formal credit is always limited by poverty and is often inaccessible to small enterprises and in rural areas.[2] To the extent that rurality, small operations, and poverty are endemic features in developing countries, the role of IFIs can be extremely important.

Policy makers, in turn, have actively encouraged IFI and have promoted its linkage with the formal sector.[3] Issues of the efficiency and distributional equity of the operation of informal credit markets have not yet been fully resolved, however.

This chapter examines the various mechanisms adopted by informal financial intermediaries to cope with structural distortions in a fragmented market environment, with the informal credit market in Philippine agriculture as a case in point. The first section, "Nature of Financial Markets Revisited," discusses some structural characteristics inherent in the nature of financial intermediation, and more specifically the role of trust in market exchanges. The empirical analysis of the Philippines in the second section, "Informal Credit Markets in the Philippines," demonstrates how informal financial intermediaries handle the issue of trust in an environment that lacks the institutional and market infrastructure that is necessary for the functioning of formal financial intermediaries. Market interlinkage and financial layering become important features of the informal credit transaction. Quantity rationing and the sorting of borrowers—implicit activities in all credit contracts—take a different form in the informal credit market. Although the second section refers to the efficiency consideration of the mechanisms adopted by IFI, the third section, "Cost of Borrowing and Equity Considerations," concentrates on equity issues by analyzing borrowing charges and comparing different types of informal credit contracts. A final section draws conclusions and presents policy recommendations.

Nature of Financial Markets Revisited

Issues of trust. Credit involves an intertemporal relationship between the borrower and the lender containing a promise to repay in the future the amount borrowed. Since there is no infallible way to gauge the true intentions of the borrower, credit transactions entail trust in a fundamental way.

The issue of trust is handled in various ways in different types of financial markets. Banks that issue credit often make their liabilities payable on demand. This imposes certain limits on banks' portfolios, putting a premium on making safe and fairly liquid loans. Safety and liquidity, in turn, can at least be partly established by a loan contract and collateral. To ensure contract enforcement and collateral liquidation and transfer, banks and other formal financial intermediaries rely on sophisticated market institutions and on a well-developed legal infrastructure.

In developed countries, such a legal infrastructure is readily available, to the extent that it is taken for granted. The high capitalization rate of the productive sector makes collateral readily available. The

availability of credit reference checks and of various market information networks effectively reduces the otherwise prohibitive costs of
information gathering. Bank regulations exist, and established court
systems make the collateral clause and other contract terms enforceable. Trust is therefore readily established in a market environment in
which specific institutions essentially crystallize confidence building
between transacting parties. In such circumstances, market exchange
for services in general, and for credit in particular, tends to be more
impersonal.

Developing countries lack such a trust-enhancing infrastructure to
facilitate information gathering and contract enforcement. Highly
skewed distribution of resources as well as generally low income levels
imply a relative scarcity of collateral, a problem that is exacerbated by
the absence of cadastral systems and the persistence of ill-defined
property rights.[4] Although bank regulations exist, their enforcement is
not always credible, and the same may be true for the court system.
These infrastructural deficiencies are reflected in imperfections of the
market, which in turn give rise to transaction costs that are not normally included in the standard neoclassical definition of the costs of
production. These include costs of information, negotiation, coordination, monitoring, and enforcement. The constraints on the growth of
the formal financial intermediaries in developing countries are thus
not merely an artificial creature of government regulation; they are also
the outcome of the inadequate development of markets and market-
support infrastructure. Unlike developed countries, the developing
world often operates under an architectural type of socioeconomic system in which prohibitive transaction costs set the operational limits of
an FFI.

The importance of trust as a variable in determining the institutional differences in credit markets between developed and developing
countries largely explains the asymmetric distribution of formal credit
in favor of certain sectors and types of loans. Studies in the Philippines,
for instance, show that despite government efforts to extend the reach
of the formal credit delivery system in rural areas, the relative share of
formal agricultural credit has in fact declined (TBAC 1985; Floro and
Yotopoulos 1991). According to the Agricultural Credit Policy Council
(ACPC), the share of formal agricultural credit has dropped from 18
percent of total loans in 1966 to 5 percent in 1975, only to increase
slightly to nearly 10 percent in 1985 and decline again to 7 percent in
1988 (ACPC 1989).

Within a sector, the bankability of projects varies widely. Asymmetry
in the allocation of formal credit is also apparent, with a concentration on
certain activities and borrower types. Floro and Yotopoulos (1991) have
shown that within agriculture, formal financial intermediaries tend to

favor the export crop subsector, especially the sugar industry, which received nearly a third of all agricultural credit. In contrast to the high rates of growth observed for the export and commercial crops, the volume of credit allocated to producers of staple food crops such as rice and corn has been shrinking continuously. The size of farm, as well as the market orientation of the output, also determines the bankability of a borrower. Microstudies have shown that "the proportion of farmers who borrow from the FFIs have diminished consistently from 37.1 percent for the period 1967–74 to 23 percent in 1981–86 and to a dismal 7.5 percent in 1988" (ACPC 1989, 1). This leaves an unfilled demand for credit for non-favored activities and borrowers. This vacuum is filled by the informal sector—explaining why informal financial intermediation is so widespread in less developed countries (LDCs).

Trust-enhancing mechanisms in the informal credit market. The *informal* in informal credit market aptly denotes its unregulated membership. This informality should not be interpreted, however, to mean that the informal sector lacks organizational structure and well-defined behavioral characteristics. On the contrary, even though the market agents involved in the credit circuit are widely heterogeneous and their activities within the informal credit sector are multifarious, they commonly evolve selected modes of behavior within the context of the market environment. More specifically, in the absence of trust-building market infrastructure and in the face of prohibitive transaction costs, they establish informal arrangements that build trust between the transacting parties. This response to intrinsic market imperfections is in fact the hallmark of the informal credit sector.

Trust in informal credit transactions tends to be based on personal relationships. In fact, personal ties often become an essential feature of the loan process. The trust on which the market relationship is built offsets to a certain extent the asymmetry of information and the moral hazard inherent in a transaction that involves a promise to pay in the future. A familial relationship among relatives and friends thus often serves as a foundation for extending informal credit. The extended family and kinship institutions forge strong personal ties that allow simple loan processing to take place, thereby making burdensome and time-consuming documentation and other paperwork unnecessary.

The lender's familiarity with the borrower's economic behavior constitutes the foundation of the personal economic relationship. At the same time, it limits the domain of credit to a small number of individuals who are personally known to the lender. Although these ex ante ties internalize the cost of borrower screening and selection, the lender still faces the risk of default unless borrower monitoring and loan collection are effectively implemented.

The informal sector enhances trust, that is, confidence in the borrower's delivery of payment in the future, by making existing ties an integral component of credit contracts. The extensive practice of interlinking markets and credit layering further cements the personal foundation of the informal credit relationship. This ability of the informal sector to evolve alternative modes of economic behavior in response to market imperfections will be examined empirically by drawing from the Philippine experience.

Informal Credit Markets in the Philippines

Our study of the informal credit market in the Philippines (Floro and Yotopoulos 1991) highlights the personal character of these credit transactions and the innovative means by which the informal sector internalizes the externalities inherent in credit markets. The study is based on a survey sample of 111 farmer-borrowers and 16 informal lenders (8 trader-lenders and 8 farmer-lenders).

The survey, which was conducted during the first half of 1984, involved respondents from five municipalities (or townships) in the Philippines: Solana in the province of Cagayan, Talavera and Jaen in the province of Nueva Ecija, and Tigbauan and Oton in the province of Iloilo. To isolate the possible effects of modern technology and commercialization on credit relationships, our study distinguished between marginal and developed areas. Developed areas contained mostly irrigated and highly productive land with villages that were quite commercialized. The marginal areas were characterized mostly by rainfed agriculture with low-productivity lands and less commercialized villages.

The respondents in our study had a heterogeneous composition, reflecting the diversity in the economic activities of the informal lenders and the large variance in the economic status of the borrowers. As the following analysis reveals, we found a wide variety of credit contracts. In the discussion that follows they are organized around issues of trust and the innovative methods to enhance trust that are adopted by the informal lenders in an inadequately developed market.

Interlinking of contracts. Market interlinkage involves the process of contracting between two parties that relates two or more market exchanges, the transactions being linked in an essential manner (Braverman and Srinivasan 1980). The interlinking of two or more market transactions serves to increase information and improve contract enforcement. It also has organizational ramifications. The interlinkage of the credit transaction improves the lender's forecast of the individual's behavior, and hence his ability to select risks appropriately from a pool of potential borrowers. In addition, it expands the control variables and strategies available to a lender and enables him to influence the borrower's actions. Interlinking of contracts across markets ensures control over related activities so that incentive problems resulting from the high cost of information are minimized.

The decrease in uncertainty through market interlinkage of credit affects the complementary contract as well. Most of the microstudies on rural credit have noted that the majority of the informal lenders consider the credit-complementary activity, whether farming, trading, rice milling, or input dealership, as their primary economic activity and principal source of income (TBAC 1981; Serrano 1983; TBAC 1985). The risk and uncertainty associated with the regular and reliable supply of inputs for their primary economic activities provide an additional motive for interlinking credit. Landlords are uncertain about the level of tenants' effort and are wary of any shirking that might reduce their share of the harvest. Traders, including rice millers and wholesalers, have no assurance regarding their share of the farmers' output, which in turn determines their supply of selling inventories. Input dealers are not certain of the level of expected demand for their merchandise. Rich farmers, wishing to expand their area under cultivation, operate in an environment of undeveloped land markets and thus lack prior information on the farmers who are likely suppliers of land occupancy or usufruct rights. These agents, therefore, have an incentive to link one market transaction with another, and particularly with credit, if the interlinked contract improves their forecast of the anticipated input supply and therefore their ability to plan.

A wide variety of interlinked contracts arises in the informal sector, reflecting both the diverse economic activities in which the market agents are involved and the complexity of their gaming behavior in response to the market environment. With interlinked contracts, lenders offer various combinations of interest rate, collateral, and other noninterest terms to different types of borrowers. Interlinkage allows for nonstandardization of credit transactions, which accounts for the observed fragmentation of credit markets. The availability and acceptability of various forms of interest substitutes in informal markets play an important role in screening and sorting borrowers. As our empirical study shows, these functions have several welfare implications; for example, to the extent that collateral acceptability plays an important role in the gaming behavior of lenders and borrowers, income inequality may be promoted intergenerationally.

Our survey identified two main types of informal lenders who provide either unlinked or linked loans, and five types of interlinkage for the latter. As Table 9.1 shows, the linked loans dominate the informal credit market, accounting for over 80 percent of the total volume.

TABLE 9.1   Distribution of Linked and Unlinked Loans by Lender Type, Total, and Mean Size (Philippine pesos)

Loan type	Trader-lenders	Farmer-lenders	All informal lenders[a]
Marginal area			
Unlinked loans			
Total volume	2,981	24,580	35,128
Mean loan size	650	456	538
% of total	4.5	33.8	21.2
Linked loans			
Total volume	63,206	48,224	130,330
Mean loan size	1,999	1,976	1,945
% of total	95.5	66.2	78.8
All informal loans			
Total volume	66,187	72,804	165,458
Mean loan size	1,985	1,448	1,307
% of total	100.0	100.0	100.0
Developed area			
Unlinked loans			
Total volume	0	45,597	75,328
Mean loan size	0	970	1,045
% of total	0	37.2	17.6
Linked loans			
Total volume	255,390	76,834	352,369
Mean loan size	3,165	2,883	3,004
% of total	100.0	62.7	82.4
All informal loans			
Total volume	255,390	122,434	427,697
Mean loan size	3,165	2,326	2,867
% of total	100.0	100.0	100.0

a. All informal lender loans include loans provided by landlords, businesses, local government officials, school teachers, as well as those provided by moneylenders.
SOURCE: Floro and Yotopoulos (1991).

Five types of interlinkage are distinguished in Table 9.2, depending on whether the loan is tied to

- the provision of intermediation services in relending and/or procuring output

- the sale of output to the lender

- the purchase of inputs or lease of farm equipment from the lender

- the transfer of rights over the usufruct of the land to the lender

- the provision of labor services to the lender

The evidence presented in Table 9.2 indicates that the first three types are prevalent among trader-lenders, while the last two occur among farmer-lenders. This relationship is only slightly blurred by the existence of another category of trader-lender loans that are tied to in-

TABLE 9.2   Distribution of Linked Loans by Lender and Linkage Type and by Study Area, Total, and Mean Size

Linkage type	Trader-lenders			Farmer-lenders		
	Total loan volume (pesos)	Mean loan size (pesos)	% of total	Total loan volume (pesos)	Mean loan size (pesos)	% of total
Marginal area						
1. Intermediation services	25,914	6,957	41.0	0	0	0
2. Sale of output[a]	36,091	2,103	57.1	7,605	774	15.8
3. Purchase of inputs[b]	0	0	0	1,180	376	2.4
4. Both 2 and 3	1,162	1,162	1.9	21,293	2,529	44.1
5. Transfer of land rights	0	0	0	18,000	3,568	37.3
6. Labor services	0	0	0	145	145	0.3
All linked loans	63,167	1,999	100.0	48,223	1,976	100.0
Developed Area						
1. Intermediation services	101,576	13,500	39.8	0	0	0
2. Sale of output[a]	142,325	3,247	55.8	32,873	2,717	42.8
3. Purchase of inputs[b]	0	0	0	2,280	427	3.0
4. Both 2 and 3	9,194	1,129	3.6	10,431	2,563	13.6
5. Transfer of land rights	2,000	2,000	0.8	28,250	4,628	36.8
6. Labor services	0	0	0	3,000	1,500	3.9
All linked loans	255,095	3,165	100.0	76,834	2,883	100.0

a. Also called "tampa" loans.
b. Includes lease of machinery.
SOURCE: Floro and Yotopoulos (1991).

termediation services. These loans represent informal financial layering and create a special subcategory of farmer-lenders, the middlemen farmer-lenders. They merit additional comment.

Two-fifths of the total amount of informal credit documented in our sample was extended by farmer-lenders. Part of that credit was advanced with a tie-in to land-rights transfer that serves as ex-ante collateral. Farmer-lender loans tied to land are more complex transactions, because they imply the borrower's default for at least one period of production, which is normally the agricultural year. There are two types of loans linked to land, depending on the amount lent, the economic status of the borrower, and the quality of the land offered in collateral. *Sanglang-patay*, or "dead mortgages," are offered to the few rich borrowers who can advance as collateral highly productive land. During the fixed period of the loan (usually three to five years) the lender enjoys the usufruct rights of the mortgaged land, which he cultivates, or receives an agreed-upon portion of the borrower's harvest from that land. Once the stipulated period is over, the usufruct rights are returned to the borrower, and the loan is considered repaid in full, both principal and interest. In effect, the present value of the stream of the returns of the land for the specified period is capitalized in the amount of principal plus interest.

More frequent are transactions with poor borrowers and loan amounts that are disproportionate to the expected returns from relatively small parcels of mortgaged land of low quality. *Sanglang-buhay*, or "live mortgages," become applicable then; they entitle the lender to the usufruct rights on the land for an indefinite period, until the loan principal is paid in full. In this case, the stream of returns that accrues to the lender from the cultivation of land during the period is considered as the capitalized value of the interest, which also reflects the rate of inflation.

Table 9.2 shows that more than one-third of farmer-lender credit was connected to some type of transfer of usufruct rights over land. The advantage of both types of linked loans extended by farmers lies in circumventing the restrictions imposed on the transfer of the ownership of land, which range from high transaction costs to outright prohibition. The transfer of usufruct rights, on the other hand, fully satisfies the lender who is interested in the land's input-augmenting effect on production, especially where economies of scale exist. Moreover, debt accumulation that takes place over several loan cycles and successive defaults may also lead to the eventual transfer of land ownership.

Table 9.1 also shows that farmer-lenders provide a significant amount of unlinked credit. These loans are usually small, with an average value much smaller than that of linked loans. Such credit may be extended to accommodate the timing of farmer-lender cash flows. It is also possible that such loans are a prelude to a linked loan and the eventual transfer of the usufruct of land. This supposition is based on the practice among farmer-lenders of rolling over small defaulted loans, presumably until the relative size of the amount outstanding, in comparison to the value of the collateral, warrants the establishment of a live mortgage, as described above. This hypothesis, however, cannot be tested rigorously with the cross-section data used in the analysis, since those reflect specific moments in long-term personalized credit exchange relations that span several production periods.

Credit layering in imperfect markets. A corollary of the personal relationships of informal credit is that the number of contracts a lender can handle is limited. There are severe diseconomies of scale in monitoring personal behavior and in collecting information. Hence information costs increase faster as the number of borrowers rise beyond a certain limit. This limitation is evident from the extent of the agency relationship we observed in our sample.

The trader-lender loans attached to middlemen services represent informal financial layering and create a subcategory of farmer-lenders, the marketing-agent lenders, or *mga piyudor*. These lenders assume dual roles as farmers on their own account and as intermediaries for a trader who entrusts them with substantial amounts of capital to relend. In this dual role, they may link a loan to the transfer of land rights, acting on their own account; or they can accept loan repayment in kind at the time of harvest, acting as the trader's agents. Their access to traders' loanable funds explains why the mean size of loan tied to intermediation services is significantly greater than the mean size of any other linked loan. Financial layering becomes an empirical implication of the personalistic character of informal credit, since it reduces the borrowers served by a lender to a manageable number who can be observed closely and can be known well.

Indirect evidence and partial quantification of the agency relationship between the trader-lender and his intermediaries is available from our sample survey. Five of the eight farmer-lenders in our sample were recipients of credit capital from big trader-lenders (Table 9.3). About 40

TABLE 9.3   Principal Sources of Credit Capital for Farmer-lenders by Study Area

Source of credit capital	Marginal area		Developed area	
	Number of farmer-lenders	Percentage	Number of farmer-lenders	Percentage
Trader	2	40	3	100
Large landowner	1	20	0	0
Others[a]	2	40	0	0
Total	5	100	3	100

a. Other sources include retained earnings and foreign remittances from abroad.
SOURCE: Floro and Yotopoulos (1991).

percent of the total volume of credit extended by trader-lenders was received by farmer-borrowers who are required to provide intermediation services such as acting as marketing and lending agents to trader-lenders (Table 9.2). Moreover, the loans received by these borrowers were significantly larger than the average farmer's loan, the result of the ultimate intent of relending.

Quantity rationing in the informal sector. Quantity rationing is an important consequence of asymmetrical information and of the highly personal nature of transactions in the informal sector.[5] Quantity rationing implies that the lender allocates his credit funds by establishing his own criteria of creditworthiness, instead of clearing the market by charging what the traffic will bear. As we have already mentioned, the majority of the informal lenders consider an activity other than lending, such as farming, trading, rice milling, and input dealership as their primary economic activity and principal source of income. Few, however, place any emphasis on the relationship between the constraints faced by lenders in their principal economic activity and their participation in the credit market. The different economic considerations of informal lenders explain to a large extent their different behavior in the credit circuit. Trader-lenders, for example, want to maximize returns to their trading activities, while farmer-lenders are more interested in collaterized loans, especially those with land collateral (see Table 9.4). The particularity of trading activity under high transaction costs and intense market competition and the difficulties associated with land acquisition under conditions of inadequately formed land markets lead these groups of informal lenders to sort their borrowers by different criteria of creditworthiness and to offer a variety of credit terms. We now examine in detail the criteria selection process by heterogeneous types of lenders.

Economic considerations of informal lenders. The rapid expansion of trading activity in rural areas as a result of the dramatic increase in the marketed surplus has intensified competition for grain among traders. High volumes of grain are necessary to maintain high utilization rates of the traders' marketing-related facilities, including trucks, warehouses, and rice mills. The bigger the milling and distribution network of the trader, the greater is the pressure to procure a larger share of the output market.

Since time is an important element in the circulation of goods, traders are concerned with the velocity of capital turnover. The longer it takes the farmer to sell his output, the longer is the completion of the goods circulation cycle. It is therefore in the traders' interest to have farmers sell their output right after harvest, and in the case of traders who also lend, it is in their interest to have farmers pay their loans in terms of output as soon as possible. Trader-lenders are therefore

TABLE 9.4   Profile of Major Informal Lenders

Characteristics	Trader-lenders	Farmer-lenders
Economic activities	Trading Lending	Farming Lending
Liquidity constraint	Need to maintain highly liquid assets	Not applicable unless capital is borrowed
Collateral		
Land	Not acceptable	Acceptable
Output	Acceptable	Acceptable
Information source		
Rich borrower	Regularity in dealing with trader leads to personal ties	Proximity in the village or kinship ties lead to personal relationship
Poor borrower	Irregular dealing with trader; need for third-party guarantor	Proximity or kinship ties lead to personal relationship
Credit terms		
Timing of loan release	Start of production cycle	May be given at any time
Timing of loan collection	Strictly at harvest time	At harvest time but allows for rollover
Enforcement of loan payment	Present at first day of harvest; threat of credit line termination	Physical proximity and social pressure
Tie-in clause	Tied-in output sale or tied-in input purchase by farmer	Tied-in output sale and/or land rights transfer
Default	Termination of credit line	Allow for rollover if defaulted loan is small; land mortgage if loan is large

SOURCE: Floro and Yotopoulos (1991).

concerned with the borrower's repayment capacity, while the same is not necessarily true for farmer-lenders.

Farmer-lenders engage in lending activity not only to augment their earnings with interest income but also to acquire more land for cultivation. Moneylending becomes an important complementary activity to farming, since it gives the lender leeway in influencing not only another person's decision to give up access to his land but also the land's implicit acquisition price. Credit provision, therefore, may serve as a means of acquiring land. The survival of the practice of indirect land transfer through the debt mechanism can be attributed to several factors. One is the failure of land reform to abolish tenancy, especially in the marginal areas. Another reason is the inadequately developed land market juxtaposed with the developed output market.[6] As a result, the more common method of acquiring land is not through the open market but through the extension of credit. A third explanation is the economic vulnerability of the majority of Philippine farmers. Their general inability to make ends meet, especially during prolonged periods of drought, persistent crop failures, or unexpected emergencies requiring large cash outlays, means that farmers are sometimes compelled to give up a portion of their landholdings to pay accumulated debts or to acquire an unusually large loan.

The difference in the objective functions of trader-lenders and farmer-lenders implies, therefore, different perceptions of risk. For a trader-lender, a creditworthy borrower is a farmer with low default risk. Moreover, the trader-lender requires his borrower to pay the loan in terms of output. This assures the trader-lender of a future supply of trading inventories, which in turn reduces his market risk and at the same time lowers his transaction costs.

In contrast, a farmer-lender considers as an attractive credit risk the farmer who will default under certain conditions and who is willing to bear the consequences of the default. A farmer-lender's direct involvement in the production process, moreover, makes land a desirable form of collateral. The profit maximization behavior of farmer-lenders thus emphasizes gaining control over the usufruct of land, along with maximizing profits through the secondary activity of moneylending. This divergence in the objective function between traders and rich farmers leads to predictable behavioral differences in dealing with rich and poor borrowers.

Sorting behavior of informal lenders. Trader-lenders are expected to behave so as to maximize their inventories of tradable output right after harvest by converting all cash and loans directly or indirectly into output. This implies not only interlinking credit with output but also sorting potential borrowers positively with respect to their repayment capacity and negatively with respect to their probability of default.

Suppose that rich farmers with large landholdings are less susceptible to default than poor farmers. This assumption is reasonable, since rich farmers have relatively more collateral to offer in the form of standing crops than do poor farmers. Given the distinction between the two types of borrowers, trader-lenders tend to concentrate on good credit risks, that is, rich borrowers, since they are more likely to have marketable output, given their sizable landholdings. This decreases the per-unit supervision costs of the trader-lender. Rich farmers also deal more often in output, reducing the lender's transaction costs in assessing personal economic behavior (see Table 9.4). The economic consideration of trader-lenders, therefore, leads them to prefer transactions with rich farmers.

Farmer-lenders, on the other hand, maximize joint returns from two activities: farming and lending. The specific role of default in land collateral transfer affects the borrower preference of farmer-lenders. Since access to collateral occurs only in the event of nonrepayment of loans, farmer-lenders are more likely to lend to farmers who are more likely to default and who are willing to bear the consequences by forgoing the collateral.

The following pertinent characteristics of poor farmers illustrate why poor borrowers who are deemed "risky" by trader-lenders are considered attractive credit targets by farmer-lenders. Poor farmers not only have a high propensity to default, but also have a smaller marketable surplus to offer in interlinkage and are more likely to offer the usufruct of land in the transaction instead. They are also more vulnerable to the fluctuations of the market or the weather and are more likely to seek distress loans.

The inaccessibility of other loan sources, such as trader-lenders, aggravates the poor farmer's vulnerability by weakening his bargaining position. Moreover, the monopoly position of a farmer-lender, by virtue of credit layering within a lender's immediate physical and economic sphere of influence, further weakens the poor borrower's position. Finally, poor farmers are also politically weak and thus less likely to increase the lender's contract enforcement costs if default occurs and foreclosure becomes necessary. Under these conditions, acceptance of the tendered terms of contract with farmer-lenders, especially the transfer of land usufruct rights in case of foreclosure, becomes a signal that the borrower is likely to be a more disadvantaged farmer.

Empirical tests of the sorting behavior. The predictions of the sorting hypothesis described above are specifically tested using the data sample of 111 Philippine borrower-farm households, which have been differentiated on the basis of income (rich and poor households) and the level of agricultural productivity of the area in which they operate (developed and marginal areas). Since each of the households in our survey had contracted a number of loans, normally with more than one lender, we can rigorously test for the correspondence between different types of lenders and types of borrowers to investigate sorting patterns. Similarly, by making the size of the loan granted in each transaction a function of the household's observable characteristics, we can test for the rationing rules that apply in our sample.

The first set of tests for the sorting behavior of lenders is based on estimating conditional probabilities. Conditional probabilities regarding credit disbursements of farmer-lenders and trader-lenders are computed using our sample survey.[7] We want to know the probability, for example, that a farm household borrows from a trader-lender (event A), given that the household belongs to the lowest income category (event B)—or, alternatively, the probability that an informal lender provides a loan to a poor farmer (event A), given that the source of the loan is a trader-lender (event B). A skewed pattern of conditional probabilities would suggest that credit allocation is not random among different classes of borrowers.

The estimated conditional probabilities presented in Table 9.5 illustrate the pattern of borrowing by different household categories. In both marginal and developed areas, the probability that poor borrowers obtained their loans from farmer-lenders is higher than the probability of their having borrowed from any other source. The converse is true for rich borrowers. The probability that they received their loans from farmer-lenders is relatively low, while the probability that they borrowed from traders is fairly close to 1. This pattern suggests that as one moves up the income ladder, there is a shift in borrowing from farmer-lenders to trader-lenders.

Table 9.6 presents the estimated probabilities regarding credit disbursements of farmer-lenders and trader-lenders. The results suggest

TABLE 9.5   Estimated Probabilities of a Household's Receiving a Loan, by Lender Type, Income Class, and Study Area

	Lender type		
Income class	Farmer-lender	Trader-lender	Others[a]
Marginal area			
Poor	0.648	0.073	0.280
Middle	0.391	0.481	0.125
Rich	0.056	0.943	0.000
Developed area			
Poor	0.515	0.317	0.165
Middle	0.354	0.529	0.118
Rich	0.117	0.766	0.115

a. Other types of informal lenders include landlords, government officials, businessmen, and schoolteachers.
SOURCE: Floro and Yotopoulos (1991).

TABLE 9.6   Estimated Probabilities of Lender Types' Granting a Loan to a Household, by Income Class and Study Area

	Lender type	
Income class	Farmer-lender	Trader-lender
Marginal area		
Poor	0.748	0.096
Middle	0.205	0.193
Rich	0.046	0.711
Developed area		
Poor	0.557	0.167
Middle	0.247	0.194
Rich	0.196	0.640

SOURCE: Floro and Yotopoulos (1991).

that in general farmer-lenders tend to allocate a greater volume of their loans to poor farmers, and trader-lenders allocate a greater volume to rich farmers. This finding further confirms the existence of implicit sorting of borrowers by the lenders.

The statistical results just presented lend empirical support for the validity of the sorting proposition. They do not explain, however, how lenders ration credit within an observationally equivalent group of borrowers, given the excess demand that characterizes the credit market. The specific borrower pattern described in the previous section is also reflected in the credit terms that lenders offer to certain types of borrowers. The following test revolves around the relation between the size of the loan and borrower characteristics that proxy his repayment capacity, such as income and the agricultural environment in which he operates.

More specifically, since trader-lenders are concerned with the ability of borrowers to service outstanding debts, they make the size of the loan an increasing function of the borrower's income. This is captured in a loglinear regression model in which the size of loans provided by trader-lenders is the dependent variable, W_{st}, and the borrower's income, Y_i, is the explanatory variable. Regional differences in environmental and technical conditions are also taken into account using dummy variable A. Our regression equation is

$$W_{st} = C_0 + C_1 Y_i + C_2 A + u \tag{1}$$

All variables are in logarithmic form.

The estimated equation is given in equation 1 of Table 9.7. The positive income coefficient (at the 1 percent level of significance) suggests that there is a strong positive relationship between the size of loan a trader-lender is willing to make and the income level of the borrower. This implies that traders tend to offer bigger loans to farmers with higher income. Since this is a logarithmic function, the regression coefficient C_1 represents loan elasticity with respect to income. The sign of the second regression coefficient, C_2, suggests that traders in the two areas do not differ significantly in their credit allocation pattern.

From the viewpoint of traders, poor farmers are considered high risks so that, in most cases, traders avoid lending to this group of borrowers even if they are willing to pay a higher interest rate. The previous tests indicate that not many traders grant loans directly to poor borrowers. There are some cases, however, in which trader-lenders lend to poor borrowers. This occurs whenever an increase in interest rate is not offset by its adverse effect on default, or when the poor borrower is also a relative or friend, in which case the trader has personal knowledge of his activities and repayment performance. The existence of trust enables the trader in this case to provide a loan, although he will charge a higher interest rate to compensate for the borrower's riskiness.

TABLE 9.7   Results of Least-Squares Regression Analysis for Trader-Lender Loans, All Households

Equation	Dependent variable[a]	Intercept	Y_i	k_i	D
1.	W_{st}	2.42	0.41*		−0.30
	(7.92)	(1.79)	(3.24)		(−1.18)
	$F = 5.64*$				
	(2,86 d.f.)				
	Adj. $R^2 = 0.15$				
2.	r_m	28.46*	−2.18*		3.20
	(14.65)	(3.83)	(−2.90)		(1.53)
	$F = 5.66*$				
	(2,86 d.f.)				
	Adj. $R^2 = 0.11$				
3.	r_m	6.93		1.17	1.62
	(14.65)	(6.25)		(1.93)	(0.72)
	$F = 3.37*$				
	(2,86 d.f.)				
	Adj. $R^2 = 0.05$				

Explanatory variables (column span: Intercept, Y_i, k_i, D)

NOTES: Blank cell = not applicable.
There were 97 trader loans in total. Because of missing values, however, only 89 observations were used.
a. All variables are in natural log form except for r_m. Starred coefficients are significant at the 95% level. Numbers in parentheses indicate the mean values for the dependent variable, t-ratios for the explanatory variables, and the degrees of freedom for F.
Variables are defined as
W_{st} = Size of loan provided by the trader-lender in pesos.
r_m = Effective monthly rate of interest on the loan.
Y_i = Household income for the period in pesos.
k_i = The incidence of default.
D = Dummy variable taking the value 0 for developed areas and 1 for marginal areas.
SOURCE: Floro and Yotopoulos (1991).

To test this postulate, we estimate two single-equation models for all loans granted by trader-lenders to determine the causation between (1) the borrower's income, Y, and the effective interest rate charged by lenders, r_m, and (2) the incidence of default, k, and r_m. Variation in area location is also taken into account using dummy variable A. Our regression equations are

$$r_m = B_0 + B_1 Y_i + B_2 A + u \qquad (2)$$

$$r_m = B_0 + B_1 k_i + B_2 A + u \qquad (3)$$

A semilog transformation regression analysis of the effective interest rate is applied to each of the models. The results suggest that trader-lenders differentiate their interest rate charges on the basis of the borrower's income. In estimated equation 2 of Table 9.7, the coefficient of

Y has the anticipated negative sign for trader-lenders. The regression co-efficient of the default rate, on the other hand, has the expected positive sign shown in equation 3 estimates.[8] The latter implies that from the trader-lenders' viewpoint, higher income borrowers are not only less risky but also less costly to supervise and to monitor; hence, they charge lower interest rates to rich than to poor borrowers. Given the calculated t-ratio for the dummy variable, the regional variation effect between marginal and developed areas was found to be not statistically significant.

Farmer-lenders, in contrast to trader-lenders, are willing and able to lend to poor borrowers. The potential gains consist not only of interest earnings, but more important, of the opportunity to gain access to the borrowers' land. Since land transfer can take place only upon default, farmer-lenders are inclined to deal with borrowers who have a high default propensity. These are the poor farmers who, in Table 9.8, are shown to be highly susceptible to land foreclosure, thus making them "creditworthy" to farmer-lenders.

Three regression models are estimated for all farmer-lender loans to analyze this lender group preference and their lending behavior. The first regression model examines the causation between borrower's income Y and the effective interest rate charged by farmer-lenders r_m.[9] The second model determines whether any negative relationship exists between the incidence of borrower default k and the effective interest rate r_m. A third model is estimated in order to test whether the size of the loan granted by farmer-lenders, W_{sf}, is positively correlated to a borrower's propensity to default k. The dummy variable A is introduced in each of

TABLE 9.8   Percentage Distribution of Household Land Mortgages by Income Class and Study Area

Income class	Number of households with mortgage	Percentage
Marginal area		
Poor	15	94
Middle	1	6
Rich	0	0
Total	16	100
Developed area		
Poor	5	56
Middle	3	33
Rich	1	11
Total	9	100

SOURCE: Floro and Yotopoulos (1991).

the equations to explain as much of the environment-related behavior as possible. The regression equations to be estimated are the following:

$$r_m = B_0 + B_1 Y_i + B_2 A + u \tag{4}$$

$$r_m = B_0 + B_1 k_i + B_2 A + u \tag{5}$$

$$W_{sf} = B_0 + B_1 Y_i + B_2 k_i + B_3 A + u \tag{6}$$

The results of a semilog transformation regression analysis are presented in Table 9.9. There is a positive and statistically significant

TABLE 9.9   Results of Least-Squares Regression Analysis for Farmer-Lender Loans, All Households

Equation	Dependent variable[a]	Intercept	Y_i	k_i	D
		Explanatory variables			
4.	r_m	−17.40*	4.24*		1.39
	(18.82)	(7.29)	(3.65)		(1.41)
	$F = 6.71^*$				
	(2,96 d.f.)				
	Adj. $R^2 = 0.14$				
5.	r_m	16.63*		−4.70*	3.03
	(18.82)	(7.29)		(−6.18)	(1.82)
	$F = 7.11^*$				
	(2,96 d.f.)				
	Adj. $R^2 = 0.16$				
6.	W_{sf}	7.71*	−0.27*	0.51*	0.89*
	(6.83)	(3.66)	(−1.22)	(2.51)	(−2.54)
	$F = 4.57^*$				
	(3,95 d.f.)				
	Adj. $R^2 = 0.16$				

NOTES: Blank cell = not applicable.
There were 107 farmer-lender loans. Because of missing values, however, only 99 observations were used. Mortgage loans were included with a zero effective interest rate.
a. All variables are in natural log form except for r_m. Starred coefficients are significant at the 95% level. Numbers in parentheses indicate the mean values for the dependent variable, t-ratios for the explanatory variables, and the degrees of freedom for F.
Variables are defined as
W_{sf} = Size of loan provided by the farmer-lender in pesos.
r_m = Effective monthly rate of interest on the loan.
Y_i = Household income for the period in pesos.
k_i = The incidence of default.
D = Dummy variable taking the value 0 for developed areas and 1 for marginal areas.
SOURCE: Floro and Yotopoulos (1991).

relationship between the interest rate and borrower's income in equation 4. Concomitantly, the relation between the rate of interest and the default propensity is significant and negative in equation 5. The regional-variation effect is statistically insignificant. In other words, there is no difference in the interest rates between marginal and developed areas, once income and the propensity to default have been controlled for.

These results have some interesting economic implications. The regression analyses indicate that farmer-lenders offer bigger loans at relatively low interest rates to farmers with higher propensity to default. Such behavior is rational if the returns to lending also include transfer of the collateral land rights. Low interest rates and lenient overall credit terms that allow for rollover of defaulted loans may also deter the borrower from spreading his loan demand over several lenders in the expectation of avoiding land transfer. In other words, the evidence suggests that farmer-lenders offer accommodating terms to high-risk borrowers in order to weaken their resistance to land mortgage.

Cost of Borrowing and Equity Considerations

The previous discussion focused on the resilience of IFI and its adaptability to prevailing market conditions. Credit layering, market interlinkage, and the process of screening and sorting borrowers are based on a situational foundation of trust that is specific to the informal credit sector. By internalizing externalities that are intrinsic in the highly imperfect residual credit market, the informal sector can extend credit beyond the narrow confines of "bankability" that exist for the rigid and overregulated formal financial intermediaries. There is, indeed, general agreement that the informal sector is more efficient than the formal credit sector in the absence of developed markets and market-support infrastructure.

As distinct from efficiency issues, equity considerations relate to the cost of borrowing and the terms of access to credit in informal markets.

Cost of borrowing in the informal sector. Table 9.10 shows a wide range of interest rates applicable in our sample. The stipulated monthly interest rate ranged from 6.3 percent to 26.1 percent, depending on the type of loan and on the relationship established with the borrower. More specifically, we find in our study sample of 297 informal, commercial loans that unlinked loans bear significantly higher nominal interest rates than linked loans. In addition, for both linked and unlinked loans the nominal interest rate is lower in the more developed areas surveyed, which have greater wealth and higher levels of agricultural productivity. Interest charges are higher in the poor areas surveyed. These trends reflect, as expected, the risk premium that is incorporated in nominal

TABLE 9.10   Stipulated and Effective Monthly Rates of Interest by Loan Type and Study
Area (percentage)

| | Marginal area | | Developed area | |
Type of loan	Stipulated rate (r_c)	Effective rate (r_m)	Stipulated rate (r_c)	Effective rate (r_m)
Unlinked loans[a]	20.0	19.2	14.6	14.4
Linked loans[a]	12.7	17.7	9.7	16.5
1. Intermedia- tion services	8.7	9.2	6.3	6.2
2. Sale of out- put	11.8	17.0	8.4	15.3
3. Purchase of inputs[b]	13.5	18.3	19.1	21.1
4. Both 2 and 3	14.4	20.7	12.4	15.2
5. Transfer of land rights to lender	—	—	—	—
6. Labor services	13.8	26.1	9.2	31.9

NOTE: Dash = not available.
a. Mean for each loan type is the weighted average interest rate for all loans under each category with size
of loan as weight.
b. Includes lease of machinery.
SOURCE: Floro and Yotopoulos (1991).

rates of interest: The risk of default is greater in unlinked loans and, other things being equal, it is greater in poorer agricultural areas.

The stipulated rate of interest is not fully representative of the cost of borrowing in the case of linked loans. Market interlinkage increases the scope of hidden charges that can encumber a loan and requires a more comprehensive approach to the measurement of returns to lending. Effective rates of interest are therefore estimated and also include implicit charges, such as input overpricing, output underpricing, and so on. Once these charges are taken into account, the interest rate differential between unlinked and linked loans decreases dramatically and so does the variance in stipulated rates of interest by type of loan and borrower. Moreover, if one abstracts from the two special cases of provision of intermediation services and of provision of labor services,[10] it appears that in the most frequent type of interlinkage, credit with the sale of output, it is the adjustment in the price of output that makes up for the extremely low stipulated interest rate.[11]

In conclusion, the analysis suggests a well-functioning market in which nominal and effective interest rates tend to converge, with the existing differentials in favor of linked loans and developed areas being consistent with a priori expectations about the risk premium.

A well-functioning market does not necessarily rule out the existence of monopoly returns accruing to the sellers. For that purpose, effective competition and/or regulation is also necessary. Although entry into the informal credit market is not regulated and the capital requirements for lenders are relatively low, the importance of personal transactions as a basis for trust sets the boundaries in which competition takes place. In certain cases, such as interlinkage of credit with the transfer of usufruct rights to land, locational proximity between the lender and the borrower further restricts the scope of competition. Finally, lack of regulation of stipulated interest rates in the informal market (and the virtual impossibility of regulating effective interest rates) leaves the lenders a broad range of discretion in setting the terms of the contract so that they can enjoy substantial economic rents. Moreover, informal lenders are also more likely to use this discretion to their advantage, since the personal relationship that develops makes it unnecessary to treat the borrower's willingness to pay a high interest rate as a signal that he intends to default. As a result, self-regulation of interest rates, which is common in the case of formal financial intermediaries, is rather unlikely in informal financial intermediaries.

Besides these IFI-specific equity considerations, the general equity issues that arise in all credit markets are also applicable. Other things being equal, the degree of competition in each segment of the informal credit market varies according to the borrower's status and his resource endowments. Even where there are many lenders, a poor farmer-borrower can face a situation similar to that of confronting a monopolistic lender. A rich farmer, on the other hand, is likely to face a more competitive market with both trader-lenders and middlemen farmer-lenders willing and able to offer credit. Both FFI and IFI take place not within a continuous and uniform market, but in a market with gradations of bankability, with the smaller and poorer borrowers who do not possess acceptable collateral falling off the scale of bankable risks.[12] On the other hand, when informal agricultural credit is concerned, land represents both wealth for collateral and potential output to link with the credit transaction. Accessibility to credit and potential resistance to land transfer become, therefore, increasing functions of land ownership, and the effective interest rate charged decreases correspondingly.

Conclusions and Policy Implications

Any transaction that involves the promise to deliver (in the future and/or according to certain specifications) entails trust in a fundamental way. FFI relies heavily on the institutional and market infrastructure that builds trust, while IFI, operating mostly at the edge of the formal and organized market, uses a web of interpersonal relationships and credit interlinkage to other markets as vehicles for creating and enhancing trust. Transaction costs, quantity rationing, and sorting rules in the informal credit market of the Philippines have been analyzed with reference to the trust characteristics of the credit contract.

The trust requisite of the credit contract is reflected in all-pervasive asymmetries in the allocation of credit, whether by FFI or IFI. It is therefore simplistic to single out the formal credit sector and to attribute its limited reach to "financial repression" associated with government acts of commission or omission (McKinnon 1973; Adams 1983). The "repressed" credit markets are not repressed because of regulation of financial intermediaries, government intervention in the credit market, or mandatory ceilings on the rate of interest, since the unregulated and unsupervised informal sector also mirrors such asymmetries. Although many of the issues raised by critics of financial regulation are valid, their exclusive preoccupation with government myopia instead of a broader interest in institutional structure and in farmer creditworthiness often leads to the wrong type of policy recommendations. Attributing the restrained growth of financial markets not to inherent characteristics of credit transactions but to government repression leads to recommending unrealistic "set-the-prices-right" reforms.

An alternative approach to extending the reach of credit is to infuse into FFI some of the flexibility of IFI while also strengthening the structure of the informal credit market. The widespread use of informal financial markets for meeting credit needs has given rise to a growing consensus that informal credit is well suited to most rural conditions (Von Pischke et al. 1983, 8). Moreover, there are lessons that can be gleaned from the informal market operations that are useful for making policy adjustments affecting the formal sector. The result is a number of creative policy schemes that propose:

- to increase the reach of the informal sector

- to apply certain strategies of the informal market agents in the formal sector as part of the financial institutions' revitalization scheme

- to integrate the informal sector into formal financial intermediation in an effort to enhance the overall performance of the financial system

Three recent credit programs in the Philippines make use of the informal sector as a conduit of government loanable funds or of credit extended by the formal sector.

The Quedan Guarantee Fund Board (QGFB) is an agency attached to the Ministry of Agriculture and Food (MAF) that uses the *quedan,* or warehouse receipt, as a loan guarantee. Traders and millers who borrow from participating banks qualify for the guarantee of 80 percent of the loan value on the basis of grain stocks they hold in a bonded warehouse. The traders and millers in turn extend production loans to farmers, subject to the tie-in provision that (a portion of) the grain harvest be sold to a specified *quedan* operator. Presently, QGFB serves grain merchants and farmers who are engaged in the small-scale trading of output. By providing access to government funds, the QGFB augments the capital base of trader-lenders and farmer-lenders. Although the QGFB receives no government subsidies, it has been able to expand its operations and to leverage its relatively small capital base of P150 million into covering loans totaling four times that amount—largely because of the 99 percent loan repayment record it has achieved, as shown in Table 9.11.

Two other low-cost special financing schemes are targeted mainly to input suppliers who are used as conduits for lending to farmers with loan interlinkage provisions. The Philippine Planters' Product Credit Scheme (PPC) makes available to input suppliers a special credit line at 12 percent annual interest on the condition that they organize distribution channels for fertilizer and pesticide credit to farmers. The credit

TABLE 9.11   Summary Performance of Selected Credit Programs, Cumulative Data as of September 1986 (millions of Philippine pesos)

Credit program	Total loans released	Total loans collected	Repayment rate[a] (%)
Quedan financing			
Traders/processors	1,767.3	1,625.5	99.8
Small farmers	6.1	3.6	92.6
Subtotal	1,773.4	1,629.1	
End Users/Input Suppliers Scheme			
Intensified Rice Production Program[b]	46.8	32.2	89.0
Expanded Corn Program[c]	78.3	57.1	94.0
National Rootcrops Program[d]	6.6	1.5	—
Subtotal	131.7	90.8	

NOTE: Dash = not available.
a. Repayment rate is computed as % of loans repaid to loans matured x 100.
b. Cumulative from Phases 1–4.
c. Cumulative from Phases 84B to 86B.
d. Cumulative from Phases 1(1985) to 2(1986).
SOURCE: Esguerra (1987).

extended by the dealer is tied to the purchase of the modern inputs of production with the purpose of encouraging the adoption of high-yielding technologies. The End-Users/Input-Suppliers Assistance Scheme, on the other hand, extends production loans to farmers using traders, rice millers (end users), and input dealers (input suppliers) as intermediaries. The latter have access to subsidized government loans (at 6 percent per annum inclusive of service charges), which they relend to farmers at 15 percent per annum.

The policy of channeling formal credit to informal lenders has been justified on the grounds of efficiency and increased financial integration, especially among small farmers. Informal lenders can build a personal relationship with their borrowers that can ensure an extremely low loan default rate. Table 9.11 attests to the programs' high repayment rates. The relative success of these programs, however, does not necessarily translate into wider credit accessibility and to increased financial integration of small farmers. Our study suggests that such programs may only increase the layering of agricultural credit, an intrinsic feature of the informal sector. An initial evaluation of the PPC and End-Users/Input-Suppliers Scheme provides no direct verification that the funds channeled through the informal conduits reached more farmer-borrowers and gives no information on the terms at which credit was extended. Moreover, the study found evidence that trader-lenders tended to favor rich borrowers. It is therefore possible that any additional funds made available through informal conduits could possibly result in bigger loans for the same number of farmers.

Credit layering is another corollary of the personal relationship of informal intermediaries. The loans trader-lenders extended to their farmer *sukis* and linked to intermediation services represent informal financial layering and create a subcategory of farmer-lenders, the marketing-agent lenders. Credit layering therefore implies that capital passes through several hands before finally reaching the small farmer-borrowers. A legitimate question that needs to be answered in this regard is what proportion of the credit subsidy under the End-Users/Input-Suppliers' Scheme, for example, is captured by the trader-recipient and the marketing agent-lenders. Moreover, given the fungibility of credit, does the likelihood of credit-diversion to unauthorized uses increase?

Another concern is the outcome of credit transactions under adverse conditions. One can make a persuasive case that the broad availability of agricultural credit on terms that are affordable by small farmers and that do not lead to default has a positive value for social welfare and overall economic growth. But these positive effects could also be reversed when lack of credit leads to default and the land is transferred to another operator who has access to credit at better terms.

This usually implies land consolidation in countries that already face wide income disparities, and may therefore exacerbate political instability. In this regard, the informal lenders' conduit schemes must be carefully reexamined to determine whether they are efficient and equitable instruments for channeling credit.

Undoubtedly, both government assistance and government regulation are required to improve the performance of financial markets, especially in developing countries. But any rehabilitation policy package, whether it involves the formal institutions alone or includes the informal sector as well, must take into account the crucial impact that the general economic environment and the specific institutional infrastructure has on financial markets. Conditions typical of underdeveloped countries make lending to small farmers in particular both risky and costly. Asymmetries in credit distribution are often the outcomes of existing market conditions as well as of the skewed distribution of resources. For any proposed solution to have permanent effects, it must address the lenders' problems, including the lack of market information and of infrastructural support services that reduce transaction costs, and the problems faced by borrowers that involve their economic viability and translate directly into their creditworthiness.

Chapter 10   Tyler S. Biggs

Heterogeneous Firms and Efficient Financial Intermediation in Taiwan

Credit has been a long-standing concern of those interested in promoting greater participation of small and medium-sized firms in industrial sectors of less developed countries (LDCs). The oft-stated problem is how to finance the emergence and growth of smaller enterprises, given their unequal access to formal financial institutions. Two ideas form the core of most advice about how to solve this problem. The first is that "supply-leading" concessional credit programs are necessary to give small enterprises (especially new start-ups) adequate access to credit. The second is that financial market integration and liberalization are required to ensure adequate flows of financial resources at reasonable cost to the private sector and particularly to small firms. On this second point, the literature on financial development is adamant that fragmented markets (fragments of the market with substantially different interest rates, excluding risk premiums and transaction costs) discourage credit use in some parts of the economy and encourage its use in others, reducing the efficiency of capital allocation and thus economic growth.

This chapter examines how the problem of financing small-scale enterprise was solved in Taiwan, a country with one of the world's most successful records of small enterprise development. The discussion focuses on how Taiwan dealt with the problem of credit intermediation in an industrial setting characterized by heterogeneous, family-owned firms and extraordinarily high information costs. Were supply-leading concessional credit programs and special banks for small enterprises essential to Taiwan's success? What about the nature of the financial system: Did integration and liberalization of financial markets play a role in channeling more funds to small and medium enterprises and in raising the efficiency of credit allocation?

The answer to the first question can be stated simply.[1] Supply-leading credit programs played only a minor role in the development of small enterprise in Taiwan. Many developing countries, especially India, have done far more to promote small enterprise than has Taiwan. Only a small proportion of domestic credit flowed through specialized banks to small and medium firms, and most of these loans were to medium-sized establishments for working capital to finance exports. Moreover, government–supported credit guarantees and other such programs have been relatively small in number. Since most successful firms in Taiwan have grown from small beginnings in the past three decades, it is questionable whether, at least in a country where entry barriers are low and incentives favor the reinvestment of profits, financial institutions and programs that specially serve small enterprises are really necessary.

The answer to the second question, which addresses the nature of the financial system, is more complex and is the subject of the remaining sections of this chapter. Put simply, our main conclusion is that Taiwan's experience calls into question the conventional wisdom, which prescribes everywhere greater financial market integration, through financial liberalization, to increase the allocative efficiency of investable resources. It may be true that substantial differences in interest rates (adjusted for risk and transactions costs) across markets reduce allocative efficiency; but Taiwan's experience suggests that decentralization of lending and fragmentation of borrowing groups, to optimize screening and monitoring of loans, can reduce intermediation costs and increase investment efficiency in LDCs with information-imperfect financial markets. A call to eliminate fragmentation of financial markets in countries where industrial competitiveness depends on innovative small enterprises, and where there are significant information constraints and imperfections in financial markets, might entail prohibitive adjustment costs. On the basis of field surveys in Taiwan in 1987, I found that a dualistic financial system helped Taiwan solve several important development problems. First, the government-controlled banks helped policy makers limit private economic power, foster industrial policy, and control inflation. Second, the curb market helped credit intermediaries allocate funds to "information-intensive" borrowers at a lower cost and more efficiently than would have been possible if all investable resources were channeled through formal sector banks.

This chapter begins with a description of the size structure of Taiwanese industry, together with an analysis of how a heterogenous firm structure affects the efficiency of credit intermediation. I then examine how Taiwan managed to overcome its significant credit intermediation problems by allowing the development of a dualistic financial system—with one fragment serving "full-information" borrowers, the other (the curb market) serving "information-intensive" borrowers. Succeeding sections survey Taiwan's curb markets and discuss why the curb market matters in a developing country like Taiwan.

Efficient Intermediation and the Size Structure of Industry

Taiwan's businessmen have a preference for family-controlled, independent companies. As one businessman in Taipei put it, "If you stood in the middle of this city and tossed a stone in any direction, you'd probably hit a boss." This proclivity for family ownership and independence plus the historical absence of state policies encouraging large enterprises (and many factors that have eased entry) have produced an industrial firm structure heavily weighted toward small and medium-sized companies.

In 1986, Taiwan had almost 115,000 firms.[2] More than 98 percent of these establishments had fewer than 300 employees, and 48 percent of these employed fewer than 5 workers. The evolution of Taiwan's firm size structure over the last two decades is summarized by the following statistic: Between 1966 and 1986, the number of establishments in Taiwan grew by 315 percent, while average firm size, as measured by the number of employees, increased by only 15 percent. In terms of production, small and medium-sized firms contributed about 50 percent of manufacturing value added, much of it for export, and employed about 62 percent of the work force. Interestingly, the largest enterprises, those with 500 or more employees, actually saw their share of net value added decline, from 46 percent to 37 percent, in the past twenty years.

Although small firms multiplied in number, it was the medium-sized companies that performed best in many industries. Between 1966 and 1986, medium-sized establishments raised their net value of production per enterprise at an annual rate of 23 percent, compared with 18 percent for larger firms, and 14 percent for small ones. Total factor productivity in 60 percent of Taiwan's industries grew fastest in the middle of the size distribution of firms. Medium-sized enterprises also created jobs at a rate of more than 20 percent per year, while small enterprises raised employment by 11 percent and large enterprises by 10 percent.

Small and medium-sized firms in Taiwan produce about half of gross manufacturing value added, albeit in many industries they are responsible for the major part of output. Table 10.1 shows the share of small and medium firms (those with fewer than 300 employees) in the value of sales of twenty manufacturing industries for the year 1985. As expected, these enterprises play a relatively minor role in highly capital-intensive industries such as chemical materials, electrical machinery, beverages, and transport equipment. In most other industries, however, smaller enterprises make a major contribution to total sales.

More important still, small and medium enterprises contribute significantly to the total value of Taiwan's exports. According to figures from Taiwan's Medium and Small Business Administration (1987), small and medium enterprises were responsible for 65 percent of total

TABLE 10.1   Share of Small and Medium-sized Enterprises in Total Industry Sales Value, 1985

Industry	Sales value (%)
Food	33
Beverage	22
Textile	41
Wearing apparel	76
Leather	80
Lumber	80
Printing	58
Chemical materials	11
Chemical products	61
Coal products	50
Rubber products	55
Plastic products	79
Nonmetallic mineral products	58
Basic metal	39
Metal products	78
Machinery	70
Electrical machinery	34
Transport equipment	38
Precision equipment	70
Misc. manufacturing	75
Total (small and medium-sized enterprises)	50

SOURCE: Medium and Small Business Administration (1987, 115).

export value in 1985. (In the same year, small and medium trading companies were responsible for 55 percent of the value of export trading business.) Independently and in tight subcontracting networks, with flexible production technology, small firms have facilitated a product-differentiated niche strategy in international markets. Taiwan's firms have been quick to move into fast-growing product areas and to redesign products to meet the changing demands of the world market. All of these strategic factors have helped Taiwan offset any competitive disadvantage that would have resulted from limited economies of scale.[3]

Imperfect information and credit rationing. With industrial competitiveness dependent on the success of small and medium firms, Taiwan's financial institutions faced enormous problems. To provide the financing necessary for new start-ups, working capital, and expansion, financial intermediaries had to find a way to overcome exceptionally high information costs. Information costs (or screening costs) are the costs a lender incurs in trying to distinguish between the risk and potential profitability characteristics of different borrowers. In an industrial setting with many new and heterogeneous firms, which are family-owned and follow unreliable accounting practices, information costs can be prohibitive. Under such conditions, banks generally ration credit and discriminate against small borrowers. I turn now to a detailed discussion of the problems of credit intermediaries in markets with imperfect information.

Financial markets with imperfect information do not operate in the same smooth Walrasian fashion as do financial markets with full information. Where no information problems exist, competitive equilibrium involves clearing supply and demands for loanable funds through collateral and interest rate movements. Borrowers with different characteristics can be charged differential market-clearing interest rates, or can be asked to provide collateral based on information about their riskiness and potential income streams. Where information costs are significant, however, lenders (banks) have difficulty distinguishing good borrowers from bad borrowers. As a result, loan contracts cannot be written in a way that discriminates among borrowers. Nor will lenders be able to monitor the behavior of borrowers effectively after they have received loans. In this situation, credit rationing and inefficient credit allocation turn out to be the "efficient" outcome of the unfettered rational behavior of lenders (Stiglitz and Weiss 1981).

To understand how banks operate in the presence of imperfect information, one has to know something about the production and information environment that lenders face. It is convenient to begin our discussion by setting out a stylized representation of Taiwan's environment.[4]

By and large, banks in Taiwan deal with broad, observationally distinguishable groups of borrowers, characterized by firm size. Within each group, the net profits of individual firms are determined by three important variables: a production function (group-specific),[5] which relates a firm's profits to the value of purchased inputs; a collection of firm-specific assets (management ability, technological capability, reputation in the business and social community), which fix the level of technical and allocative efficiency; and a stochastic term, which defines firm-specific effects of exogenous shocks (government policy changes, business cycles, input supply shocks, and so on). Net profits measure the firm's debt repayment capacity.

Each firm has a good estimate of the *specific* distribution of its net expected profits, as well as its expected returns on investments, based on historical experience, knowledge of firm-specific assets, and its production function. Bank lending officers, on the other hand, know the *average* characteristics of each group, but because information costs are high, they cannot distinguish between members of each group (particularly at the small end), nor can they monitor the individual behavior of group members. In such an environment, banks are vulnerable to changes in the group composition and shifts in the behavior of individual group members.

Banks correctly perceive several differences in the *average* characteristics of each group. First, the probability density function of the risk parameter for small firms differs from that of large firms. Small firms (particularly new firms) have, on average, a much higher probability of failure, and, because they are vulnerable to exogenous shocks, exhibit more erratic fluctuations in average profits. In short, small firms, as a group, are riskier borrowers from the lenders' point of view. Second, in some industries the average profit rate of small firms is less than that of larger firms. Third, the level of firm-specific assets, on average, is higher among larger firms than among small ones.[6] It is these perceived group characteristics that form the basis for lending decisions when banks have imperfect information about individual group members.

Banks offer loan contracts to maximize their expected profits. Two terms are specified in these contracts: collateral requirements and interest rates. If banks are permitted to vary both terms freely, and if they have enough information to discriminate among individual borrowers (that is, if they know firm-specific risk parameters, monetary and nonmonetary assets, and productivity), a credit market equilibrium will ensue in which there is no excess demand for loanable funds and intermediation is allocatively efficient. In equilibrium, every borrower will be willing to pay the contractual terms necessary to yield the bank its expected profit. Small firms that display average group characteristics (higher risk, lower productivity, and fewer firm-specific assets) will be offered less favorable terms than large firms.[7] Small firms that perform at a higher level and are less risky will be offered terms equivalent to those offered large firms.

Credit market equilibrium with high information costs. What happens to credit market equilibrium when information costs are high and bankers have imperfect knowledge about individual borrower characteristics? The answer depends on the lender's credit allocation procedures and on whether borrower behavior responds to changes in the terms of credit contracts. We may begin with the case of fixed borrower behavior.

Having information only on the *average* characteristics of borrower groups, banks will offer firms with equal characteristics different loan terms if they are members of different size groups. Even when a small firm is above average in terms of risk and productivity, banks will "tag" the firm according to its group characteristics. Because loan officers rely on firm size as an (imperfect) signal of individual firm characteristics, banks will "statistically discriminate" against the progressive small enterprise. Relatively productive, low-risk small firms will be offered discriminatory loan contract terms, resulting in reduced credit use.

The by-product of discouraged credit use is a distorted equilibrium allocation of credit away from high-productivity small enterprises. If, as in Taiwan, progressive small enterprises are important for industrial competitiveness, such distorted credit allocation could slow growth. Correction of this allocative inefficiency requires credit intermediaries that can collect and process information more efficiently than banks.

When borrower behavior can respond to changes in the terms of loan contracts, the negative effect of high information costs on efficient credit market equilibrium is increased. Stiglitz and Weiss note two ways that loan contract terms can influence borrower behavior, assuming that borrowers can freely decide whether to apply for credit and can choose how to use the credit once they receive it.[8] First, raising the interest rate (or collateral requirements) has an incentive effect. As rates rise, the incentive for borrowers to choose riskier projects increases. To cover the higher cost of debt, borrowers will often divert credit to higher return, but often riskier, investments, raising the probability of default. Borrowers can respond to changing contract terms in this way because lenders find it too costly to obtain the necessary information to monitor borrower behavior. Second, raising the interest rate causes an adverse selection effect. As interest rates increase, good borrowers self-select out of the credit market in a way that worsens *average* borrower characteristics (from the lenders' viewpoint). Because they have asymmetric information about group member characteristics, banks are vulnerable to such changes in group composition.

The result of these effects is to reduce the lender's expected return as the interest rate rises. As a consequence, unfettered credit market equilibrium can exhibit self-imposed interest rate (and collateral) restrictions and nonprice quantity rationing, resulting in an excess demand for loans. Irrespective of this excess demand, banks will find it unprofitable to raise the rate of interest because of the deterioration of average borrower characteristics. Thus, if either the adverse incentive or selection effect from raising interest rates is strong, interest rates will not be used to equilibrate the loan market. Increases or decreases in the loan supply function may have no effect on the interest rate charged. The market rate of interest may also change with changing economic circumstances, but not necessarily in a way that will be stabilizing, or in a manner that would be suggested by conventional supply-and-demand analysis (Stiglitz and Weiss 1988).

If the possibility of direct voluntary default is added to borrower behavior, the bank's credit offer curve and the nature of credit market equilibrium would change still more from the case in which borrower behavior is fixed, particularly if incentives for default vary positively with contract terms. Formal financial institutions are generally limited in the types of indirect controls they can use to raise the cost of voluntary default and lessen adverse incentive effects. Correcting for the effects of borrower behavior is accomplished in informal credit markets by such devices as interlinking credit transactions with transactions in product markets and strictly constraining access to future credit (more on this point later).

When there is quantity rationing in credit markets, small firms are the first to be cut out. Even if adverse selection and incentive effects are the same in both groups, differences in the expected profitability of loans to each group (because of average group characteristics) cause small firms to be rationed out of the market. If banks perceive adverse selection and incentive effects to be larger in the small firm group, their rationing of small firms will be even greater.

It is likely that conditions in credit markets with imperfect information largely work to ration economically viable small firms out of the formal sector. When this occurs, the return on the excluded group's investments may be higher than the investments of some of those borrowers that have access to credit. In such cases, credit rationing clearly leads to allocative inefficiency.

Credit market equilibrium with restriction on loan contracts. In Taiwan, as in many other countries, loan contract terms are restricted by government policy. Banks (in part because they are government controlled) are not free to vary collateral at will because of political sensitivities (although bank collateral requirements have been stiff). In addition, interest rate controls have been in place since the late 1950s. Such restrictions on the terms of loan contracts can impinge on efficient financial market equilibrium.

With interest rate controls and a collateral ceiling, there may be no combination of collateral and interest rates that banks can offer to offset the higher risk and lower profitability of many smaller enterprises. In this situation, banks simply refuse to lend to small firms and shift their lending to the better collateralized and, on average, safer and more productive large firms. As in the case of self-imposed bank interest rate restrictions, credit market equilibrium will involve nonprice quantity rationing and allocative inefficiency. Liberalization of interest rate controls would eliminate this discriminatory rationing and lead to a more equitable and efficient equilibrium. But the resulting equilibrium would only be second-best. In the presence of significant information costs, abolishing interest rate repression is not sufficient to achieve optimal allocative efficiency of investable resources.

Financial regulation in Taiwan. Intermediation problems caused by industrial size structure and imperfect information have been aggravated in Taiwan by strict financial regulation, by selective credit controls, and by repressed interest rates.[9] Taiwan's formal financial system has been rigidly controlled over the last three decades. Banks are government owned and bureaucratically regulated, and the authorities have largely inhibited competition from foreign banks. Nonbank financial institutions have also been highly constrained. One result of this rigid government regulation has been that banks (the dominant credit institutions) operate through very bureaucratic and conservative procedures.

In simple fact, banks in Taiwan have functioned as little more than a chain of pawnshops: Three-quarters or more of what they lend must be secured by collateral, generally in fixed assets. Administration of banks has been mired in red tape and often inefficiency. Because bank officials have been held personally responsible for every penny of "the state's money" by government auditors, they have taken few risks; their main object being to avoid errors and to advance through the bureaucracy (Gold 1981). In such an atmosphere, the propensity for credit rationing and inefficient intermediation substantially increases.

Two of the most important elements of financial regulation have been controlled interest rates and selective credit controls. Bank interest rates in Taiwan have been subject to direct government control, and government has consistently exercised this control as an important factor in monetary policy. Throughout the 1960s and 1970s, official interest rates were controlled at levels well below the natural rate that would have cleared the market. The large 10 to 20 percentage point gap in the 1960s and 1970s between official loan rates and curb market rates is evidence of this disequilibrium.[10] Undoubtedly, controlled interest rates have aggravated credit rationing and allocative inefficiencies in official loan markets and have been responsible for a diversion of savings into the unregulated financial sector. Unlike many other developing countries, however, Taiwan managed to reduce some of the worst effects of repressed interest rates by maintaining positive, albeit disequilibrium, real rates for most years.

Since the 1950s, concessional selective credit programs have also been part of the government's financial policy. Exporters, "strategic industries," and other types of enterprises have, through special discount windows at the central bank, received bank loans at less than general loan rates (which were already controlled at levels below the equilibrium rate). With the addition of special interest rates (and outright channeling of bank credit to favored borrowers) a three-tiered credit market emerged. At the top were enterprises such as exporters, which could get subsidized interest rates, in the middle were other privileged borrowers—mostly larger firms—which paid the bank general loan rates, and on the bottom were the majority of small and medium companies, which had to seek relatively high-cost finance in the informal credit market.

Quantity rationing, discriminatory lending, and intermediation inefficiency in Taiwan. Many authors writing about Taiwan's industrial growth mention the limited access of small firms to formal financial intermediaries. For example, Erik Lunberg (1979, 299) remarks that a high annual rate of growth of private investment from 1965 to 1975, which averaged about 20 percent, together with Taiwan's imperfect credit and capital markets, "suggests a relatively high share of self-financing, particularly for the great number of small and medium-sized firms in manufacturing and trade." Banks unquestionably have rationed small borrowers in Taiwan and offered discriminatory loan contracts to those having access to the financial system. A recent study by Shea and Kuo (1984) shows the extent of this bias. From 1965 to 1982, large firms obtained five times more bank credit per dollar of sales revenue than small firms and secured approximately four times more credit per unit of value added.

Interviews I conducted in the fall of 1987 with more than 100 manufacturing enterprises of all sizes in five industries further substantiate these statistics. In more than 90 percent of the cases interviewed, firms had no access to bank credit when starting the business. Short-term loans for working capital were extended to the firm only after a record of business success was established and after the firm had grown to a respectable level of sales (and in many cases a certain level of exports). Some small companies did obtain access to start-up loans through personal credit to the company owner. These were generally collateralized loans based on home mortgages. Until the mid-1970s, however, even mortgage-based personal loans were limited. Only as bank liquidity grew rapidly with increasing trade surpluses in the late 1970s did mortgage lending increase substantially.

Table 10.2 illustrates the magnitude of allocative bias in domestic bank lending for 1974–1986.[11] A mild bias in the direction of exporters and heavy industry is indicated, together with a substantial bias toward large manufacturing firms. In the early 1970s, the bias toward large firms was especially extreme. As Taiwan's trade surplus accumulated and bank liquidity increased in the late 1970s and early 1980s, however, statistical discrimination and credit rationing of smaller firms diminished somewhat.

TABLE 10.2   Access to Domestic Borrowing by Manufacturing Sector in Taiwan, 1974–1986 (percentage)

	1974–1977	1978–1982	1983–1985	1986
Total manufacturing[a]	63.9	48.3	38.2	31.1
Export industry[b]	34.4	23.9	20.5	18.4
Domestic industry[c]	29.5	24.3	17.7	12.7
Domestic-export	−4.9	0.4	−2.8	−5.7
Heavy industry[d]	33.8	29.0	22.5	18.3
Light industry[e]	30.2	19.1	15.7	12.8
Light-heavy	−3.6	−9.9	−6.8	−5.5
Large manufacturing enterprises	49.5	32.9	24.8	19.8
Small and medium manufacturing enterprises[f]	14.4	15.3	13.4	11.3
Small-large enterprises	−35.1	−17.6	−11.4	−8.5

NOTE: Figures are percentages of total domestic bank loans (foreign bank lending averaged about 10% of total lending 1972 to 1986).
a. Includes public and private manufacturing enterprises. The decline in manufacturing loans is mirrored by a similar increase in mortgage-based loans to individuals.
b. Export industries are classified as textiles and apparel, wood products, metal products, export food processing, and miscellaneous manufacturing on the bases of sales-export ratios (20% of sales).
c. Domestic industries are classified as domestic food processing, paper and publishing, chemicals and chemical products, and transportation equipment.
d. Heavy industries are classified as chemicals and chemical products, nonmetallic mineral products, basic metals, metal products and petroleum, and transportation equipment.
e. Light industries are those not classified as heavy.
f. Based on Small and Medium Business Administration, "Trend Outstanding Loans Extended by Domestic Banks to Small and Medium Enterprises." These figures include industry, agroindustry, commerce, and services. We use the administration's percentages to estimate the totals for manufacturing enterprises. Small and medium-sized enterprises are those with less than 300 employees.
SOURCES: *Financial Statistics Monthly*, various issues, and *Flow of Funds in Taiwan District, 1965–1985* (Economic Research Department, Central Bank of China, ROC, Taipei).

Comparison of debt-to-equity ratios for large and small firms gives a rough indication of the effect of discriminatory bank lending. For the 1970s and early 1980s, the top 500 private enterprises in Taiwan had average debt-to-equity ratios (290) that were twice the average for all private enterprises (155) and approximately three times the average for smaller enterprises (102).[12]

It is important to note that, although bank lending may have had interindustry and intraindustry allocative biases, Taiwan's financial system consistently favored private over public sector borrowers. Although the state has strictly controlled financial intermediaries and interest rates, it did not exercise this control, as did the governments of so many other developing countries, to expropriate increasing amounts of seigniorage. Conservative fiscal policy in Taiwan meant that the real cost of financial restriction—"squeezing out" private sector credit demands—never materialized. By the mid-1960s, 70 percent of domestic credit went to accommodate the private sector, and this proportion increased to almost 80 percent in the early 1970s (Table 10.3). Given the high positive correlation

TABLE 10.3   Private Sector Share of Domestic Credit in Taiwan, 1961–1986 (percentage)

	Private sector	Private enterprise	Individuals and others	Government employees	Government agencies
1961–1969	70	56	14	25	5
1970–1979	79	65	14	19	2
1980–1986	75	47	28	22	3

NOTE: All figures are outstanding balances at the end of the year.
SOURCE: *Financial Statistics Monthly*, various issues.

between the share of domestic credit flowing to the private sector and the level and efficiency of aggregate investment, favoring the private sector doubtlessly had considerable positive influence on Taiwan's rate of economic growth.[13] Chief among the benefits of high real growth rates has been the large proportion of enterprise finance that has come from accumulated profits, particularly in the case of small and medium firms. Surveys show that on average about 45 to 55 percent of private enterprise investment has been financed from internal sources over the past three decades (Liu et al. 1984, 23–25). For smaller firms, internal financing has been even higher, averaging 60 to 65 percent.[14]

Because small and medium enterprises produced about 50 percent of value added in the 1970s and early 1980s and received only a fraction of outstanding loans, there is good reason to believe that some allocative inefficiency accompanied bank lending. The allocative efficiency of the financial system can be measured in several ways, the best of which is probably to compare marginal returns on capital investments across different sectors and industries (interindustry efficiency) and across firms of different sizes within an industry (intraindustry efficiency). Abstracting from risk, uncertainty, and transaction costs, if marginal returns across different sectors, industries, and firm size groups are approximately equal, the condition for allocative efficiency is met.

Unfortunately, accurate estimates of marginal returns to credit to different industries and firms are difficult to obtain. To assess intraindustry returns to credit, we calculated a proxy measure using total factor productivity for different firm size categories at the International Statistics Industrial Classification (ISIC) 4-digit level for the late 1960s, 1970s, and early 1980s.[15] Firms with 50–299 employees were found to have slightly higher total factor productivity than either larger or smaller firms in 65 percent of Taiwan's industries in the late 1960s and 1970s. In the 1980s, larger firms (those with 500 workers or more) increased their productivity and slightly outranked medium-sized firms, but smaller firms with fewer than 50 employees remained in third place. The relatively high productivity of firms with 50–299 employees in the 1960s and 1970s suggests intraindustry inefficiency in credit allocation for those years, considering how little credit these firms actually received (about 15 percent).

To develop a proxy for interindustry returns to credit, we calculated both the marginal capital output ratio and the gross rate of return to capital for eleven ISIC 3-digit industries between 1976 and 1981. Correlation of these measures with allocated shares of total loans and discounts of domestic banks indicate that bank lending preferences did not coincide closely with a ranking of industries based on marginal returns on investment. But the match of loan allocations with marginal returns to capital in each industry was only mildly eccentric, the correlation coefficient for both efficiency measures being roughly .5. We also examined the variation of marginal returns to capital across industries (see Table 10.4). Over the six years included in the analysis, the interindustry variance in each case was not extraordinary in its magnitude, but it did show a significant decline of about 30 percent from 1976 to 1981. This reduction in variance indicates a movement in the direction of greater allocative efficiency over the period.

Riegg (1979) conducted a more extensive analysis of the efficiency of bank lending in Taiwan, which attempted to incorporate dynamic industrial efficiency as well as differences between private and social efficiency. He constructed rankings of each 3-digit ISIC industry based on its contribution to the marginal efficiency of capital, as well as to exports, employment, and forward and backward linkages. Riegg suggests that although lending may not have been statically efficient across industries (in terms of the marginal efficiency of capital), static

TABLE 10.4   Costs of Borrowing of Nine Different Manufacturing Industries, 1973–1984

	Average (%)	Variance
1973	14.6	2.7
1974	19.1	4.0
1975	17.2	3.3
1976	16.8	3.0
1977	15.6	3.2
1978	15.6	3.6
1979	18.1	5.5
1980	19.7	5.0
1981	21.5	5.0
1982	17.5	1.7
1983	15.0	1.7
1984	14.3	1.3

NOTE: Data based on three-digit classification of ISIC.
SOURCE: *Financial Statements of Firms* (Economic Research Department, Central Bank of China, ROC, Taipei), December, 1986, 115–17.

inefficiency may have been offset by greater dynamic and social efficiency. In his estimation, "The banks lent a little more to agriculture, high-risk basic industries—like ship building, petrochemicals and steel—and to fledgling export industries—like electronics—than a purely private system would have lent." This, in the end, helped to promote "development potential." However, Riegg found it difficult to say much more because he lacked sufficient disaggregated data on which to base a more detailed analysis.

To recapitulate, it is clear from the evidence of outstanding bank loans that small enterprises have been subject to quantity rationing and statistical discrimination in formal credit markets in Taiwan. The evidence that such discriminatory lending patterns resulted in significant allocative inefficiency is less convincing, however, possibly for two reasons. First, allocative inefficiency is difficult to measure, given the available data. Second, although intraindustry inefficiencies in bank lending were probably significant, interindustry inefficiencies were very likely not.

Intermediaries and De Facto Intermediaries

Faced with a difficult credit intermediation problem, Taiwanese authorities pressed market forces into service of their financial policies by acquiescing to the unrestricted development of an active curb market as an efficient adjunct to regulated credit institutions. In adopting this compliant stance (and on occasion even intervening to support the curb market), the government permitted the existence of a series of "markets" for credit side by side, differing in types of borrowers and the terms of loans. These markets effectively sorted borrowers along dimensions of both "information intensity" and risk.

Borrowers with significant financial resources and reputations (for example, public enterprises and large manufacturing and commercial firms) had access to "full-information" credit markets (such as commercial banks, official money markets, and equities markets), while riskier borrowers with limited resources (mostly new entrants and many small and medium enterprises) were served by "information-intensive" credit markets (informal lenders and money markets and leasing and installment companies). The line of demarcation between different segments of the credit market in Taiwan was quite pronounced because of heavy government regulation. Unlike the conservative, government-controlled banks, curb market lenders were willing to develop new and innovative instruments for risky ventures, to offer loans when there were few assets available for collateral, and to meet the needs of borrowers when speed was essential.

As the system for credit intermediation developed in Taiwan, the commercial banks directed their loans mostly to larger public and private enterprises ("upstream" heavy-industrial suppliers, "central" factories, large trading companies, leasing and installment companies, and the like). In turn, larger firms (including some of the public enterprises) then often became de facto intermediaries, on-lending directly (through trade credit, and loans for equipment and working capital) to smaller, "downstream" customers, subcontractors, and suppliers at interest rates well above bank lending rates.[16] At the same time, de facto intermediation was facilitated officially through various credit instruments available at banks and by government legal interventions in the curb market.

At banks, credit instruments, such as the domestic letter of credit, or LC (sometimes called a back-to-back LC), were initiated to help larger firms secure commercial bank credit for their subcontractors and suppliers.[17] For example, a large, established manufacturer could use an export LC or a purchase order to his small suppliers to create a domestic LC or, in the case of a purchase order, a banker's acceptance. These financial instruments would then be discounted by the commercial bank and used to issue domestic LCs, which, in turn, would be used by the small subcontractor or supplier as collateral for loans for working capital. Similarly, loans for larger trading companies were arranged based on export LCs. On-lending to small and medium domestic manufacturers was then facilitated through back-to-back credit instruments.[18]

In the curb markets, the most important financial instrument facilitating de facto intermediation was the postdated check. Postdated checks were normally used to accommodate flows of trade credit and other financial transactions between firms. Transactions between upstream suppliers and downstream manufacturers, for example, were generally conducted with 30- to 45-day postdated checks made out for an amount equal to the principal plus interest for the agreed time period. These checks could then be discounted by the supplier through curb market brokers. Because trade credit was so important for doing business in Taiwan (anywhere from 30 percent to perhaps 80 percent of private enterprise credit, depending on firm size),[19] the government intervened to secure the postdated check market.

The Negotiable Instruments Law was enacted in the 1950s making it a criminal offense to fail to honor a postdated check. The penalty was tough: Failure to redeem a postdated check could result in as many as two years in prison. And the law was vigorously enforced. The great majority of criminal cases processed through the courts in the 1970s had to do with violations of the Negotiable Instruments Law. In fact, one of the reasons cited for abolition of the criminal penalty in 1987 was the amount of complaints from the courts regarding the number of cases that had to be prosecuted on behalf of the banks.[20] Unquestionably, the Negotiable Instruments Law increased confidence in curb market transactions. Businessmen in Taipei say that postdated checks are widely used because "they are the only legal financial instrument."[21]

Government involvement in the curb market to facilitate de facto intermediation also took other forms. In Taiwan, as in other East Asian countries, firms rely heavily on debt to finance business activities. This tends to make firms more vulnerable to economic downturns. As a consequence, government authorities often intervened in financial markets to foster greater stability, and the curb market was no exception. In 1985, for example, the government initiated a program entitled Special Provisions for Redeeming Bad Checks. Under this program, strategic industries, important exporters, enterprises with publicly traded securities, automated industries, and firms involved in the Center-satellite program were granted "a (six-month) grace period for redeeming bad checks (read postdated checks) issued by them, leaving no bad records, and without referring them to courts for prosecution, provided their petitions, together with necessary documentary evidence, is submitted and approved by the Industrial Development Bureau of the Ministry of Economic Affairs" (Small and Medium Business Assistance Center 1985).

The government-owned banks also played their part. Borrowers were often required to deposit loan funds in checking accounts, which had to be managed as current working capital accounts. The bank then issued the borrower a prescribed number of checks. Loans (which were granted for three to six months) could then be drawn down by writing checks up to certain limits. The number of checks handed out by banks was strictly limited to control credit in the postdated check market.

Checking accounts could not be drawn down all at once. As checks were written and cashed, drawing down the loan, repayments to the account were made as postdated checks were received by the borrower from his business transactions, and so on.[22] If the loan-based checking account was not managed in this fashion, the usual renewal of the loan, every three to six months, was not granted. Many borrowers with access to such loans maintained relations with three or four banks in this manner.

Through de facto intermediation and direct credit operations of other curb lenders, the curb market developed rapidly in both size and sophistication. Table 10.5 shows that by 1970, curb market assets represented almost 30 percent of total financial assets in Taiwan. At the time, this was larger than all the financial assets of regulated financial institutions. Even by 1980, the importance of curb market financing continued to be almost equivalent to financing by formal financial intermediaries. It wasn't until the late 1970s, when the official money market was given the freedom to expand, that curb market financing began to diminish somewhat. By 1985 curb lending had declined to about 26 percent of total financial assets.

A Reconnaissance of Taiwan's Curb Markets

The unregulated financial market in Taiwan is made up of fragments that evolved from "traditional" financial intermediaries and others that have

TABLE 10.5   Composition of Financial Assets, Taiwan, 1965–1985 (percentage)

	1965	1970	1975	1980	1985
Source of loans					
Financial institutions	31.1	28.5	36.7	31.9	33.5
Enterprises and households[a]	19.6	29.0	29.2	30.9	26.5
Government agencies	9.7	4.6	1.8	1.5	1.8
Securities					
Government	2.6	2.7	1.0	.6	1.1
Enterprises					
Long-term	35.4	32.3	27.8	28.8	26.8
Short-term	—	—	—	2.1	3.8
Other domestic assets (net)	1.5	2.9	3.5	4.2	6.5
Total	100.0	100.0	100.0	100.0	100.0

NOTE: Dash = not available.
a. Includes enterprise borrowing from friends and relatives, borrowing and lending between enterprises, and trade credit (bills and accounts receivable).
SOURCES: *Taiwan Statistical Data Book*, 1987; *Flow of Funds in Taiwan District*, 1987, 103.

emerged more recently, largely in urban areas.[23] Institutions such as moneylenders, pawnshops, rotating credit associations, and loans from friends and relatives, which flourished before establishment of modern banks, continue to play an important role. Postdated checks, deposits with firms, private savings cooperatives, financial lease companies, installment companies, and enterprise trade credits arrived on the scene much later. This mix of traditional and modern forms of credit intermediation allows the curb market to provide an assortment of financial instruments, tailored to a wide spectrum of savers and investors.

The size and nature of the curb market also means that a great deal of personal and business finance in Taiwan is conducted on a one-to-one basis. Most transactions are governed by personal relationships that are part of the fabric of Chinese culture.[24] Even those transactions conducted at arms length in the curb market are carried out in submarkets, segmented by forms of social connection that allow for close screening of borrowers: by industry, by company, by social clubs, by family connections, and so on. To help the reader understand more about how the curb market operates in Taiwan, a description follows of some of the most important institutions and financial instruments.

Postdated checks: Dee-Hua Street and other informal money markets. Trade credit in Taiwan is normally extended in three ways: on a straight accounts receivable plus daily interest basis from one enterprise to another, on the basis of the purchaser paying a higher product price to the supplier but at some specified later date, and, most commonly, by the purchaser issuing a postdated check (based on the normal time limits of trade credits) on his business or personal bank account (or, if the businessman has no bank account, a simple promissory note) in favor of the supplier. In the majority of cases, suppliers are larger "upstream" firms extending credit to smaller "downstream" manufacturers; however, since supplier credit is a ubiquitous part of doing business in Taiwan, firms of all sizes transact business with postdated checks.

The postdated check and the third-party check have come to be the most common curb market financial instruments. They are so pervasive that Taiwanese businessmen use the words "paying by check" synonymously with getting credit: Bills are either "paid at once" or "by check." The third-party check (*dyan-pyan*, exchange of third-party checks) sometimes called check transferring, is a preferred form of payment or collateral. Two parties will often exchange checks, endorsing each, so that they can then each approach third-party curb lenders (brokers) or suppliers, with checks guaranteed by two people.

Just as in a conventional regulated money market, a discounting market of small private brokers has grown up to facilitate the use of postdated and third-party checks for supplier credit and other financial activities. These discounting markets are generally organized by industry to reduce information costs and are thus fragmented. Dee-Hua Street in Taipei has, for example, long served as the site for discounting postdated checks in the textile industry, because this is where many of the early textile shops were located. As the textile industry began to diversity its operations into other business activities, Dee-Hua Street also became the discounting hub for other industries.

The discounting system generally operates in this way. When large suppliers or middlemen (or any company in the industry holding a postdated check) begins piling up a large amount of postdated checks and needs additional liquid assets, these checks are endorsed and sold at a discount to the market in Dee-Hua Street. Discounted postdated or third-party checks are, in turn, generally endorsed by other parties in the market and rediscounted many times (like banker's acceptances). The market is based on tight interpersonal relationships, and everyone (or company) has a personal credit limit. One cannot enter the system without being known or personally recommended and/or secured by a known entity. Not all postdated checks brought to the market are discounted. Brokers scrutinize each issuer and, if a check looks too risky, the party that brought the check to the market is asked to issue a postdated check on his own account to replace it.

Development of the postdated check system depended on Taiwan's Negotiable Instruments Law, as noted earlier. The law specifically made all endorsers equally responsible for redeeming checks with the issuer. Government agencies policed the system, keeping records on bad check cases and referring malefactors to the courts for prosecution. Commercial banks were also involved in regulating the system by tightly controlling the number of blank checks allowed per customer and by reporting violators to government authorities.

Annualized compounded interest rates on postdated checks are set out in Table 10.6 for the period 1963–1986. In the 1960s and early 1970s, interest rate differentials between general (short-term) bank loans and loans against postdated checks averaged about 10 percent.[25] The differential increased in the late 1970s and early 1980s to as much as twenty percentage points as the economy adjusted to the effects of the second oil shock and credit tightened. In 1986 the differential was still eighteen percentage points.

Although the postdated check continues to play a prominent role in Taiwan's financial transactions, several factors are causing a decline in the use of this instrument. First, since the late 1970s the regulated money market has grown steadily, together with the average size and sophistication of business firms. Banker's acceptances and commercial paper are beginning to replace informal financial instruments. Second, after a recent financial scandal involving the curb market, government moved

TABLE 10.6   Annual Interest Rates on Loans against Postdated Checks and Commercial
Bank Rates on General Loans, Taiwan 1963–1986

	Loans against postdated checks[a]	General loans, commercial banks
1963–1969	23.0	14.9
1970	22.6	12.5
1971	22.3	12.5
1972	23.2	11.7
1973	24.3	13.7
1974	32.8	15.5
1975	28.9	13.8
1976	29.3	12.5
1977	28.5	11.2
1978	28.2	11.2
1979	32.6	14.2
1980	34.6	14.2
1981	34.6	13.0
1982	31.1	9.0
1983	28.7	8.5
1984	27.4	8.0
1985	26.2	6.2
1986	23.0	5.0

a. Based on a compounded monthly rate.
SOURCE: *Financial Statistics Monthly*, various issues.

to reduce the significance of the postdated check system. In 1987, the criminal penalty for issuing bad checks was abolished. Expecting a major credit slump as a result of this action, the government expanded short-term credit accommodation at banks by promoting the use of commercial paper and discounted time letters of credit; increased commercial banks' purchasing of accounts receivable; and eased conditions for opening commercial bank checking accounts.

"3:30 financing." Given the criminal penalty for bouncing a postdated check, there arose a market for "3:30 financing"— last-minute borrowing for deposit in checking accounts before the bank closing hour of 3:30 P.M. to cover checks written against insufficient funds. The available rates for 3:30 financing are advertised in the newspapers, and are extremely high. Local curb market lenders claim that this sort of financing has lost its popularity since the decriminalization of check bouncing.

"Car loans." The "car loan" (*chi che dai kuan*) is a very popular type of loan transaction for which the borrower's car is used as collateral. The borrower and lender bargain and agree on a certain value for the car, and the lender lends that amount less the agreed-upon interest. The borrower turns over the car keys and registration to the lender, and then has a designated number of days within which to return the borrowed funds to the lender. Both lender and borrower can sue for breach of contract for failure to perform, although the legal system is quite cumbersome in dealing with this type of case and so most problems must be settled by other means. Car loan "companies" advertise publicly, and this is one of the most popular means of raising capital in a short period of time.

"Partnerships" and "investors." In the start-up financing of new business ventures, no practice is more common than that of borrowing the necessary paid-in capital funds to comply with corporate registration laws. The law requires that a business owner have capital of NT$1,000,000 as paid-in capital for a new company in order to have the company duly registered and established. That amount of capital can be readily borrowed for deposit in the company account. Such capital is borrowed and deposited just long enough for the company accounts to be verified as complying with minimum capital requirements. Borrowers generally pay a daily percentage fee for use of the lender's money in this way: For example, for the use of the lender's NT$1,000,000 for deposit in the start-up business owner's account for one day, as in the example above, the borrower might pay a fee of 3 percent per day, or NT$30,000. It is thus often the case that the start-up business actually only has a very small percentage of the minimum start-up capital, as required by law for registration purposes, when the company is legally established.

This practice is illegal, yet so widespread as to be practically universal. A good personal relationship with a bank manager is often helpful to lenders in this business, as bank managers knowingly assist in verifying the necessary account funds to help a friend make some money. There are thriving "companies" whose business it is to act as "investor" (*jin ju*) for new companies. There are, obviously, no records kept of such business, and secrecy is maintained through the all-important integrity of the personal relationships involved.

Related to this practice is that of having friends or relatives act as "partners" or "investors" in new companies incorporated in a form that might legally require more than one shareholder. The start-up investment is most often arranged through the true sole shareholder, with the friends or relatives signing their names as partners. As one Chinese businessman put it, "Most companies have several so-called 'investors' when the true investment and management is really in the hands of one or two people."

"Byau hwei." Though less significant a factor in business finance than the postdated check system, the *byau hwei* is so nearly universal an aspect of personal and business finance in Taiwan that it is important to mention. The *hwei* has a longstanding history in Chinese society. One Chinese businessman suggested that the Chinese people have been organizing such *hweis* since the time of the Ming dynasty.

Basically, a *hwei*, or group, is organized when one person decides he or she needs some money and others, his or her personal acquaintances, have money to invest. The originator, or *hwei tou* (literally "group head") takes responsibility for the *hwei*, which works as follows:

Suppose there are ten *hwei* members, including the *hwei tou*, who has organized this group because he needs NT$20,000 in a hurry. Each participant pays in NT$2,000 for use by the *hwei tou* during this, the first month of the *hwei*. (The "lifetime" of a particular *hwei* depends on the number of members—for example, a *hwei* with ten members will continue for ten months.) One month later, the second month of the *hwei*, the remaining nine members have the opportunity to bid for that month's pool. By secret bid, they each tell the *hwei tou* how much "interest" they are willing to pay on that month's NT$2,000 plus the interest rate at which he or she bid, during each successive bid collection for the remainder of the *hwei*'s lifetime. Thus, if the *hwei tou* is Person 1, he or she receives NT$20,000 at the first *byau*, and must pay NT$2,000 into the pool each month for nine more months. The highest bidder at the second *byau* (one month later) collects the amount for which he or she bid, but then must pay in that amount plus interest each month for eight more months. Each person can only collect the *byau* once during the life of the *hwei*, and from then on pays back in at the interest rate at which he or she won the bid. Thus, the person who least needs money, and can afford not to bid or collect throughout the lifetime of the *hwei*, will end up making the most money.

Lease and installment companies. Leasing companies have grown up, particularly in the late 1970s, to finance the purchase of heavy equipment and machinery. In 1977, only three companies were registered as members of the Taipei Association of Lease Companies, and these firms were financing only about NT$700 million in equipment. By 1983, the number of leasing firms had increased to thirty-seven with a financing volume of NT$17 billion. Many of these new entrants are affiliated with large manufacturing companies and nonbank financial institutions. As much as 50 percent of the usable assets of leasing companies comes from commercial bank loans. In effect, leasing firms have become de facto intermediaries for the commercial banks, providing a financial channel to small and medium enterprises without access to regulated financial institutions.

Installment companies operate like leasing companies but generally deal in consumer durables, mainly cars. Specialized installment companies did not exist formally until 1978. Commercial bank loans provide as much as 40 percent of the funds of installment companies.

Friends and relatives. Loans and investments from friends and relatives have been crucially important in Taiwan, particularly for start-up capital. In interviews with Taiwanese businessmen we found that more than 90 percent had received start-up capital from friends and relatives. In addition, new infusions of loans and investments from friends and relatives were important as small companies faced cyclical business problems or as they needed finance for expansion.

Since under Taiwan's bankruptcy law there is no such thing as subordinated credit, friends, relatives, and investors who would normally be simple company shareholders have preferred lending to firms rather than paying in capital. Because of the "insider" status of friends and relatives, their loans for all practical purposes were privileged. In the event of financial distress, they were often paid back first, as if their debt were subordinated. Many investors also preferred to lend firms money rather than to buy equity because interest income is treated more favorably than dividends by Taiwan's Internal Revenue Service: Interest is tax deductible and is not double taxed by corporate income tax. For all of these reasons, equity finance is only about 35 percent of assets in Taiwan, though a large portion of loans are from would-be "shareholders."

Bankers in Taiwan argue that these "shareholder loans" show up in statistics as curb market lending, inflating curb market volume. Small and medium enterprises are defined by government according to their paid-in capital (less than NT$40 million of paid-in capital). Because "shareholders" keep paid-in capital low by lending money, many firms defined as small and medium are in fact much larger.

Why the Curb Market Matters in Taiwan

Emergence of a large and thriving curb market has been enormously important to Taiwan's industrial development for at least four reasons. First, the curb market complemented the formal credit market by providing information-intensive, efficient credit facilities, what Scitovsky (1986) has called the "small loans" function of the curb market. Second, the curb market helped to mobilize domestic savings by offering high returns (although riskier) on investable funds. Third, the presence of an active curb market increased the "fungibility" of financial resources by offering an alternative market-determined interest rate on investment funds: the "safety valve" function of the curb market (ibid.). Fourth, many curb market transactions facilitated business dealings ("contracting modes") between heterogeneous firms. Each of these salutary effects of the curb market is described in greater detail in the next section.

The "small loans" function. By extending credit facilities to small, riskier borrowers more cheaply and efficiently than formal financial institutions could have, the curb market made a net contribution to allocative efficiency. There is little doubt that judgments of creditworthiness based on long-standing personal contacts among relatives and friends, and between small businessmen and equally small lenders or credit brokers who live nearby, can be more accurate and less costly than those based on expensive investigation by loan officers at large commercial banks. This was particularly true in Taiwan's case, inasmuch as bank lending officers tended to be overly conservative because of heavy government interference.

The efficiency of the curb market as a lender to small and medium-sized enterprises has been noted at different times in many countries. Timberg and Aiyar (1984), for example, found in a study of India four characteristics of curb lenders that explain their lower administrative and default costs:

- Curb lenders are closer to and therefore know their clients better than do commercial bank lenders.

- Curb lenders have lower overall operating costs because they work from less elaborate establishments, pay lower wages, and require less paperwork.

- Nonprice competition in curb markets is lower because interest rates are market determined.

- Curb markets are not subject to the regulations of commercial banks, such as reserve requirements.

All of these characteristics are as descriptive of Taiwan's curb lenders as they are of India's. It is ironic that the characteristics of curb lenders that are often said to cause financial inefficiency (fragmented markets, the bilateral nature of transactions, high interest rates, and the short-term nature of most loans) in fact seem to ensure their efficiency as intermediaries to small and medium enterprises.

In addition to its contribution to allocative efficiency, an important aspect of the curb market's small loans function was that it eased firm entry and exit. Easy entry and exit were at the heart of Taiwan's competitive success. Analysis of industry- and firm-level data shows that the industries with the fastest productivity growth rates also had the highest rates of entry-exit turnover (Biggs and Lorsch 1989, 35–37). In Taiwan, curb markets enabled entrepreneurs to start businesses with almost no assets. After serving a short apprenticeship in a larger (often foreign) company to learn about production skills, technology, and potential customers, aspiring Taiwanese entrepreneurs had only to obtain an export order from a foreign or local trading firm to go into business. With an order in hand, an array of informal credit possibilities opened up.

Start-up funds most often came from friends and relatives and/or, beginning in the late 1970s, a mortgage-based private bank loan. In some cases larger firms financed start-ups of small subcontractors. With an LC from a foreign buyer, working capital could be raised through friends and relatives, curb market moneylenders, and postdated or third-party checks. Thirty- to forty-five-day supplier credit based on a postdated check was standard practice. And land, machinery, and factory space could easily be leased or rented.[26] Rental of capital equipment also reduced start-up risk substantially, as it made it easy to exit business if sales did not materialize. Finance to do all this was provided quickly and flexibly with low collateral requirements.

Mobilization of domestic savings. By offering lenders and savers a higher return than they would have received in formal financial markets, curb markets in Taiwan helped stimulate mobilization of domestic resources. This occurred in two ways. First, by virtue of their lower transaction costs, and by avoiding the implicit taxation imposed by commercial banks (through controls on lending and deposit rates and reserve requirements), curb markets mediated savings that otherwise would not have been saved at all. Second, the curb market induced very small savers to save amounts that otherwise would have been spent on trivial consumption, as evidenced by the *byau hwei*, which, as indicated earlier, are important vehicles for personal savings and investment in Taiwan.

The "safety valve" function. The extent to which the curb market discharges its safety valve function depends on the degree of formal financial sector regulation and repression. As a safety valve, the curb market helps contribute to allocative efficiency by accommodating those borrowers rationed out by lower return projects because of government-imposed restrictions on loan contracts and credit rationing. If the credit of formal financial institutions is initially channeled to certain uses, in conjunction with disequilibrium interest rates or selective government controls, and those uses are less profitable than other opportunities, the curb market will assist with the reallocation of credit from less to more profitable uses at market-equilibrium rates of interest. This "safety valve" has been extremely important in countries like Korea, where government-directed financial subsidies have been large. In Taiwan, where interest rate repression and financial subsidies were moderate, the "safety valve" played a smaller role. On the other hand, Taiwan has benefited more from the small loans function of the curb market.

The presence of an active curb market in Taiwan added materially to the fungibility of financial resources. Coupled with the fact that curb market interest rates were market determined, added fungibility meant that the prevailing opportunity cost of investable funds was ultimately guided by the higher curb market interest rate. Firms with access to commercial bank loans at controlled interest rates inevitably had to weigh returns on planned investments against returns from on-lending the funds at higher curb market rates. Accordingly, the higher opportunity cost (determined by the curb market) of investable funds often deterred entrepreneurs from undertaking lower yielding investments, even when they had access to cheap bank funds. This factor kept the average efficiency of aggregate investment high in Taiwan. In turn, higher aggregate investment efficiency resulted in higher rates of economic growth.[27] Shea and Kuo (1984) have estimated conservatively that the allocative efficiency contribution of the curb market in Taiwan raised the gross domestic product annually by an average of more than 1 percent during 1965–1982.

By the same token, the "safety valve" function of the curb market played a key role in making effective the subsidies implicit in low interest rates and concessional selective credit policies (Cole and Park 1983; Cole and Patrick 1986). If the banks issuing low-interest loans did not extract all the rents from the original borrowers through collateral requirements, compensating balances, and side payments, firms with access to loans at preferential interest rates had the opportunity to on-lend these funds in the curb market. Effective interest rate differentials between markets varied from 15 to 30 percent, depending on the type and year of the loan. Without the curb market, the effective subsidy would have depended on the investment return in the firm's business activities or on the short-term savings deposit rate in commercial banks, which was much lower than the curb lending rate.[28] In an outward-oriented country like Taiwan, exporters reaped most of the subsidies made effective by an active curb market, because government loan programs were generally aimed at tradable goods.

Interlinkage of credit and production transactions. The flexible niche strategy pursued so successfully by Taiwan's firms in many export industries has depended crucially on the country's industry structure. To reduce costs, and most of all to enhance flexibility in the face of capricious international markets, Taiwan's businessmen specialized to the maximum degree and took up many forms of subcontracting in both supplier and producer activities. Most export producers became linked to tight networks of small independent "job-shoppers," each producing small parts of a product that would be finally assembled by the central factory and exported through foreign or local trading companies. Such an industry structure relies heavily on markets rather than hierarchies to organize production and thus calls for ways to facilitate "contracts" that link players (firms) in the economy and that connect factor and product markets.

Williamson (1985) argues that the main purpose served by economic organization is economizing on transaction costs. Different modes of contracting have different costs, and it is the magnitude of these transaction costs that determines whether transactions take place. Where transaction costs are too high, or where the risk is such that the parties are reluctant to invest in transaction-specific assets, there is a tendency to underinvest (that is, transactions will not take place). Transaction costs comprise the costs of establishing and administering contracts, such as the costs involved in gathering and processing information, search costs, legal costs, organizational costs, and opportunity costs attributable to sunk assets, among others.

Two fundamental problems that arise in transactions (contracting) are bounded rationality and postcontracting opportunism.[29] *Bounded rationality* is a term used to convey the point that people have limited information and limited ability to process it. This implies incomplete information about market opportunities, limited ability to predict the future and derive implications from prediction, and limited ability to specify in advance responses to future events. Opportunism follows from bounded rationality plus self-interest. *Opportunism* refers to the possibility that mutually reliant parties may mislead, distort, disguise, or confuse in order to expropriate wealth from one another. A contract promises future performance, typically because one party makes an investment, the profitability of which depends on the other party's future behavior. In the circumstances, the party making the investment wants to protect against the possibility of being exploited by the other party (either wilfully or because of an honest disagreement). Accordingly, transaction costs include costs incurred in making contracts enforceable by law or by self-enforcement and extend to precautions against potential expropriation of the value of investments relying on contractual performance, as well as the costs of informing and administering the terms of contractual relations.

With a legal system that limited their ability to enforce property rights, Taiwan's businessmen had to find creative ways to overcome high transaction costs. Integration of the production chain (vertical integration) under the roof of a single company was one possibility. Vertical integration reduces transaction costs by limiting the number of market transactions. But the Taiwanese preference for family-owned, independent firms rules out extensive vertical integration, as does the flexible-niche strategic orientation of Taiwanese firms, which requires relatively small, fast-moving production establishments. Alternative mechanisms thus had to be improvised that could support innumerable and varied market transactions between heterogeneous enterprises. One of the most conspicuous vehicles in Taiwan for reducing transaction costs (that is, reducing the possibilities of such factors as postcontract opportunism) was the linking of financial and production transactions.

Curb market financial activities were tremendously important in this respect and had at least two major affects on production transactions. First, the bilateral character of curb market finance reduced complexity and uncertainty in product market transactions: The existence of contracts (financial) in one market was an enabling condition for contracts (production) in the other.[30] Second, the availability of particular types of curb financial instruments, which eased firm entry and exit, also reduced the magnitude of transaction-specific (sunk) investments.

In the first case, exercising some control over the other contractual party's assets, through some form of dependence or side payment (incentive), can be a way to reduce the possibility of postcontract opportunism, and thus to reduce transaction costs. Accordingly, in Taiwan, where larger, well-established enterprises have access to bank credit and small firms do not, transactions between producers and suppliers and between large factories and subcontractors are almost always accompanied by finance. Motivation for these loans, apart from maintaining good relations within the industry, is to ensure subcontractor loyalty and dependability in terms of specifications of the production contract, product quality, timing of delivery, and so forth.

Loyalty and dependability of subcontractors are very important, particularly when larger firms invest in training subcontractors and when product quality and delivery schedules are crucial. Curb finance, in the form of extensive (and often preferential) trade credits, direct loans for equipment and working capital, acceptance of postdated checks, recommendations and credit guarantees for small subcontractors at banks, and so on, was used to buy loyalty and dependability. Interlinkages between finance and production were found in each of the five industries studied.[31] Linkages were found to be particularly strong in industries producing products of high complexity, requiring greater fixed entry costs in terms of physical and human capital. The machine tool industry is a good example. Many machine tool firms indicated that the main reason Taiwan was competitive in international markets was the tight networks of highly skilled subcontractors in and around the city of Taichung. Competition for good suppliers and subcontractors in this industry is substantial. To ensure subcontractor loyalty and dependability, both loans and equity investments were therefore made by the larger firms in the smaller subcontractors. Production contracts also facilitated financial contracts. More important still were the inescapable social sanctions. On the large producer's side, financial transactions were facilitated by strong social sanctions, thus reducing postcontract opportunism. That is, credible commitments (Williamson often uses the term *trading hostages*) had to be created by both parties in order for large producers to enter into financial contracts with subcontractors. Large firms commit themselves to lend money, and small subcontractors put their *hsin-yung* ("reputation," "reliability," or "credit rating") on the line. A businessman (or firm) in Taiwan who for whatever reason fails to meet his obligations, immediately loses his *hsin-yung*. *Hsin-yung* is the most important "currency" in Taiwanese business (the word also refers to the quality and reliability of a firm's products), and a small firm's most valuable asset. To start and run a business one needs capital, but capital isn't enough. One must also have *hsin-yung*, and to have *hsin-yung*, one must know and be respected by people in one's industry. If someone loses his *hsin-yung*, no one will advance him any more money (postdated checks, and so on) or goods, and his creditors start demanding immediate repayment: "That's the end—the firm goes bust."[32]

Last, curb market finance also reduced transaction costs and facilitated contracting by substantially lowering transaction-specific (sunk) investments and asset specificity. Large sunk investments and assets that are nonredeployable, in that their value crucially depends on the other contracting party's future behavior, increase transaction costs because they make the contracting parties vulnerable to holdup and moral hazard. Each of these factors affects expectations about the costs of postcontract opportunism. Unregulated financial institutions, such as leasing companies, which allow firms to set up with rented factories and equipment, reduce vulnerability attributable to sunk investments because investments are much smaller. Likewise, extensive trade credit, postdated checks, lease companies, and loans and deposits from friends and relatives all substantially ease firm entry and exit, making assets more easily redeployable.

In summary, production and financial transaction linkages were crucially important in Taiwan because they facilitated contracting in a market-based (as opposed to hierarchical-based) economy. The ability to make contracts allowed small firms to participate in production and provided a "glue" that held together Taiwan's heterogeneous enterprise structure. Put simply, interlinked transactions supported industry structure, industry structure in turn facilitated competitive strategy, and strategy made possible Taiwan's competitive edge in international markets.

Conclusion

The fact that banks do not think of themselves as auctioneers, offering loans to the highest bidder, but rather as screening and monitoring institutions is important: It means that, when banks lack perfect information about borrowers, interest rates do *not* play the simple allocative role ascribed by conventional microeconomics, and as a result the equilibrating forces provided by market mechanisms can be weak or virtually absent. Credit market equilibrium under these circumstances can be characterized by discrimination against smaller borrowers, quantity rationing, and interest rate rigidities.

In an economy such as Taiwan's, in which government intervention in financial markets is extreme and market structure is dominated by heterogeneous firms, formal credit market equilibrium can be characterized by even greater discrimination and quantity rationing. Taiwan solved its intermediation problem by allowing (and at times promoting) the development of a bifurcated financial system. The central core was rigidly regulated to serve government's policy interests—limit economic power, promote industrial policy, and control inflation—and the flexible curb market edges took care of the information-intensive small borrowers that were so important to the country's competitive strategy in world markets. I question whether financial market integration through liberalization would have been the best solution for the combination of credit intermediation and macroeconomic problems Taiwan faced.

There are four good reasons to be wary of the orthodox prescription of financial market integration when market structure is characterized by heterogeneous firms and high information costs.

First, as I have argued in this chapter, abolishing interest rate controls may not be enough to reduce the discrimination and quantity rationing of banks and raise the allocative efficiency of investable resources.

Second, neostructuralist models of the financial system, which include active curb markets, show that liberalization can cause stagflation (Taylor 1985; van Wijnbergen 1983). If liberalization brings an increase in real deposit rates, attracting investable funds into banks and away from the curb market, the fact that banks have reserve requirements (and curb lenders do not) can reduce the total supply of loanable funds to business. This contractionary impact on credit can reduce economic growth. Moreover, as the analysis has pointed out, curb market intermediaries in an economy with market distortions and imperfect information generally operate with lower transaction costs and higher investment efficiency than formal financial intermediaries. Channeling funds into formal institutions away from curb markets in a country like Taiwan could raise intermediation costs and result in a net decrease in available investable funds.

Third, linkages between curb market financial transactions and production transactions in a "transactions-based" economy like Taiwan's reduce costs on both sides of the market—that is, linkages reduce the transaction costs of lenders, facilitating financial contracts, and reduce the transaction costs of producers, facilitating production contracts. Such informal ways to make transactions possible and reduce their costs are crucial for competitiveness in an economy in which the legal system is not yet well established and in which fast, flexible production decisions are required to meet the conditions of capricious international markets. Premature disruption of informal financial activities because of financial liberalization could result in high adjustment costs and reduced economic growth.

In short, Taiwan's rigid financial system with a flexible curb market appears to be a "second-best" solution for the intermediation problem it confronted. This is an important lesson from Taiwan's experience that other developing countries interested in expanding the economic contribution of small and medium-sized enterprises might heed. In many countries, the formal financial sector has expanded through a buildup of specialized development banks or special finacial programs to provide an alternative to informal credit. Although the formal sector and its special programs may have succeeded in dealing with the more bankable borrowers in some cases, it has not generally been able to compete with curb market lenders in terms of transaction cost or coverage. Taiwan's experience indicates that policy makers should consider solving credit intermediation problems by enlisting (and assisting) active curb markets as an efficient, complementary adjunct to formal financial institutions.

Part 4   The Black Economy

Omkar Goswami
Amal Sanyal
Chapter 11   Ira N. Gang

Taxes, Corruption, and Bribes:
A Model of Indian Public Finance

The concept of black market income usually relates to any one or more
of three criteria: that which (1) is illegal or originates from illegal activities, (2) evades tax, and (3) escapes inclusion in the annual national
income accounts (Acharya et al. 1986, 6). This discussion pertains only
to income that meets part of the second criterion, namely, potentially
taxable income that evades personal income tax.

Irrespective of the niceties of definition, the black market economy
in India has been a matter of concern to policy makers since the late
1960s. Its sheer size is quite astounding in absolute as well as relative
terms. In the fiscal year April 1980–March 1981, the amount of income
that evaded all manner of taxes accounted for anything between 4.23
percent and 8.59 percent of India's gross domestic product at factor
cost.[1] More significantly, after all permissible tax deductions were accounted for, it was found that 41 percent to 58 percent of potentially
taxable income succeeded in escaping the tax net (ibid., 133).

To a large extent, the reason for the persistence of such immense
cheating is a hierarchy of rampant corruption among politicians and
sections of the bureaucracy, especially within the Income Tax Department. A 1985 study conducted on behalf of the Ministry of Finance

201

concluded that 76 percent of the government auditors accepted bribes to reduce tax liabilities. Furthermore, 68 percent of the taxpayers covered by the study readily admitted to paying bribes to get a clean chit on their returns. The going bribe rate was around 20 percent of the extra tax demanded.[2]

Furthermore, extremely high average and marginal tax rates of the 1960s and 1970s played their parts in nourishing corruption. In 1984, to create "a salutary effect on our tax culture, and induce the maximum number of tax payers to come forward and voluntarily declare their true income" (Government of India, 1984), the government of India sharply reduced tax and penalty rates and also raised the exemption limits. Subsequently, exemption limits have been steadily increased and tax rates reduced. Moreover, fines and penalties on undisclosed incomes have been brought down. Finally, there has also been a reduction in the intensity or probability of audit.[3]

It was believed that these incentives would bring about a sharp increase in income tax revenues; however, except for a single year, 1986, personal income tax revenues actually declined, after adjustment for population and income growth.[4] One explanation for such a seemingly perverse result is that compliance had actually increased, but revenues fell because the government got its elasticities wrong; however, it is also possible that, instead of increasing, compliance fell. The compliance data for India are highly confidential, and only senior bureaucrats can confirm whether or not taxpayers chose to become more honest. In the absence of such data, our objective is to set up a simple theoretical model in which *fiscal liberalization might lead to a fall in income tax compliance and revenues.*

This chapter attempts to analyze some of the problems of tax collection in economies where potential income tax evaders interact with corrupt government auditors. In the next section we outline a simple model involving taxpayers, auditors, and the government, which seeks to capture the essential aspects of such interaction. Some policy-oriented results are derived in the section "Comparative Statics." This is followed by a section that indicates areas of future theoretical and empirical research and states the basic conclusions. The mathematical aspects of the model are relegated to an appendix.

The Model

The model summarized in this section extends the works of Reinganum and Wilde (1985) and Graetz, Reinganum, and Wilde (1986) by incorporating corrupt auditors who take bribes. Most models of tax evasion assume an asymmetry between taxpayers and government auditors—

the former may or may not be corrupt, but the latter are uniformly honest.[5] This is an unreal assumption for many countries, including India. To accommodate corruption, we have assumed that the proportion of corrupt government auditors is exogenously given. The going bribe rate, however, is the outcome of a bargain struck between a corrupt income tax officer and a taxpayer who has been caught cheating.

In the model each taxpayer earns a true income $Y_i(i = 1,2, \ldots ,N)$, and chooses to declare Z_i, where $0 \leq Z_i \leq Y_i$. For simplicity, there are no "habitually honest" compliers. This assumption does not affect the results in any qualitative way. There are, however, some habitually honest auditors, though they may constitute a small fraction. Further, we assume that if a person is audited, the auditor—be he honest or corrupt—learns the true income, Y_i. The notations used are

p: the probability of being audited

k: the proportion of corrupt auditors, given exogenously.

t: the proportional tax rate, given exogenously.

f: the proportional fine rate, also exogenously given.

b: the bribe rate finally agreed upon between the taxpayer and the auditor.

c: the unit cost of auditing, which is the same over all audits and is not so high as to trivialize the maximization problem

The different outcomes are characterized by the game tree in Figure 11.1.

Let us analyze the second stage of the game. At this point, a taxpayer has been picked for audit by a corrupt auditor. The auditor demands a bribe on the hidden income, which is $b_i(Y_i - Z_i)$, and this is his net gain from the deal. If the taxpayer agrees to give a bribe, his disposable income falls by $b_i(Y_i - Z_i)$; otherwise, he has to pay the tax and fine on his undisclosed income, that is, $(t + f)(Y_i - Z_i)$. This interaction can be characterized as a two-person, fixed threat bargaining process, for which the Nash solution is a bribe rate that maximizes the product gains from negotiation.[6] Given Y_i and Z_i, bargaining yields an equilibrium bribe rate, b_i^*, which is simply one half of the tax plus fine rate, or $b_i^* = (t + f)/2$ (see Appendix).

We now examine the taxpayer's problem. Any taxpayer will cheat if the expected disposable income from evasion is greater than from honesty. Given t, f, k, b_i^*, and anticipated probabilities of audit, the gains from cheating consist of three parts: (1) what is obtained without audit, namely, $(1 - p)(Y_i - tZ_i)$; (2) what is left behind if the evasion is caught by an honest auditor, that is, $p(1 - k)\{Y_i - tZ_i - (t + f)(Y_i - Z_i)\}$; and (3) the disposable income if the evasion is caught by a corrupt

FIGURE 11.1 The Interactive Game

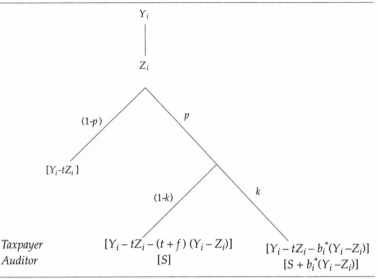

Taxpayer $[Y_i - tZ_i - (t+f)(Y_i - Z_i)]$ $[Y_i - tZ_i - b_i^*(Y_i - Z_i)]$
Auditor $[S]$ $[S + b_i^*(Y_i - Z_i)]$

SOURCE: Authors.

auditor, $pk\{Y_i - tZ_i - b_i^*(Y_i - Z_i)\}$. To make cheating worthwhile, the sum of these three parts has to exceed $Y_i(1 - t)$.[7]

Solving this yields an expression for the probability of audit that induces full income revelation by all taxpayers (denoted as p^*). Formally, $p^* \equiv (2t)/\{(t + f)(2 - k)\}$ (see Appendix). If the government happens to choose a probability of audit that is less than p^*, all taxpayers cheat to the hilt and declare zero income; equally, if the probability is greater than or equal to p^*, then honesty is the best policy for each and every taxpayer.[8]

It is not enough to devise a truth-revealing audit probability; it must also lie within zero and unity. In other words, $p^* \leq 1$, which implies that $(2t)/\{(t + f)(2 - k)\} \leq 1$. Given the tax and penalty rates, $p^* \leq 1$ clearly delineates the maximum corruption that can be supported by any revenue-collecting economy: this is $k \leq 2f/(t + f)$ (see Appendix). An example from the Indian case serves as a rather sad illustration. In India the average proportional tax rate is around 26 percent, and penalties are levied at 5 percent of hidden income. This implies that if audits are used to induce truth telling, no more than 32 percent of the government auditors can be corrupt. In fact, 76 percent of the auditors accept bribes. It is not surprising, therefore, that audits scarcely encourage honest declarations. Conversely, given the Indian t, f, and k, $p^* = 1.35$.

Let us now turn to the government's objective function. We have assumed that the government wishes to maximize expected aggregate revenue net of auditing costs, which consists of (1) what it gets with certainty, $t\Sigma Z_i$, and (2) the income obtained by unearthing hidden-income through audits carried out by honest auditors, or $p[(1 - k)(t + f)\Sigma(Y_i - Z_i) - Nc]$. The government's task is to choose a probability of audit that maximizes the sum of these two parts.

In a zero-one, "bang-bang" model such as ours, the government essentially has a very limited number of options. It can either

- choose a probability of audit that is less than the truth-telling one ($p < p^*$), have all the taxpayers declare zero income, and then rely upon its honest auditors to obtain some revenue through audits (option 1) or

- choose the higher truth-revealing audit probability with higher aggregate audit costs (option 2)

In the first instance, the government gets $p[(1 - k)(t + f)\Sigma Y_i - Nc]$ through auditing; and in the second, it gets $[t\Sigma Y_i - p^*Nc]$, where $p^* \equiv (2t)/\{(t + f)(2 - k)\}$. Now, a priori, one does not know whether these net revenues are positive or negative (nonpositive). So, in determining the revenue-maximizing probability of audit, the government has to examine four cases, each consisting of a pair drawn from the subcases $p < p^*$ and $p = p^*$. From each of these pairs $\{(p < p^*),(p = p^*)\}$, the government will choose the audit probability that gives greatest net revenue. The Appendix provides a complete characterization of these pairs and the government's choices. Here we give an intuitive explanation.

State I. Option 1 yields nonpositive net revenue, and option 2 gives positive net revenue. Here, if p^* is feasible ($p^* \leq 1$), then the government clearly maximizes revenue by choosing p^*. If, however, p^* is greater than unity (as in India), the highest probability that the government can feasibly choose is $p = 1 < p^*$. But this implies that p is less than p^*, and in such a state the government gets nonpositive net revenue (since option 1 is in force). Thus, although $p = 1$ is feasible, it is not optimal. So, if $p^* > 1$, the best strategy for the government is to opt for a zero audit probability. This state may be described as an *intermediate cost regime*: either the government is able to sustain a full income revelation audit probability (if $p^* < 1$) or, failing that, the costs force an equilibrium at zero audit.

State II. Options 1 and 2 both yield positive net revenue. Here, the government will maximize net revenue by choosing either p^* (if $p^* < 1$) or $p = 1$ (if $p^* > 1$). This is clearly the best scenario for the government, and may be described as the *low audit-cost regime*.

State III. Options 1 and 2 both yield negative net revenue. Here, it makes no sense for a government seeking to maximize net revenue to audit in either case ($p = p^*$ or $p < p^*$)—for auditing only generates greater losses than does letting sleeping dogs lie. This is the worst case, the *high audit-cost regime*.

State IV. Option 1 produces positive net revenue, and option 2 produces nonpositive net revenue. This is an absurd outcome, for it is impossible to have a situation where truth telling yields a negative (nonpositive) net revenue, whereas cheating does not. Hence, this case need not be explored at all.

The government's problem can be summarized in Table 11.1.

TABLE 11.1   The Government's Choice Problem

	Low cost (state II)	Intermediate cost (state I)	High cost (state III)
$p^* \le 1$	Choose $p = p^*$ to obtain a revenue of $(2 - k)$ $(t + f)Y - 2Nc$	Choose $p = p^*$ to obtain a revenue of $(2 - k)$ $(t + f)Y - 2Nc$	Choose $p = 0$ to obtain zero revenue
$p^* > 1$	Choose $p = 1$ to obtain a revenue of $(1 - k)$ $(t + f)Y - Nc$	Choose $p = 0$ to obtain zero revenue	Choose $p = 0$ to obtain zero revenue

SOURCE: Authors.

Comparative Statics

We now examine the impact of changes in the tax rate, the fine rate, and the proportion of corrupt auditors on three relevant variables: (1) the truth-revealing probability of audit (p^*), (2) the equilibrium bribe rate (b^*), and (3) the government's net revenue. In these exercises, we assume that p^* is feasible, in the sense of $p^* \le 1$. As earlier, this section summarizes the results and provides the intuition behind each outcome. The formal proofs are in the Appendix.

A rise in the tax rate. As the tax rate rises, people wish to cheat more than before. In an interactive setting, not only does the government know this, but the taxpayers also know that the government knows this. To counteract the tendency that people wish to cheat more than before, the government has to raise the risk of being caught by an honest auditor, which it does by increasing the truth-revealing probability of audit,

p^*. Moreover, if the government chooses the tax rate optimally by enforcing p^*, then a rise in the tax rates results in an increase in the equilibrium net revenue (see Appendix). Further, if p^* is adopted, no one cheats and, hence, the effect of taxes on the equilibrium bribe rate is trivial.

In reality there is no reason to believe that governments do, indeed, choose their optimal audit probabilities. More often than not, governments pick an arbitrary probability of audit, and then tinker with tax rates; and such situations have important policy implications for revenue as well as for the equilibrium bribe rate. Suppose the government fixed a suboptimal probability of audit ($\tilde{p}$) and then started raising the tax rate. As long as $\tilde{p}$ exceeds p^*, the taxpayers will declare their full income, net revenue will increase, and nobody will pay a bribe. As t rises, however, so does p^*; and there must come a point after which $\tilde{p}$ is equal to, and then less than, p^*. When this occurs, every taxpayer starts cheating and declaring zero income—hoping to get away by paying a bribe—and net revenue will begin to decline. In this milieu, the corrupt auditors will move into the act and, in fact, charge higher bribe rates with every rise in t (recall that $b^* = (t + f)/2$). Thus, if the government fixes $\tilde{p}$ and increases t, b^* will effectively be zero until p^* equals $\tilde{p}$ and will increase when p^* exceeds $\tilde{p}$.

This suggests an important result. *Whether a rise in the tax rate increases revenue depends upon whether or not the government has optimally chosen its probability of audit.* In general, there can be an outcome that adheres to a Laffer curve in cases where the audit probability is chosen in a purely random manner. As t rises, so long as $p^* < \tilde{p}$, the government's revenue will increase, and bribe rates are irrelevant; once t is such that $p^* \geq \tilde{p}$, everyone will cheat, the revenue will fall, and corrupt auditors will demand increasing bribe rates. Therefore, if net revenues are plotted against the tax rate, there will be an inverted U-shaped curve.

A rise in the fine rate. Raising the fine rate is undoubtedly the best option for the government, irrespective of the probability of audit chosen. For one thing, an increase in the fine rate unambiguously reduces the optimal truth-revealing audit probability p^* (see Appendix). Further, if the government chooses the optimal p^*, net revenue increases, since the number of people to be audited in equilibrium (p^*Nc) falls while all else remains the same. And, despite the equilibrium bribe rate's increasing, the increase has no operational significance, since all taxpayers reveal their full income. Even if the audit probability is chosen capriciously, increases in the fine rate cannot worsen things for the government. Suppose $\tilde{p} \geq p^*$; here, a rise in f will further reduce p^*, continue to force truth telling, and leave government no worse off. On the other hand, if $\tilde{p} < p^*$, then the government clearly improves its net revenue position when f rises sufficiently to reduce p^* to $\tilde{p}$. Once this occurs, the equilibrium bribe rate becomes discontinuous. When p^* is above $\tilde{p}$, not only are bribes taken, but the bribe rate also increases with f; however, once p^* falls to $\tilde{p}$, everyone starts declaring truthfully, bribes disappear, and the bribe rate becomes irrelevant.[9]

A rise in the proportion of corrupt auditors. Once again, we need to analyze what happens when the government chooses the audit probability optimally and when it does not. As k rises, p^* increases and approaches $\{2t/(t+f)\}$. In the optimal-choice case, p^* rises and government revenue clearly falls. When the government chooses an arbitrary $\tilde{p} > p^*$, then all is well as long as this inequality is maintained; however, if k rises enough for p^* to equate or overtake $\tilde{p}$, then everybody starts cheating, bribes come into play, and government revenue falls. The equilibrium bribe rate, however, remains unchanged.

Conclusions

The objective of this chapter was to analyze some of the problems of compliance in a rampantly corrupt milieu. In particular, we have wanted to examine whether seemingly well-meaning policies such as lowering tax and penalty rates could lead to counterproductive outcomes. The comparative static exercises show that in certain instances, fiscal liberalization can result in a fall in tax revenues. Such reductions might have little to do with elasticities and might instead reflect a decline in tax compliance. Although the data are almost impossible to find, this may well be a fiscal problem in India. In particular, India might be in an intermediate cost regime with $p^* > 1$.

   Our model is undoubtedly quite simple, and there are several areas for further research. First, risk neutrality is a convenient assumption but not necessarily a realistic one across a wide menu of audit probabilities, tax, and penalty rates. Second, we need to examine the efficacy of different carrot and stick mechanisms that may reduce a government auditor's incentive to take bribes.[10] Third, maximizing net revenue is really not an appropriate objective of government. Presumably, governments wish to maximize some kind of social welfare, with revenue as an instrument. Fourth, we need to examine the theoretical and empirical feasibility of delegating the audit procedure to agencies in the private sector that have less incentive to take bribes.[11] Fifth, and most important, models such as these have to be empirically tested using panel data. A few things, however, are clear. It is no longer possible to analyze black market income generation in developing (and perhaps some developed) economies without addressing the problem of symmetric corruption. Further, it is better for governments to recognize the effects of bureaucratic corruption and devise instruments to minimize its impact than to ignore it and face the greater embarrassment of chronic failures of fiscal policy.

Appendix to Chapter 11

The Mathematical Aspects of the Model

A. The equilibrium two-person, fixed threat, Nash bargaining solution

The problem is

$$\text{Max}_{b_i} V = [S + b_i(Y_i - Z_i) - S] \left[(Y_i - tZ_i) - b_i(Y_i - Z_i) - (Y_i - tZ_i) - (t + f) \right. $$

$$\left. (Y_i - Z_i) \right] \quad (1)$$

The first order condition yields an equilibrium bribe rate (b_i^*) such that

$$b_i^* = \left(\frac{t + f}{2} \right) \quad (2)$$

B. A taxpayer's maximizing decision

Any taxpayer will cheat if

$$(1 - p)(Y_i - tZ_i) + p[k\{Y_i - tZ_i - b_i^*(Y_i - Z_i)\} + (1 - k)\{Y_i - tZ_i - (t + f)$$

$$(Y_i - Z_i)\}] > Y_i(1 - t) \quad (3)$$

After substituting b_i^* from (2), we get that cheating is worthwhile if

$$p < \left(\frac{2t}{(t+f)(2-k)} \right) \equiv p^* \tag{4}$$

If, however, $p \geq p^*$, then every taxpayer will declare truthfully; p^* is the truth telling probability of audit.

C. Condition for a feasible truth-revealing audit probability

For (4) to be feasible, $p^* \leq 1$. This implies that

$$k \leq \left(\frac{2f}{t+f} \right) \tag{5}$$

D. The government's problem

The government attempts to choose a probability of audit that maximizes total net revenue,

$$\text{Max } \Pi = t\Sigma Z_i + p[(\Sigma Y_i - \Sigma Z_i)(1-k)(t+f) - Nc] \tag{6}$$

Define $\Sigma Y_i \equiv Y$ and $\Sigma Z_i \equiv Z$. The government has a choice:

- Choose $p < p^* \rightarrow$ everyone cheats $\rightarrow$ government gets $p[(1-k)(t+f)Y - Nc]$. Now, the term $[(1-k)(t+f)Y - Nc] \leq 0$ (denoted as $\int_1$), or $[(1-k)(t+f)Y - Nc] > 0$ (case $\int_2$).

- Or choose $p = p^* \rightarrow$ nobody cheats $\rightarrow$ government gets $[tY - p^*Nc]$. Again, this term can be nonpositive (case ω_1) or positive (case ω_2).

The possibilities to examine are $(\int_1, \omega_2)$, $(\int_2, \omega_2)$, $(\int_1, \omega_1)$, and $(\int_2, \omega_1)$.

I. $(\int_1, \omega_2)$: $(1-k)(t+f)Y \leq Nc$ and

$$[tY > p^*Nc] \rightarrow [(2-k)(t+f)Y] > 2Nc$$

Here, if $p^* \leq 1$, government maximizes revenue by choosing p^*; however, if $p^* > 1$, then no feasible p (including $p = 1$) can yield strictly positive net revenue. Therefore, if $p^* > 1$, the government should optimally choose $p = 0$. So, the solution is $p = p^*$, if $p^* \leq 1$, and p = 0 otherwise. This is the *intermediate-audit-cost regime*.

II. $(\int_2, \omega_2)$: $(1-k)(t+f)Y > Nc$ and

$$[(2-k)(t+f)Y] > 2Nc$$

Here, if $p^* \leq 1$, choose p^*; or else choose $p = 1$. The solution is $p = \min (p^*, 1)$. This is the *low-audit-cost regime*.

III. ($\mathfrak{z}_1$, ω_1): $(1 - k)(t + f)Y < Nc$ and

$$[(2 - k)(t + f)Y] \leq 2Nc$$

Here, for $k \neq 0$, the optimal solution is $p = 0$, that is audit nobody. This is the *high-audit-cost regime*.

Finally, the last case, ($\mathfrak{z}_2$, ω_1), is an absurd one, for it is not possible to have a situation where truth revelation yields nonpositive net revenues while cheating generates positive revenues.

E. Comparative static results

A rise in the tax rate:
From (4) we get

$$\frac{\partial p^*}{\partial t} = \left(\frac{2}{2-k}\right)\left[\frac{f}{(t+f)^2}\right] > 0 \qquad (7)$$

So, a rise in tax raises the optimal truth telling audit probability p^*. Now, if the government chooses p^*, the net revenue is $[tY - p^* Nc]$. This increases because $(\partial^2 p^* / \partial t^2) < 0$; p^* rises with t, but at a decreasing rate. As long as p^* is chosen (assuming that it is feasible), the bribe rate has no meaning, although technically it rises with increases in t. However, if a $\tilde{p}$ is arbitrarily picked by the government then all is well as long as $\tilde{p} > p^*$. But, with t rising, p^* increases, and soon $\tilde{p} \leq p^*$. Now, everyone cheats, bribes come into play, the rise in bribe rate is meaningful, and the government loses net revenue. This is a Lafferian outcome: with $\tilde{p} > p^*$ revenue rises as t rises; but from the point where $\tilde{p} = p^*$ and thereafter, revenue falls as t increases.

A rise in the fine rate:
Here, $p^* = 2t/(t + f)(2 - k)$ falls. So, if p^* is chosen, then revenue rises, since $[tY - p^* Nc]$ increases. As long as p^* is chosen, $Y_i = Z_i$ for all i, and the bribe rate's rising has no real significance. If $\tilde{p}$ is picked, and $\tilde{p} \geq p^*$, then a rise in f—leading to a fall in p^*—results in strict inequality, and the government is no worse off. Alternatively, if $\tilde{p} < p^*$, then a falling f must lead to a state where $\tilde{p} \geq p^*$; and, here, the government is strictly better off in opting for an increase in the penalty rates.

A rise in the proportion of corrupt auditors:
A rise in k unambiguously increases p^*. In turn, this raises the total cost of audit, $p^* Nc$, which lowers the government's equilibrium revenue. If

the arbitrary $\tilde{p} > p^*$, and if k rises such that p^* can equal or overtake $\tilde{p}$—subject to the maximal value being $(2t)/(t + f)$—then the cheating phase comes into play, and the government also loses in this instance. The equilibrium bribe rate is unaffected by k; but once cheating appears, the equilibrium amount of bribe taken increases.

Part 5   Conclusion

Chapter 12

Michael Roemer
Christine Jones

What Have We Learned about Policy?

One of the main aims of the HIID workshop on parallel markets was to alert officials of developing country governments and the major aid agencies to the impact of parallel and fragmented markets on policy reform and implementation. It is appropriate to conclude this volume by recalling what the workshop has enabled us to learn about policy.

Parallel markets generally ameliorate ill-advised policies such as controls over prices or quantities. As discussed in Chapter 2, such unofficial markets are likely to improve welfare by encouraging increases in output and avoiding real costs of access for consumers. Attempts by government to enforce controls by suppressing illegal trading not only make it more difficult for parallel marketers to serve their useful social function but also add real costs of enforcement to society's burden. David Bevan, Paul Collier, and Jan Willem Gunning show in Chapter 5 how strong enforcement not only makes parallel markets more costly but can prevent them from clearing, leaving unsatisfied consumers at the prevailing parallel market price.

In some circumstances, however, parallel markets can reduce welfare if they do not add substantially to total output and if traders or consumers incur high costs in those markets. Moreover, the payment of fines and bribes probably tends to concentrate income. Detlev Peutz and Joachim von Braun found in their study of Gambian groundnut markets (Chapter 3) that wealthy farmers were much more likely to operate in, and benefit from, parallel markets than were poor farmers.

Parallel markets offer an escape from bad policies that cannot be reformed. In this era of worldwide economic reform, it hardly needs to be said that the best prescription for government is to deregulate the market and seek other means to achieve the economic aims that are not well served by free markets. If political or bureaucratic pressures make it difficult to deregulate markets, parallel markets offer the possibility of a second-best prescription: relax enforcement of controls and let parallel markets operate to allocate resources more efficiently.

Controls can be enforced in ways that retain some benefits of parallel markets. Even the approach of letting parallel markets work may seem too calculating and cynical, especially as an explicit official policy. Then, as we pointed out in Chapter 2, there is still scope for policies to reduce the welfare costs of controls. First, enforcement should be especially lenient on those parallel market traders who also offer substantial quantities at controlled prices on official markets. The simplest form of this enforcement regime would be to allocate official market quotas to producers and to ignore (or even to encourage) unofficial market sales if the quotas have been fulfilled.

Second, when government agricultural marketing boards are charged with the task of establishing below-market prices for basic foods, there should be no quantitative restrictions on competitive marketing channels. Parallel marketers who can operate within the limits established by farmer and consumer prices should be permitted to obtain price-controlled produce—and in this way to benefit both farmers and consumers. As private dealers take on more of the volume traded, marketing board costs (and the number of people the boards employ) need to be curtailed.

Third, the research summarized in Chapter 2 suggests that consumer costs can be reduced if something approaching a costless rationing scheme can be devised. One approach is to supply ration coupons with entitlements that do not fully exhaust supplies, then allow competition for the balance of supplies. This reduces search and queuing costs by limiting them to the surplus of supplies over coupon entitlements and ensures that consumers with the highest marginal valuations will obtain the surplus quantities.

Models of parallel or black markets call into question some widely held beliefs about government policy. In Chapter 6, David L. Lindauer uses a parallel market approach to invalidate the conventional wisdom that high government wages lead to high private wages. Once government's budget constraint is considered and the private market is seen as a (legal) parallel market in labor, it becomes evident that higher government wages lead to a greater supply of workers—hence *lower* wages—in the private market.

Omkar Goswami, Amal Sanyal, and Ira N. Gang question a different conventional wisdom in Chapter 11. Modeling tax enforcement in India, they demonstrate that the decision to lower tax rates leads government also to lower audit frequencies, since it no longer pays to audit as much as before. Then, when most tax officials are likely to be corrupt, as in India, this leads to a *decline* in revenue, contrary to the experience with tax reforms in other countries.

Parallel markets in a general equilibrium setting can confound policies that make sense without them. Once controls and parallel markets are considered in the context of general equilibrium, linkage effects between markets can yield some unexpected results. This volume adds several instances to those in the literature (see Chapter 2). In Chapter 4, Jean-Paul Azam shows how the parallel market for the inconvertible Nigerian naira locked Niger's price level to that of its much larger neighbor. When Niger undertook restrictive monetary and fiscal policies at the same time as Nigeria, the latter's policies reinforced those of Niger and exacerbated the recessionary impact in the smaller country.

Using a computable general equilibrium model incorporating the United States' parallel market for illegal alien labor, Trien T. Nguyen demonstrates in Chapter 7 that a relatively small number of illegal workers can *raise* legal employment and tax revenue significantly, contrary to expectations.

The existence of parallel markets reduces the expected benefit from deregulation. Until recently, analyses of market liberalization proceeded as if the official market told the entire story, in which case deregulation brings net benefits. Once we acknowledge that parallel markets are likely to increase welfare under controls, the net benefit from liberalization is likely to be smaller. In the case of pure parallel markets, those engendered only by government intervention, there still remains some net benefit from deregulation because the parallel market cannot fully replace the unfettered market: there are likely to be some real costs to operating the parallel market, and the total quantity marketed through both markets will be less than under a single uncontrolled market.

When markets are fragmented, controls themselves may improve welfare by driving resources from the formal market into the preexisting informal market, as happens with curb markets in repressed financial systems. In that case, deregulation will channel resources back into the formal market without fully incorporating the informal market fragment—because of its high operating costs, lack of information, and other inherent characteristics. Then those who purchase on the informal market are worse off; and they tend to have lower incomes than the gainers, who purchase on the formal market. If we allow for interpersonal comparisons using welfare weights, deregulation can cause a net loss in welfare.

When markets are fragmented, the best policy is to develop new institutions that will integrate markets, and only then to deregulate. The three chapters on informal credit markets provide examples of market fragmentation that exists, not because of government policies, but because of inherent characteristics of the markets. Parker Shipton describes in Chapter 8 how, in The Gambia, rural credit markets can lack the most rudimentary of modern financial institutions, such as time-based interest rates. It is easy to see why the banking system would not incorporate these rural borrowers, even in the absence of government restrictions.

The informal credit markets in the Philippines and Taiwan are far more sophisticated than those of The Gambia, but the policy conclusion is similar. In Chapter 9, Pan A. Yotopoulos and Sagrario L. Floro identify two different kinds of rural informal moneylenders with different aims: traders who lend to larger farmers to facilitate purchases of inputs or outputs, and the larger farmers who lend to smaller farmers, often in the hope of default that leads to acquisition of land. The authors conclude that the credit attached to these specialized functions would not be replaced by banks in a deregulated market.

A more advanced but still fragmented market is described by Tyler S. Biggs in Chapter 10. In Taiwan, the credit needs of small, family-run firms are not served by modern banks because credit to those firms entails excessive risk and loan administration costs. These firms borrow instead from the informal curb market, which has developed its own set of tailored debt instruments. In Taiwan the government recognized the important role of the curb market and supported it by giving legal sanction to its most innovative institution, postdated checks.

The Taiwan case points the way to the most basic policy conclusion of the section on fragmented markets. In the face of fragmentation, the optimal policy is not to deregulate markets but to work first on institutions that can help to integrate informal markets more closely into formal ones. In Indonesia, for example, government developed a highly successful rural credit system operated by one of its own banks, which lends to farmers and small traders at commercial (and profitable) rates of interest. Rural savers and borrowers were integrated into the bank's widespread operations. When Indonesia deregulated its financial sector, these rural customers benefited along with everyone else in the formal credit market. Similar programs should be possible in other countries, including the three discussed in this volume.

NOTES AND REFERENCES

Chapter 1 Christine Jones, David L. Lindauer, and Michael Roemer, "Parallel, Fragmented, and Black: A Taxonomy"

Notes

1. See Roemer (1986).
2. The definitions and descriptions of markets employed in this paper are based on the paper by Lindauer (1989), written for the HIID workshop.
3. Development economists employ a large lexicon of terms to describe market structure. Other commonly used expressions include *curb, dual, gray, segmented*, and *informal markets*. See Lindauer (1989) for a more extensive account of alternative characterizations of market structures in developing economies.
4. For reasons given in the next section, curb markets may not be pure examples of a parallel market.

References

Acharya, S., and S. Madhur. 1983. "Informal Credit Markets and Black Money: Do They Frustrate Monetary Policy?" *Economic and Political Weekly* 18, no. 41 (October): 1751–56.

Bevan, D., P. Collier, and J. Gunning. 1989. "Black Markets: Illegality, Information and Rents." *World Development* 17, no. 12 (December).

Boulding, K. 1937. "A Note on the Theory of the Black Market." *Canadian Journal of Economic & Political Science* 13 (February): 115–18.

Gönensay, E. 1966. "The Theory of Black Market Prices." *Economica* 33, no. 130 (May): 219–25.

Lindauer, D. 1989. "Parallel, Fragmented or Black?: Defining Market Structure in Developing Economies." *World Development* 17, no. 12 (December).

McKinnon, R. 1973. *Money and Capital in Economic Development*. Washington, D.C.: The Brookings Institution.

Michaely, M. 1954. "Communications: A Geometrical Analysis of Black-Market Behaviour." *American Economic Review* 54, no. 4 (September): 627–37.

Nowak, M. 1985. "Black Markets in Foreign Exchange." *Finance and Development* 22, no. 1 (March): 20–23.

Peattie, L. 1987. "An Idea in Good Currency and How It Grew: The Informal Sector." *World Development* 15, no. 7 (July): 851– 60.

Roemer, M. 1986. "Simple Analytics of Segmented Markets: What Case for Liberalization?" *World Development* 14, no. 3 (March): 429–39.

Stiglitz, J. E., and A. Weiss. 1981. "Credit Rationing in Markets with Imperfect Information." *American Economic Review* 73: 393–410.

Timberg, T., and C. Aiyar. 1984. "Informal Credit Markets in India." *Economic Development and Cultural Change* 33, no. 1 (October): 43–59.

Chapter 2:   **Christine Jones and Michael Roemer, "The Behavior of Parallel Markets in Developing Countries"**

Notes

This chapter is a revised version of Jones and Roemer (1989), used with permission from Pergamon Press plc.

1. See Chapter 1, in this volume, by Jones, Lindauer, and Roemer.

2. Nine of the papers from the workshop dealing with parallel markets have been published in Jones and Roemer (1989).

3. The costs of operating include the normal return on capital and on managerial and entrepreneurial effort.

4. Real resource costs involve increased use of productive factors, labor and capital, or of goods and services to trade in the parallel market. Fines and bribes are transfers from sellers to government or its officials, and are not real costs to the economy.

5. Though private costs in the form of bribes or penalties are not real resource costs, their subsequent expenditure may distort the economy and reduce welfare. We discuss below the conditions under which parallel markets improve welfare by reducing consumers' search and queuing costs on official markets.

6. The Senegal case suggests a possible broadening of the definition of a parallel market. Illegal traders may attract buyers not only by reducing the costs of trading but also by offering nonprice advantages such as better quality grain, more convenient locations, more timely purchases and sales, and so forth.

7. This section is adapted from Devarajan, Jones, and Roemer (1989).

8. This effect was first noted by Pitt (1981).

9. In some circumstances, this might be a legitimate approach. Biggs, in his article in this volume on the curb market in Taiwan, relates how the government promoted the parallel credit market as a way to reach small manufacturers in whom the banks showed little interest. In this and similar cases, a parallel market can help to correct the distortions of a fragmented market.

References

Acharya, Shankar, and Srinivasa Madhur. 1983. "Informal Credit Markets and Black Money." *Economic and Political Weekly* 18, no. 41: 1751–56.

Alderman, Harold, and Joachim von Braun. 1984. *The Effects of the Egyptian Food Ration and Subsidy System on Income Distribution and Consumption*. Washington, D.C.: International Food Policy Research Institute.

Azam, Jean-Paul, and Tim Besley. 1989. "Economies of Scope in Two-Way Smuggling: Theory and Application to Ghana." *World Development* 17, no. 12: 1921–30.

Bevan, David, Paul Collier, and Jan Gunning. 1989. "Black Markets: Illegality, Information and Rents." *World Development* 17, no. 12 (December): 1955–63.

Bhagwati, Jagdish, and Bent Hansen. 1973. "A Theoretical Analysis of Smuggling." *Quarterly Journal of Economics* 87: 172–87.

Bhagwati, Jagdish, and T. N. Srinivasan. 1973. "Smuggling and Trade Policy." *Journal of Public Economics* 2: 377–89.

Biggs, Tyler. 1988. "Financing the Emergence of Small and Medium Enterprise in Taiwan: Heterogeneous Firm Size and Efficient Intermediation." *USAID EEPA Discussion Paper no. 16*. Cambridge, Mass.: Harvard Institute for International Development, August.

Boulding, Kenneth E. 1937. "A Note on the Theory of the Black Market." *Canadian Journal of Economics and Political Science* 13: 115–18.

Bronfenbrenner, Martin. 1947. "Price Control under Imperfect Competition." *American Economic Review* 37: 107–20.

Browning, Edgar K., and William Patten Culbertson, Jr. 1974. "A Theory of Black Markets under Price Control: Competition and Monopoly." *Western Economic Journal* 12: 175–89.

Chinn, Dennis L. 1978. "Farmer Response to Foodgrain Controls in Developing Countries." *Quarterly Journal of Economics* 92, no. 4: 697–703.

Cole, David, and Yung Chul Park. 1983. *Financial Development in Korea, 1945–1978*. Cambridge, Mass.: Council on East Asian Studies.

Deacon, Robert T., and Jon Sonstelie. 1985. "Rationing by Waiting and the Value of Time: Results of a Natural Experiment." *Journal of Political Economy* 93, no. 4: 627–47.

———. 1989. "Price Controls and Rent-Seeking Behavior in Developing Countries." *World Development* 12, no. 17 (December): 1945–54.

Devarajan, Shanta, Christine Jones, and Michael Roemer. 1989. "Markets under Price Controls in Partial and General Equilibrium." *World Development* 17, no. 12 (December): 1881– 93.

Edwards, Sebastian. 1988. "Financial Deregulation and Capital Markets: The Case of Korea." *World Development* 16, no. 1 (January): 185–94.

Gönensay, E. 1966. "The Theory of Black Market Prices." *Economica* 33, no. 130 (May): 219–25.

Jones, Christine, and Michael Roemer. 1989. "Modeling and Measuring Parallel Markets in Developing Countries." *World Development* 17, no. 12 (December): 1861–70.

————, eds. 1989. *Parallel Markets in Developing Countries.* Special issue of *World Development* 17, no. 12.

Krueger, Anne O. 1974. "Political Economy of the Rent-Seeking Society." *American Economic Review* 64, no. 3: 291–303.

May, Ernesto. 1985. "Exchange Controls and Parallel Market Economies in Sub-Saharan Africa: Focus on Ghana." World Bank Staff Working Papers, no. 711. Washington, D.C.

McKinnon, Ronald I. 1973. *Money and Capital in Economic Development.* Washington, D.C.: The Brookings Institution.

Michaely, Michael. 1954. "A Geometrical Analysis of Black Market Behavior." *American Economic Review* 54: 627–37.

Morris, Michael L. 1988. "Parallel Rice Markets: Policy Lessons from Northern Senegal." *Food Policy* 13, no. 3 (August): 57–269.

Morris, Michael L., and Mark D. Newman. 1989. "Official and Parallel Cereals Markets in Senegal." *World Development* 17, no. 12 (December): 1895–1906.

Mukherji, Badal, Prasanta K. Pattanaik, and R. M. Sundrum. 1980. "Rationing, Price Control and Black Marketing." *Indian Economic Review* 15, no. 2: 99–117.

Nowak, Michael. 1984. "Quantitative Controls and Unofficial Markets in Foreign Exchange." *IMF Staff Papers* 31, no. 2 (June): 404–31.

Nguyen, Trien T. 1989. "The Parallel Market for Illegal Aliens: A Computational Approach." *World Development* 17, no. 12 (December): 1965–78.

Nguyen, Trien T., and John Whalley. 1986. "Equilibrium under Price Controls with Endogenous Transactions Costs." *Journal of Economic Theory* 39 (August): 290–300.

Pinto, Brian. 1988. "Black Markets for Foreign Exchange, Real Exchange Rates and Inflation: Overnight vs. Gradual Reform in Sub-Saharan Africa." World Bank, Washington, D.C., May. Revised draft.

Pitt, Mark. 1981. "Smuggling and Price Disparity." *Journal of International Economics* 11: 447–58.

Shaw, Edward. 1973. *Financial Deepening and Economic Development.* New York: Oxford University Press.

Sheikh, Munir A. 1976. "Black Market for Foreign Exchange, Capital Flows and Smuggling." *Journal of Development Economics* 3: 9–26.

————. 1989. "A Theory of Risk, Smuggling and Welfare." *World Development* 12, no. 17 (December): 1931–44.

Timberg, T. A., and C. V. Aiyar. 1984. "Informal Credit Markets in India." *Economic Development and Cultural Change* 33, no. 1 (October): 43–59.

van Wijnbergen, Sweder. 1983."Credit Policy, Inflation and Growth in a Financially Repressed Economy." *Journal of Development Economics,* 13, no. 2: 45–65.

Chapter 3:   Detlev Puetz and Joachim von Braun, "Parallel Markets and the Rural Poor in a West African Setting"

Notes

1. For details on the survey, see von Braun, Puetz, and Webb (1989).

2. Estimates by von Braun and Puetz (1987) show, for example, in groundnuts, a marginal fertilizer productivity of 2.4 kilograms for each additional kilogram of fertilizer applied. In 1985 this was equivalent to an additional revenue of more than 5 dalasi (the Gambian currency) for each dalasi spent on fertilizer (in 1987 prices, about D 4).

3. Cash prices in 1987 (prices for 1985 in brackets) on the parallel market were D 0.71 (D 0.39) compared with D 0.84 (D 0.57) on the official market. For fertilizer acquired on credit, farmers paid D 0.92 (D 0.54) on the parallel market and D 1.01 (D 0.62) officially.

References

Bardhan, P. 1980. Interlocking Factor Markets and Agrarian Development: A Review of Issues. *Oxford Economic Papers* 32: 82–90.

Bevan, David, Paul Collier, and Jan Gunning. 1989. "Black Markets: Illegality, Information, and Rents." *World Development* 17 (December): 1955–63.

Binswanger, H. P., and Mark R. Rosenzweig. 1986. Behavioural and Material Determinants of Production Relations in Agriculture. *The Journal of Development Studies* 22, no. 3: 503–39.

Devarajan, Shantayanan, Christine Jones, and Michael Roemer. 1989. "Markets under Price Controls in Partial and General Equilibrium." *World Development* 17 (December): 1881–93.

Jones, Christine, and Michael Roemer, eds. 1989. Parallel Markets in Developing Countries. Proceedings of a workshop on parallel markets sponsored by the Harvard Institute for International Development, Cambridge, Massachusetts. *World Development* 17 (December): 1861–70.

Lindauer, David L. 1989. "Parallel, Fragmented or Black? Defining Market Structure in Developing Economies." *World Development* 17 (December): 1871–80.

Morris, Michael, and Mark D. Newman. 1989. "Official and Parallel Cereals Markets in Senegal" *World Development* 17 (December): 1895–1906.

Porath, Yoram Ben. 1980. F-connection: Families, Friends, and Organization of Exchange. *Population and Development Review* 6, no. 1: 1–31.

von Braun, Joachim, and Detlev Puetz. 1987. An African Fertilizer Crisis: Origin and Economic Effects in The Gambia. *Food Policy* 12, no. 4: 337–48.

von Braun, Joachim, Detlev Puetz, and Patrick Webb. 1989. *Technological Change in Rice and Commercialization of Agriculture in a West African Setting: Effects on Production, Consumption, and Nutrition.* Research report no. 75. Washington, D.C.: International Food Policy Research Institute.

Chapter 4:   Jean-Paul Azam, "Cross-Border Trade between Niger and Nigeria, 1980–1987: The Parallel Market for the Naira"

Notes

This chapter has benefited from discussions with Sylviane Guillaumont and various informants in Niamey (Niger) and from helpful comments by Michael

Roemer, which are gratefully acknowledged. But responsibility for the chapter, including any shortcomings, is entirely mine.

1. These data have been "scrambled" on purpose with respect to measurement units, since the informant did not wish the facts to be published. The order of magnitude is such that the outflow to Switzerland of "H" notes was roughly equal to one-fifth of the inflow of BEAC notes in 1982.

References

Arnoult, E. J. 1983. "Cross-Border Trade between Niger and Nigeria." In *Joint Program Assessment of Grain Marketing in Niger*, ed. Elliot Berg et al. Niamey, Niger: USAID.

——. 1986. "Merchant Capital, Simple Reproduction and Underdevelopment: Peasant Traders in Zinder, Niger Republic." *Canadian Journal of African Studies* 20, no. 3: 323–56.

Azam, J. P., and T. Besley. 1989. "General Equilibrium with Parallel Markets for Goods and Foreign Exchange: Theory and Application to Ghana." *World Development* 17: 1921–30.

Frelastre, G. 1986. "Le troupeau nigérien en péril." *Le mois en Afrique* 247–48 (September): 97–105.

Grégoire, E. 1986. *Les Alhazai de Maradi (Niger)*. Paris: Editions de l'Orstom.

Igué, O. J. 1983. "L'officiel, le parallèle et le clandestin." *Politique Africaine* 9: 29–51.

Johnson, O. E. G. 1987. "Trade Tax and Exchange Rate Coordination in the Context of Border Trading." *IMF Staff Papers* 34, no. 3: 548–64.

Pinto, B. 1988. "Black Market Premia, Exchange Rate Unification, and Inflation in Sub-Saharan Africa." World Bank PPR Working Article Series, no. 37. Washington, D.C.

Quirk, B., V. Christensen, K. M. Huli, and T. Sasaki. 1987. *Floating Exchange Rates in Developing Countries*, Occasional Paper no. 53. Washington, D.C.: International Monetary Fund.

Chapter 5:   **David Bevan, Paul Collier, and Jan Willem Gunning,**
"The Persistence of Shortages in Rural Black Markets"

Note

This chapter is a revised version of Bevan, Collier, and Gunning (1989b), used with permission from Pergamon Press plc.

References

Azam, J. P., and J. J. Faucher. 1987. *Offre de biens manufacturés et développment agricole: le cas du Mozambique*. Paris: Organization for Economic Cooperation and Development.

Azam, J. P., T. Besley, D. L. Bevan, P. Collier, P. Horsnell, and J. Maton. 1989. *Supply of Manufactured Goods and Agricultural Development: The Cases of*

Ghana, Tanzania and Rwanda. Paris: Organization for Economic Cooperation and Development.

Bevan, D. L., A. Bigsten, P. Collier, and J. W. Gunning. 1987a. "Peasant Supply Response in Rationed Economies." *World Development* 15, no. 4: 431–40.

———. 1987b. *East African Lessons on Economic Liberalization.* Aldershott, England: Gower, the Trade Policy Research Centre.

Bevan, D. L., P. Collier, and J. W. Gunning. 1989a. *Peasants and Governments: An Economic Analysis.* Oxford: Oxford University Press.

———. 1989b. "Black Markets, Illegality, Information and Rents," *World Development* 17, no. 12: 1955–63.

———. 1990. *Controlled Open Economies: A Neoclassical Approach to Structuralism.* Oxford: Oxford University Press.

Cooksey, B., A. Fowler, and C. Kwayu. 1987. "Incentive Goods for Development in Tanzania." CDP Consultant Report. Nairobi.

Sharpley, J. 1983. *The Impact of External and Domestic Factors on Tanzania's Agricultural Surplus and Foreign Exchange Earnings in the 1970s.* Paris: Organization for Economic Cooperation and Development, Development Centre.

Tanzanian Industrial Studies and Consulting Organisation. 1985. *Soap Industry Study.* TISCO. Dar es Salaam.

Chapter 6:   David L. Lindauer, "Government Pay and Employment Policy: A Parallel Market in Labor"

Notes

I would like to acknowledge the support I received from the World Bank to pursue the research on which this chapter is based. Thoughtful comments were provided by Mark Leiserson, Robert Goldfarb, Oey Meesook, and Len Nichols.

1. Kannappan (1983, 168–75), and Webb (1977) review traditional arguments relating government wage policies to urban wages.

2. A review of recent empirical trends in government pay and employment in Africa appears in Lindauer, Meesook, and Suebsaeng (1988).

3. Among the institutional works are Segal's (1971) review of civil service pay determination in Ceylon, and Fogel and Lewin's (1974) discussion of government compensation in the United States. Smith (1977a, 1977b) and Venti (1985) offer econometric treatments of U.S. public/private pay differentials. Similar approaches have been employed by Johnson (1971) for Kenya, Lindauer and Sabot (1983) for Tanzania, and van der Gaag, Stelcher, and Vijverberg (1989) for Côte d'Ivoire and Peru. A theoretical model based on political considerations is described by Reder (1975); it employs vote-maximizing behavior on the part of government officials.

4. The framework shares much in common with the parallel markets approach developed in Roemer (1986). Roemer addresses a number of market contexts. His emphasis is on traditional labor market regulations, e.g., minimum wages, and not on the pay and employment policies of the public sector itself.

5. A review of this literature focusing on the supply of government output rather than on government demand for inputs can be found in Mueller (1979), chap. 8.

6. The product market analogy is the case of price leadership in oligopoly theory, where a dominant firm is portrayed as facing a demand curve equal to the difference between market demand and the sum of the supply schedules of all smaller firms. See, for example, Scherer (1980), chap. 8.

7. This is true, of course, by construction. Recall, the supply of labor facing the public sector is defined as, $S_L^p = \bar{S}_L - D_L^p$, and, hence, $\bar{S}_L = S_L^p$ At an intuitive level, while any point on the private labor demand schedule equates wages with marginal revenue products, only one wage clears the labor market. In Figure 6.1, $w > w_1$ creates an excess supply of labor facing private firms. Under competitive conditions this excess supply, which includes public employees, would lead workers to bid for private jobs and should result in a fall in the private wage offer to w_1. Similarly, at $w < w_1$ an excess demand for workers exists, and competition between private firms for scarce labor would be expected to restore the competitive equilibrium at $w = w_1$.

8. In the United States, Smith (1977a, 1977b) and Venti (1987) find that government wages often fail to match "prevailing wages." Given the difficulties encountered in measuring "prevailing wages" for specific occupational groups, ceteris paribus, some observed differentials may result from information problems. If such problems were purely random, the prevailing wage model would be expected to hold on average; however, both authors find systematic differentials for specific worker groups suggesting that government pay policies in the United States reflect other objectives. Johnson (1971) and Lindauer and Sabot (1983) have reported similar results for Kenya and Tanzania, respectively. See also Lindauer, Meesook, and Suebsaeng (1988) for recent estimates of public/private earnings differentials in Africa.

9. A commitment to "living wages" in Zambia has maintained real earnings for unskilled government workers relative to other civil servants. Between 1975 and 1983, government servants with university training witnessed a decline in real starting salaries of over 50 percent while unskilled laborers experienced only a 13 percent decline. As a result, government laborers enjoyed an approximately 20 percent wage premium over their private sector counterparts in the early 1980s.

10. Anecdotal evidence on this point is abundant. See Lindauer, Meesook, and Suebsaeng (1988) for a fuller discussion. One of their examples follows:

> In Uganda in 1982, the Public Salaries Review Commission found that [as a result of precipitous real wage declines] "the civil servant had either to survive by lowering his standards of ethics, performance and dutifulness or remain upright and perish. He chose to survive." It has been observed that government employees in Uganda spend only one-third to one-half of normal working hours on government work; the rest of the time is devoted to other jobs . . . such as farming or trading. (P. 21)

11. Wage fixing in the private sector may also result from the strength of labor's bargaining position. If wage labor has some monopoly power in the labor market, because of unions or the backing of a prolabor government, firms may be compelled to pay wages above market-clearing levels. This may help account for wage determination in enclave sectors—for example, the traditionally high earnings of copper workers in Zambia relative to most other wage earners with comparable labor skills.

12. Roemer (1986) develops the concept of a parallel and informal market in labor arising from evasion by private agents of wage regulations, including social welfare legislation and taxes.

References

Berg, E. 1970. "Wages, Policy and Employment in Less Developed Countries." Paper presented to the Conference on Prospects for Employment Opportunities in the 1970s, Cambridge University.

Fogel, W., and D. Lewin. 1974. "Wage Determination in the Public Sector." *Industrial and Labor Relations Review* 27, no. 3: 410–31.

Harris, J., and M. Todaro. 1970. "Migration, Unemployment and Development: A Two-Sector Analysis." *American Economic Review* 60, no. 1: 126–42.

Johnson, G. E. 1971. "The Determination of Individual Hourly Earnings in Urban Kenya." Institute for Development Studies Discussion Paper no. 115. University of Nairobi.

Kannappan, S. 1983. *Employment Problems and the Urban Labor Market in Developing Nations.* Ann Arbor: Division of Research, University of Michigan Graduate School of Business Administration.

Lindauer, D. L., Oey A. Meesook, and Parita Suebsaeng. 1988. "Government Wage Policy in Africa: Summary of Findings and Policy Issues." *World Bank Research Observer* 3, no. 1: 1–25.

Lindauer, D. L., and R. Sabot. 1983. "The Public/Private Wage Differential in a Poor Urban Economy." *Journal of Development Economics* 12, no. 3: 137–52.

Mueller, O. 1979. *Public Choice.* Cambridge: Cambridge University Press.

Reder, M. 1975. "The Theory of Employment and Wages in the Public Sector." In *Labor in the Public and Nonprofit Sectors,* ed. Daniel Hammermesh. Princeton: Princeton University Press.

Roemer, M. 1986. "Simple Analytics of Segmented Markets: What Case for Liberalization?" *World Development* 14, no. 3: 429–39.

Scherer, F. 1980. *Industrial Market Structure and Economic Performance,* 2d ed. Chicago: Rand McNally.

Segal, M. 1971. *Government Pay Policies in Ceylon.* Geneva: International Labour Organization.

Smith, S. 1977a. *Equal Pay in the Public Sector: Fact or Fantasy.* Princeton, N.J.: Industrial Relations Section, Princeton University.

———. 1977b. "Government Wage Differentials." *Journal of Urban Economics* 4, no. 3: 248–71.

van der Gaag, J., M. Stelcher, and W. Vijverberg. 1989. "Wage Differentials and Moonlighting by Civil Servants: Evidence from Côte d'Ivoire and Peru." *World Bank Economic Review* 3, no. 1: 67–96.

Venti, S. 1987. "Wages in the Federal and Private Sectors." In *Public Sector Payrolls*, ed. David Wise. Chicago: University of Chicago Press for the National Bureau of Economic Research.

Webb, R. 1977. "Wage Policy and Income Distribution in Developing Countries." In *Income Distribution and Growth in the Less Developed Countries*, ed. Charles Frank and Richard Webb. Washington, D.C.: The Brookings Institution.

World Bank. 1981. *Accelerated Development in Sub-Saharan Africa*. Washington, D.C.: The World Bank.

———. 1986. *Financing Adjustment with Growth in Sub-Saharan Africa, 1986–90.* Washington, D.C.: The World Bank.

Chapter 7:   Trien T. Nguyen, "The Parallel Labor Market for Illegal Aliens"

Notes

This chapter is a slightly modified version of my paper, "The Parallel Market of Illegal Aliens: A Computational Approach," used with permission from *World Development* 17, no. 12, copyright 1989, Pergamon Press plc. Helpful comments by Paul Collier, Shantayanan Devarajan, Santiago Levy, Michael Roemer, and other participants of the HIID Workshop on Parallel Markets, Harvard University, November 11–12, 1988, are gratefully acknowledged.

1. This assumption can be extended to the more general formulation of price controls in Nguyen and Whalley (1986, 1990) such that whether constraints on wages are binding or not is endogenously determined in the model.

2. We can further extend the model by considering both skilled and unskilled labor. Unskilled labor can then be further differentiated into unskilled legal workers and unskilled illegal aliens. This nesting structure allows substitution between skilled and unskilled labor as well as between legal and illegal labor.

3. Examples of capital factor taxes are corporate taxes (including state and local taxes), corporate franchise taxes, and property taxes.

4. Examples of labor factor taxes are social security taxes, unemployment insurance, and worker's compensation.

5. I am grateful to Michael Roemer for this suggestion.

6. Extension to the multihousehold case is straightforward and hence is omitted for expositional ease.

7. See also Ethier (1986a, 1986b).

8. For utility functions (for example, Cobb-Douglas and CES) that allow multiplicative separability of price and income effects in consumer demand functions, it is analytically possible to solve the labor market–clearing equation $ZL(r, u, T) = 0$ for the unemployment rate u. As a result, the general equilibrium system $(20abc)$ is reduced to only two factor-market excess demand equations $(20ac)$ in terms of two unknowns (r, T).

9. This is probably consistent with conservative estimates of about 9 million unemployed Mexicans, which is almost equal to the population of Mexico City. See Johnson and Williams (1981, 74).

10. Welfare measures are in terms of Hicksian equivalent variations (EV), expressed as a percentage of benchmark national income. Positive values imply welfare gains, while negative values imply welfare losses.

11. Or that they had been working on perishable agricultural crops for at least ninety days in the year ending May 1, 1986.

12. My illustrative welfare calculations are based on the assumption of an ideal situation in which there are no changes in the labor markets of nearby developing countries that can trigger a change in the number of foreign workers contemplating crossing the border into the United States illegally.

13. The high sensitivity of the agricultural sector to changes in per-unit fines precludes more dramatic simulation exercises (for example, a 50 percent increase or even a doubling of per-unit fines), since it is possible for the unemployment rate of legal workers to be pushed well below the zero level. In effect, the simulation exercise is thus confined to that of a local comparative static analysis.

14. Reynolds and McCleery (1988) considered a three-factor, two-country trade model of the United States and Mexico, but did not take into account either minimum wages or government enforcement.

References

Alessandrini, S., and B. Dallago, eds. 1987. *The Unofficial Economy*. Vermont: Gower Publishing Company.

Alm, J. 1985. "The Welfare Cost of the Underground Economy." *Economic Inquiry* 24: 243–63.

Bailey, T. 1985. "The Influence of Legal Status on the Labor Market Impact of Immigration." *International Migration Review*, 19, no. 2 (summer): 220–38.

Ballard, C. L., et al. 1985. *A General Equilibrium Model for Tax Policy Evaluation*. Chicago: University of Chicago Press.

Chiswick, B. R., ed. 1982. *The Gateway: U.S. Immigration Issues and Policies*. Washington, D.C.: American Enterprise Institute for Public Policy Research.

———. 1986. "Illegal Aliens: A Preliminary Report on an Employee-Employer Survey." *American Economic Review Papers and Proceedings* 76, no. 2 (May): 253–57.

———. 1988a. "Illegal Immigration and Immigration Control." *Journal of Economic Perspectives* 2, no. 3 (summer): 101–15.

———.1988b. *Illegal Aliens: Their Employment and Employers*. Kalamazoo, Mich.: Upjohn Institute for Employment Research.

Devarajan, S., et al. 1989. "Markets under Price Controls in Partial and General Equilibrium." *World Development* 17, no. 12 (December): 1881–93.

Djajic, S. 1987. "Illegal Aliens, Unemployment and Immigration Policy." *Journal of Development Economics* 25: 235– 49.

Ethier, W. J. 1986a. "Illegal Immigration: The Host Country Problem." *American Economic Review* 76, no. 1 (March): 56–71.

———. 1986b. "Illegal Immigration." *American Economic Review Papers and Proceedings* 76, no. 2 (May): 258–62.

Gaertner, W., and A. Wenig, eds. 1985. *The Economics of the Shadow Economy*. New York: Springer-Verlag.

Greenwood, M. J., and J. M. McDowell. 1986. "The Factor Market Consequences of U.S. Immigration." *Journal of Economic Literature* 24, no. 4 (December): 1738–72.

Harris, J. R., and M. Todaro. 1970. "Migration, Unemployment and Development: A Two-Sector Analysis." *American Economic Review* 60, no. 1 (March): 126–42.

Jones, C. W., and M. Roemer. 1987. "Microeconomics of Price Controls: A Reexamination." Development Discussion Paper no. 242. Cambridge, Mass.: Harvard Institute for International Development.

Johnson, K. F., and M. W. Williams. 1981. *Illegal Aliens in the Western Hemisphere: Political and Economic Factors.* New York: Praeger.

Kesselman, J. R. 1989. "Income Tax Evasion: An Intersectoral Analysis." *Journal of Public Economics* 38: 137–82.

Kimbell, L. J., and G. W. Harrison. 1986. "On the Solution of General Equilibrium Models." *Journal of Economic Modelling* 3, no. 3 (July): 197–212.

Mansur, A., and J. Whalley. 1984. "Numerical Specification of Applied General Equilibrium: Estimation, Calibration and Data." In *Applied General Equilibrium Analysis* ed. H. Scarf and J. B. Shoven. New York: Cambridge University Press.

Morris, M. D., and A. Mayio. 1980. *Illegal Immigration and Foreign Policy.* Washington, D.C.: Brookings Institution.

———, abridged by A. M. Carroll. 1982. *Curbing Illegal Immigration.* Washington, D.C.: Brookings Institution.

Nguyen, T. T., and J. Whalley. 1986. "Equilibrium under Price Controls with Endogenous Transactions Cost." *Journal of Economic Theory* 39, no. 2 (August): 290–300.

———. 1989. "General Equilibrium Analysis of Black and White Markets: A Computational Approach." *Journal of Public Economics* 40: 331–47.

———. 1990. "General Equilibrium Analysis of Price Controls: A Computational Approach." *International Economic Review* 31, no. 3 (August): 667–84.

North, D. S., and M. F. Houstoun. 1976. *The Characteristics and Role of Illegal Aliens in the U.S. Labor Market: An Exploratory Study.* Washington, D.C.: New TransCentury Foundation.

Pitt, M. 1981. "Smuggling and Price Parity." *Journal of International Economics* 11, no. 4: 447–58.

Pozo, S., ed. 1986. *Essays on Legal and Illegal Immigration.* Kalamazoo, Mich.: Upjohn Institute for Employment Research.

Reynolds, C. W., and R. K. McCleery. 1988. "The Political Economy of Immigration Law: Impact of Simpson-Rodino on the United States and Mexico." *Journal of Economic Perspectives* 2, no. 3 (summer): 117–31.

Rivera-Batiz, F. L. 1986. "Can Border Industries Be a Substitute for Immigration?" *American Economic Review Papers and Proceedings* 76, no. 2 (May): 263–68.

Shoven, J. B., and J. Whalley. 1984. "Applied General Equilibrium Models of Taxation and International Trade: An Introduction and Survey." *Journal of Economic Literature* 22, no. 3 (September): 1007–51.

Tanzi, V., ed. 1982. *The Underground Economy in the United States and Abroad.* Lexington, Mass.: Lexington Books.

Chapter 8:   Parker Shipton, "Time and Money in the Western
              Sahel: A Clash of Cultures in Gambian Rural Finance"

Notes

The research on which this paper is based was sponsored by the Harvard Economic and Financial Policy Analysis project in the Ministry of Finance and Trade, The Gambia, funded by the Agency for International Development. Special thanks go to my hosts and my research assistants in The Gambia, including C. Baldeh, E. Baldeh, A. Jallow, A. Jammeh, F. Janneh, F. Khan, J. Newlands, M. Sanyang, A. Sillah, M. Trawally, Y. Dem, and their families. For advice and other help I am grateful to M. Roemer and C. Jones, and to D. Cole, C. Cuevas, B. Gilman, T. Herlehy, J. Ito-Adler, M. McPherson, S. Potok, D. Puetz, S. Radelet, M. Robinson, L. Sanneh, B. Sidibe, P. Steele, and J. D. Von Pischke. Revisions were completed under a generous residential writing fellowship from the Carter G. Woodson Institute for Afro-American and African Studies, University of Virginia. All opinions expressed, however, are my own.

1. "We reckon hours and minutes to be dollars and cents," wrote T. C. Haliburton (1796–1865) in *The Clockmaker*. "Take away *time is money*, and what is left of England?" wrote Victor Hugo in 1862 in *Les Misérables*. Weber's 1904 classic, *The Protestant Ethic and the Spirit of Individualism*, was far from the first study to trace links between religious and economic ethics, but fused them most compellingly. Marx's *Capital* criticized as "commodity fetishism" the assumption that "money begets money" (part 1, chapter 1, section 4).

2. Field research was conducted in April and May 1987 and from July to October 1988. In addition to open-ended interviews, a structured survey, whose results are still being processed, was conducted with equal numbers of men and women informants, totaling about 138 in the first visit and 186 in the second, each visited repeatedly, in five randomly chosen villages among Foni Berefet District (Western Division), Niani District (MacCarthy Island Division), and Wuli District (Upper River Division). Working with experienced local enumerators and interpreters chosen for their previous ties and rapport in the particular villages, I stayed mainly in two of the villages and benefited from close contact with several key informants as well as from acquaintance with the broader field of respondents. The ethnic distribution of villagers interviewed in the surveys approximated the distribution in the nation as a whole: Mandinko (36 percent), Fula (28 percent), Wolof (21 percent), Jola (8 percent), Serahuli (4 percent), and others (3 percent)..

3. Formal and informal schooling, however, have prepared few rural Gambians for the arithmetic involved in calculating interest as rates. Those who can manage the math may be able to take advantage of neighbors who cannot, in dealings among themselves or with financial institutions.

4. For the fiscal year 1987–88, the Ministry of Finance and Trade estimated the gross domestic product at 1,257.8 million dalasis (or 479.3 million at 1976–77 prices). Gamble (1955), Haswell (1975), Kargbo (1983), and Derman et al. (1985), among others, offer descriptive measurements of Gambian poverty.

5. Radelet (1988) describes the economic reform program.

6. The formal-informal dichotomy is of course artificial, and used here only for its heuristic value. In some respects "local customs" of ordinary people can be as formal as, or more formal than, economic behavior in and around official bureaus, where it can sometimes be very informal indeed.

7. A body of recent economic surveys variously comparing the roles of formal and informal financial systems in particular West African countries includes Christensen (1988), Cuevas (1989), Graham et al. (n.d.), Hammsa (1984), Puetz and von Braun (1987), Tapsoba (1982), Tuck (1983), and Walker (1987). Most emphasize quantitative dimensions. Comparing the findings from the different countries is a task ahead, but a delicate one, given the different research methods and translations used.

8. See Haswell (1975) for detailed descriptions of the rural operations of the trading firms and their agents.

9. The Ministry of Finance and Trade calculated the inflation rate of the dalasi as 45.9 percent in 1986–87 (an unusually high rate resulting from the floating of the currency that year) and 12.5 percent in 1987–88.

10. There are now discussions in the government about deregulating the interest rates of banks and other institutions.

11. In 1986, 48 percent of The Gambia's money supply was reported to be outside of the banking system (Ramamurthy 1986, 25). See also World Bank (1985).

12. For more detailed treatments of the topics discussed in this and the next section, see Shipton (1990a; 1990b). For a few of the many ethnographic descriptions of other facets of community life in Gambian and related Senegalese societies, see Gamble (1955), Hodge (1971), Hopkins (1971), Weil (1971), Haswell (1975), and Schaffer and Cooper (1980), on the Mandinko; Diop (1981) on the Wolof; Linares de Sapir (1970), on the Jola; and Elias Scharffenberger (1982) on Gambian women of various ethnic groups.

13. Farmers give several reasons for preferring to save their wealth in stock, in addition to the subtler considerations of gender noted above. These include the fact that animals breed, the advantages of milk and manure production, the usefulness of animal traction, the ceremonial values of animals, and the prestige and other satisfactions of having herds. See also Shipton (1990b)

14. For comparisons, see Tuck (1983, 66), on Senegal; Graham et al. (1987, chapter 4, 18–21), on Niger; and Cuevas (1989, 9), on the Kindia and Nzerekore regions of Guinea.

15. Rotating savings and credit associations are also known by many other names, including *tondas* (Spanish), merry-go-rounds, or in The Gambia, *compin* ("company") groups. In Cameroon, where the Bamileke and other groups have some of the best-established practices of rotating savings and credit associations in Africa, these are called *ndjangi*. Though most Gambian and African groups are women's groups, Gambian men sometimes also belong to them, and some salaried men, for instance in the Gambian army, are known to form them.

16. See Geertz (1962), Ardener (1964), and Shipton (1990a) for more detailed discussions of rotating savings and credit associations.

17. The exception is a participant in a ROSCA whose turn falls early in the cycle. She or he benefits from inflation by repaying later small amounts totaling the amount borrowed.

18. In May 1987 the Basse branch of the GCDB (one of only two branches of the bank outside the greater Banjul area) reported that 49 percent of its 858 savings depositors had less than 250 dalasis in their accounts (that is, less than the value of one sheep). Interviews with bank staff suggested that most of the roughly 100 farmers (people whose primary source of income is farming) saving at the bank were among those with less than 250 dalasis. Only an estimated 10–15 percent of the 858 depositors were women. Only about five farmers were currently borrowing from the branch.

19. Particular choices for answers were not prompted in my surveys. Von Pischke (1983) concisely summarizes poor rural people's incentives and disincentives to save in financial institutions. His forthcoming book, tentatively titled *Finance at the Frontier*, expands on some of these ideas and suggests a balance between savings and credit.

20. The Agricultural Development Bank had tried mobile banks in the early 1980s, but it was unable to sustain them before it failed.

21. A loan or credit may be defined in English as any transfer of goods or services from one party to another, or to any of its members, for a delayed compensation in the same or another form, with or without interest.

22. Currently Mandinka, Jola, and Manjago cash bridewealth payments appear often to amount to less than 500 dalasis; but Wolof bridewealths often appear to be around 1,000 dalasis, and Fula bridewealths frequently exceed 2,000 dalasis in rural Gambian villages. Families of particularly well-educated or well-connected women may demand a much higher bridewealth. In addition to these transfers, grooms and their families are usually expected to provide cattle or other livestock and other food for the weddings, and grooms to give their new wives goods like beds, boxes of clothing, pots and pans, radios and tape recorders, watches, and sometimes animals and jewelry as they set up house.

23. Cuevas found in two regions of Guinea that about 90 percent of a sample of 250 people arranged their main informal financial loans in their own villages (1989, 8).

24. See Robertson (1987) and sources cited therein for a study of African share contracting, including a chapter on The Gambia and Senegal. See also Swindell (1978), David (1980), and Colvin et al. (1981) on these two countries.

25. Christensen (1988, 68) similarly comments on the absence of professional moneylenders in Burkina Faso. See Wellington (1955), Yusuf (1975), and Von Pischke (n.d.) on moneylenders elsewhere south of the Sahara.

26. Lebanese and Ako merchants have until now more or less confined their direct operations to the Banjul area, though some may have agents in the smaller towns.

27. Most of the larger scale traders in The Gambia are men. Among Mauritanians a particularly high proportion are male: In The Gambia, Mauritanian men outnumber Mauritanian women by over three to one (Population and Housing Census, *Provisional Report* 1983, 30). See also Haswell (1975, 188–89) on relations between traders or lenders and the rest of the rural public.

28. A main theme of Haswell (1975, 65–66 and passim).

29. The sura of "The Cow," Sura II, Part III, of the Qur'an, reads, "And if the debtor is in straightened circumstances, then (let there be) postponement to (the

time of) ease; and that ye remit the debt as almsgiving would be better for you if ye did but know" (Pickthall translation, verse 280).

30. See GPMB Annual Report 1971–72 and Jones (1986, 15); Clark (1987, table 1), gives yearly figures from 1974–75 to 1985–86. Haswell (1975) describes some changes in groundnut marketing and credit patterns up to the mid-1970s. Private groundnut traders finance crop purchases by borrowing from the commercial banks if they can, or by mortgaging urban land or other property; others purchase from farmers on credit. Gambian farmers have always had opportunities to sell their groundnuts informally in Senegal, but this trade seems seldom to involve credit.

31. Urban merchants are said to charge substantially higher interest for foreign merchants borrowing for cross-border trade, perhaps because the risks of lending are high.

32. The main government organ assisting small businesses is the Indigenous Business Advisory Service (IBAS), of the Ministry of Economic Planning and Development. Most of its clients are based in the cities and larger towns.

33. Dunsmore et al. noted moneylending rates varying between 50 percent and 150 percent (1976, 310). Haswell noted that a wealthy compound head who lent money in Genieri village charged rates between 49 percent and 157 percent over eight months in 1973–74 (1976, 186). Reports collected for the present study in 1987 suggest that these figures still represent the most common range for seasonal loans—the figure of 100 percent being the most commonly recorded—but that the rates may vary between 0 and over 1,000 percent, if calculated in monetary values and on an annual basis. As one might expect, shorter term loans reach the highest rates when calculated on an annual basis.

34. Moore (1986) discusses at greater length such historical changes in East African contract law and practice.

35. Although western church-based aid organizations like Catholic Relief Services are active in the countryside, Christian religious influence is small.

36. Some of the indigenous aspects of religious belief and practice include ancestral spirits, local celebration scheduling, and some forms of witchcraft and sorcery, house magic, and worn amulets.

37. In Mandinka, imam is *alimaamo*, and the French term *marabout* is translated *mooroo*.

38. The first relevant passages occur in Part III, Sura II, "The Cow." Verse 275: "Those who swallow [charge] usury cannot rise up save as he ariseth whom the devil has prostrated by (his) touch. That is because they say: Trade is just like usury: whereas Allah permitteth trade and forbiddeth usury. . . . As for him who [refraineth and] returneth [to usury]—Such are rightful owners of the Fire. They will abideth therein." Verse 276: "Allah hath blighted usury. . . . " Verse 282: "O Ye who believe! When ye contract a debt for a fixed term, record it in writing. Let a scribe record it in writing between you in (terms of) equity" (Pickthall translation). Elsewhere the sura of "The Cow" states: "It shall be no offence for you to seek the bounty of your Lord by trading. . . . Those that live on usury shall rise up before Allah like men whom Satan has demented by his touch; for they claim that usury is like trading. But Allah has permitted trading and forbidden usury" (*The Koran*, Dawood translation, 344, 354.)

39. See Schacht (1964, 12, 145–48) for a general treatment of *ribā* in Islamic law.

40. Some consider *ribā* ironically to be a kind of debt that the lender acquires to the borrower, for which the borrower may or may not forgive him or her on the judgment day.

41. The sura of "The Cow" states: "Believers, give in alms of the wealth you have lawfully earned" (*The Koran*, Dawood translation, 354). "Lawfully" is taken in The Gambia and elsewhere to exclude wealth earned as *ribā*, usury.

42. "Eating" or consuming the rewards of usury will give the lender a swollen belly, some Gambians say, and vultures will pull out his intestines. For parallels in other African traditions (Christian and local), in which specific prohibitions on earning are linked with specific prohibitions on spending, see Shipton (1989). For a detailed historical treatment of concepts of usury in Judeo-Christian traditions, see Nelson (1949).

43. Gambians say that trade profits become sinful, however, when a seller raises them expressly to take advantage of a particular buyer known to be in difficulty.

44. Part IV, Sura III, "The Family of 'Imran,'" verse 130: "O Ye who Believe! Devour not usury, doubling and quadrupling (the sum lent) . . . and ward off from (yourself) the Fire prepared for disbelievers." See also Part VI, Sura IV, "Women," verses 160, 161 (Pickthall translation). Though it does not explicitly say how long it takes for interest to accrue to the double, the Qur'an does tell believers, "So do not fail to put your debts in writing, be they small or big, together with the date of payment" (*The Koran*: "The Cow," Dawood translation, 355). The emphasis on the date here suggests recognition that interest may accrue, in one way or another, as time progresses.

45. Any loan arrangement involving "double profit" is likely to meet with disapproval in The Gambia. In the case of crop loans, the idea of "doubling" itself has a double meaning. As a district chief explained it, Allah gives humans profit from seeds sown, by multiplying them for harvest. If humans then lend these at interest to obtain further profits from each other, they are seeking double profit, and thus committing a sin (in Mandinka, *junubo*). Muslims are taught that only divinity should be able to make rewards multiply. The Qur'an repeatedly states that the charitable will collect back on the day of judgment: "He that gives his wealth for the cause of Allah is like a grain of corn which brings forth seven ears, each bearing a hundred grains" (*The Koran*, Sura of "The Cow", Dawood translation, 353). "That which you seek to increase by usury will not be blessed by Allah, but the alms you give for His sake shall be repaid to you many times over" (*The Koran*, Sura of "The Greeks," verse 39, Dawood translation, 191).

46. There are, of course, other reasons for lenders to keep loans short, such as the opportunity cost of capital and the possibility of borrowers' moving away.

47. Haswell's research on Genieri village in The Gambia, conducted over twenty-five years, is one of Africa's best examples of longitudinal research. She has not dealt conclusively, however, with the questions raised here about perceptions of time in interest and usury.

48. For surveys of *ḥiyal*, legal devices, in other Islamic countries, see Khan (1929), Schacht (1964, chapter 11 and pp. 208–ll, and the bibliography on p. 242), and Rodinson (1974, 36ff). In The Gambia, borrowers and lenders may not believe

that divinity can be fooled, but many say they are more comfortable following the *hiyal* strategies regardless. Schacht's classic work discusses sympathetically the relationship between theory and practice in Islamic contract law.

49. The *hiyal* principle helps explain, I think, why Haswell observed in Genieri village that "loans were not always made in cash but frequently in food grains payable in cash or groundnuts" (1975, 188).

50. Gambians likewise speak of Allah as merciful and forgiving, and they supplicate this quality. Muslims use many of the same contexts to discuss forgiveness between humans as they use to discuss divine forgiveness of humans, just as Christians supplicate their divinity to "forgive us our debts as we forgive our debtors" in the Lord's Prayer.

51. Compare this finding on courts among the Chagga of Tanzania in the 1940s and 1950s: "It seems that where the claim was promptly brought to the court, before a large debt piled up, the court was more likely to allow a high rate [of interest]" (Moore 1986, 188).

52. The findings of Puetz and Von Braun (1988, 18) agree with my own on this point: "Food loans are lower [in interest] than other loans, all other factors held constant."

53. Puetz and von Braun found in central Gambia that "the higher the loan amount the lower the interest" (1988, 18). Hill notes, in her study of Hausaland in Nigeria and Karnataka in India, that "as a general rule, bigger creditors charge lower interest rates" (1982, 215).

54. Haswell (1976, 186), Dunsmore et al. (1976, 310), and I have found the same differential in our studies in The Gambia, but Puetz and von Braun report no such difference discernable in theirs (1988, 18), leaving the general point open to question. Hill (1982, 215) found the differential in Hausaland, Nigeria, as have others elsewhere in West Africa.

55. The nearest other law that might apply is the Pawnbrokers Act.

56. For a thorough treatment of medieval European doctrines concerning usury, see Nelson (1949). Moneylending laws have appeared and disappeared in England since at least the sixteenth century. Henry VIII's statute of 1541 forbade interest of over 10 percent per year. In subsequent reigns over 170 years, usury law was scrapped and reinstated at rates that varied from 8 percent to 5 percent. By 1867 usury laws had been reabandoned.

57. Though the Gambian legal code was issued two years after internal self-government had been achieved and in the year of independence, it is unabashedly British, printed in London, and listing amounts in pounds, not dalasis, which became the national currency in 1971. It still lists the capital city as Bathurst, not Banjul, as renamed in 1973.

58. The formula given in Schedule B of the Moneylenders Act for calculating an interest rate, percent per annum, is

$$\frac{100 \times I \times 24}{(N + I) \times P \times L}$$

where I = total interest payable, N = number of installments, P = principal, and L = number of calendar months in the intervals between installments. The sense is unclear.

59. The law stipulates, however, that moneylenders may not wait more than a year after an (unspecified) "cause of action" to start legal proceedings to recover money or security (Cap. 126, sec. 30).

60. Annual interest of 48 percent after two calendar years remains just short of the "doubling" that the Qur'an expressly forbids. Since most rural loans are contracted during the hungry season and repaid during the harvest and trade season anyway, the difference between 48 percent and 50 percent is not of great importance.

61. The sums mentioned in this paragraph are Gambian pounds. From 1843 to 1913 The Gambia participated in the United Kingdom's monetary system. From 1913 to May 13, 1964, the Gambian currency was the West African pound. From then until July 1, 1971, it was the Gambian pound, divided into 20 shillings, or 240 pence. The Gambian pound replaced the West African pound at par. On July 1, 1971, the nation replaced the Gambian pound with the dalasi, at the rate of 1 dalasi = 4.00 Gambian shillings = 0.48 U.S. dollars. The Gambian dalasi is divided into 100 *butut*

62. Tellingly, the Pawnbrokers Act still in force requires the pawnbroker to exhibit, in large letters over his outer door, "his Christian name" and other names (Cap. 136, sec. 10, item 1b), even though the person is twenty times more likely to be a Muslim than a Christian.

References

Ardener, Shirley. 1964. "The Comparative Study of Rotating Credit Associations." *Journal of the Royal Anthropological Institute* 4, no. 2: 201–29.

Berman, Brian, Sambou Kinte, et al. 1983. *The Rice Industry of the Gambia.* Report to the United Nations Food and Agriculture Organization. TCP/GAM/2303 (Ma). Rome: FAO Technical Co-operation Programme.

Christensen, Garry. 1988. "Rural Credit Markets in Burkina Faso: Structure and Performance." Department of Agricultural Economics, Cornell University. Typescript.

Clark, R. H. 1987. *A Study of Agricultural Credit Operations of the Cooperative Movement in The Gambia.* Report to the United Nations International Labor Office, Co-operative Development Project. Geneva: ILO.

Colvin, Lucie, Cheick Ba, Boubacar Barry, Jacques Faye, Alice Hamer, Moussa Soumah, and Fatou Sow. 1981. *The Uprooted of the Western Sahel: Migrants' Quest for Cash in the Senegambia.* New York: Praeger.

Cuevas, Carlos. 1989. *Rural Household Finance in the Kindia and Nzerekore Regions of Guinea.* Report to the World Council of Credit Unions. Economics and Sociology Occasional Paper no. 1576. Department of Agricultural Economics and Rural Sociology, Ohio State University, Colombus.

David, Philippe. 1980. *Les navétanes: histoire des migrants saisonniers de l'arachide en sénégambie des origines à nos jours.* Dakar: Les Nouvelles Editions Africaines.

Derman, William, Frank Casey, Sarah Lynch, Cynthia Moore, and Charles Steedman. 1985. *Rural Development in the Gambia River Basin.* Ann Arbor: Center for Research on Economic Development, University of Michigan.

Diop, Abdoulaye-Bara. 1981. *La société wolof: tradition et changement.* Paris: Karthala.

Dunsmore, J. R., A. Blair Rains, G. D. N. Lowe, D. J. Moffatt, I. P. Anderson, and
  J. B. Williams. 1976. *The Agricultural Development of The Gambia: An Agricul-
  tural, Environmental, and Socio-Economic Analysis*. Land Resource Study no.
  22. Surbiton, England: Land Resources Division, Ministry of Overseas
  Development.
Elias Scharffenberger, Christine. 1982. "Socio-Economic Profile of Rural Gam-
  bian Women." Unpublished typescript, Banjul.
Franklin, Benjamin. 1958 [1748]. "Advice to a Young Tradesman." In *Autobiogra-
  phy and Other Writings*, ed. Russel B. Nye. Boston: Houghton Mifflin.
Gambia. 1966. Moneylenders Act. *Laws of The Gambia*. Bathurst: Government
  Printer.
———. 1986. *Population and Housing Census, 1983, Provisional Report*. Banjul:
  Central Statistics Department.
Gambia, Ministry of Agriculture, Program Planning and Monitoring Unit. 1987.
  "Credit Sub-Sector Paper." Unpublished draft.
Gambia Produce Marketing Board (GPMB). Annual Reports.
Gambia, Rural Development Programme. 1978. *Crop and Farm Development*.
  Banjul: Rural Development Project.
Gamble, David. 1955. *Economic Conditions of Two Mandinka Villages: Kerewan and
  Keneba*. London: Research Department, Colonial Office.
———. 1979. *A General Bibliography of The Gambia*. Boston: G. K. Hall.
Geertz, Clifford. 1962. "The Rotating Credit Association: A Middle Rung in
  Development." *Economic Development and Cultural Change* 1, no. 3: 241–63.
Graham, Douglas H., Carlos E. Cuevas, and Kifle Negash. n.d. "Rural Finance
  in Niger." Report to the U.S. Agency for International Development.
Hammsa, Sonia. 1984. *Informal Financial Circuits in West Africa*. Washington,
  D.C.: Office of Housing and Urban Programs, U.S. Agency for International
  Development.
Haswell, Margaret R. 1975. *The Nature of Poverty: A Case-History of the First
  Quarter-Century after World War II*. New York: St. Martin's Press.
Hill, Polly. 1982. *Dry Grain Farming Families: Hausaland (Nigeria) and Karnataka
  (India) Compared*. Cambridge: Cambridge University Press.
Hodge, Carleton T., ed. 1971. *Papers on the Manding*. Bloomington: Indiana
  University, Research Center for the Language Sciences; The Hague:
  Mouton.
Hogan, Edward B. 1987. "Producing and Marketing Groundnuts in The Gam-
  bia." Report to the U.S. Agency for International Development.
Hopkins, Nicholas S. 1971. "Mandinka Social Organization." In *Papers on the
  Manding*, ed. Carleton T. Hodge. Bloomington: Indiana University, Re-
  search Center for the Language Sciences; The Hague: Mouton.
Jones, Christine W. 1986. "The Domestic Groundnut Marketing System in The
  Gambia." Report to the Ministry of Finance and Trade, The Gambia.
Kargbo, Alimami M. 1983. "An Economic Analysis of Rice Production Systems
  and Production Organization of Rice Farmers in The Gambia." Ph.D. diss.,
  Michigan State University.
Khan, M. S. A. "Mohammedan Laws against Usury and How They Are
  Evaded." *Journal of Comparative Law* 1929: 233–44.
The Koran. N. J. Dawood, trans. 3d rev. ed. 1968. Harmondsworth: Penguin.

Linares de Sapir, Olga. 1970. "Agriculture and Diola Society." In *African Food Production Systems*, ed. Peter F. M. McLoughlin. Baltimore: Johns Hopkins University Press.

Marx, Karl. 1906 [1867]. *Capital*. Chicago: Charles H. Kerr.

Moore, Sally Falk. 1986. *Social Facts and Fabrications: "Customary" Law on Kilimanjaro, 1880–1980*. Cambridge: Cambridge University Press.

Nelson, Benjamin N. 1949. *The Idea of Usury*. Princeton: Princeton University Press.

Puetz, Detlev, and Joachim von Braun. 1988. "Parallel Markets and the Rural Poor in a West African Setting." Paper prepared for the Workshop on Parallel Markets, Harvard Institute for International Development, Cambridge, Mass., November 11–12.

The Qur'an. Published as Marmaduke Pickthall, trans. 1971. *The Meaning of the Glorious Qur'an*. Beirut: Dar al-Kitab Allubnani.

Radelet, Steven C. 1988. "Economic Reform in The Gambia: Policies, Politics, Foreign Aid, and Luck." Paper prepared for the Harvard Institute for International Development Conference on Economic Reform, Marrakech, Morocco, October.

Ramamurthy, G. V. 1986. "Agricultural Credit Policy and Structure: The Gambia." Report to the United Nations Food and Agriculture Organization, Technical Cooperation Program.

Robertson, A. F. 1987. *The Dynamics of Productive Relationships: African Share Contracts in Comparative Perspective*. Cambridge: Cambridge University Press.

Rodinson, Maxime. 1966. *Islam and Capitalism*. Brian Pearce, trans. London: Allen Lane.

Save the Children, Gambia Field Office. 1985. "Upper Baddibu HIP Area, Impact Area Studies Report." Save the Children (U.S.), Banjul. Mimeo.

Schacht, Joseph. 1964. *An Introduction to Islamic Law*. Oxford: Clarendon Press.

Schaffer, Matt, and Christine Cooper. 1980. *Mandinko*. New York: Holt, Rinehart and Winston.

Shipton, Parker. 1989. *Bitter Money: Cultural Economy and Some African Meanings of Forbidden Commodities*. American Ethnological Society, Monograph 1. Washington, D.C.: American Anthropological Association.

———. 1990a. "How Gambians Save." Working Paper WPS 395, Agriculture and Rural Development Department, World Bank, Washington, D.C.

———. 1990b. "African Famines and Food Security: Anthropological Perspectives." *Annual Review of Anthropology*. Palo Alto, Calif.: Annual Reviews.

Swindell, Kenneth. 1978. "Family Farms and Migrant Labor: The Strange Farmers of the Gambia." *Canadian Journal of African Studies* 12: 3–19.

———. 1981. *The Strange Farmers of The Gambia: A Study in the Redistribution of Population*. Centre for Development Studies, University College of Swansea, Monograph Series, no. 15. Norwich: Geo Books.

Tapsoba, Edouard K. 1982. *Crédit agricole et crédit informel dans la région orientale de haute-volta: analyse economique, performance institutionelle et implications en matière de politique de développement agricole*. MSU International Development Working Paper no. 2. East Lansing: Department of Agricultural Economics, Michigan State University.

Tuck, Laura. 1983. "Formal and Informal Financial Markets in Rural Senegal." Report to the U.S. Agency for International Development.

U.S. Agency for International Development. 1985. "Gambia Agricultural Research and Diversification Project." Project paper, Washington, D.C.

Von Pischke, J. D. 1983. "Toward an Operational Approach to Savings for Rural Developers." In *Rural Financial Markets in Developing Countries: Their Use and Abuse*. ed. J. D. Von Pischke, Dale W. Adams, and Gordon Donald. Baltimore: Johns Hopkins University Press.

———. n.d. *Finance at the Frontier*. Forthcoming.

Von Pischke, J. D., Dale W. Adams, and Gordon Donald. 1983. *Rural Financial Markets in Developing Countries: Their Use and Abuse*. Baltimore: Johns Hopkins University Press.

Walker, Patricia. "Savings Mobilization and Development: The Potential for Mobilizing Rural Savings in Senegal under the New Agricultural Policy." Banque Centrale des Etats de l'Afrique de l'Ouest, Agence de Dakar.

Weber, Max. 1958 [1904]. *The Protestant Ethic and the Spirit of Capitalism*. Talcott Parsons, trans. New York: Charles Scribner's Sons.

Weil, Peter M. 1971. "Political Structure and Process among the Gambia Mandinka: The Village Parapolitical System." In *Papers on the Manding*, ed. Carleton T. Hodge. Bloomington: Indiana University, Research Center for the Language Sciences; The Hague: Mouton.

Wellington, Martin W. 1955. "Aspects of Moneylending in Northern Sudan." *Middle East Journal* 9: 139–46. Republished by *Development Digest* (July 1980): 71–78.

World Bank. 1985. *The Gambia: Financial Sector Review*. Washington, D.C.

Yusuf, Ahmed. 1975. "Capital Formation and Management among the Muslim Hausa Traders of Kano, Nigeria." *Africa* 45, no. 2: 167–82.

Chapter 9: Pan A. Yotopoulos and Sagrario L. Floro, "Transaction Costs and Quantity Rationing in the Informal Credit Markets: Philippine Agriculture"

Notes

We gratefully acknowledge financial support from the Organization for Economic Cooperation and Development, Economic Development Centre, and the contribution of Tilburg University, Development Research Institute, and of Kyoto University, Institute of Economic Research, where a sabbatical year for the senior author made the completion of this research possible. We would like to thank Tim Besley and Dale Adams for valuable comments.

1. For examples, see Bell (1988) and McKinnon (1973).

2. See, for instance, ADB (1985), Burkner (1980), Ghate (1986), and Lamberte (1985).

3. The Philippines can again serve as an example, as the concluding section demonstrates.

4. In most Asian countries, tenancy is still prevalent in rural areas, so most farmers do not have legal and hence transferable rights over their landholdings.

5. Quantity rationing in markets with imperfect information has been discussed extensively by Stiglitz and Weiss (1981).

6. The persistence of tenancy in rice and corn agriculture implies that the farmers are mainly producers who have acquired cultivation rights in exchange for rent but who do not have transferability rights. Since there is no legal market for cultivation or land occupancy rights, the latter can be transferred only by means of the debt mechanism and in the event of loan default.

7. The probability $P[.]$ is said to be conditional on the occurrence of the event A defined by the information B. The frequency approach is used to estimate $P[.]$; that is, for a given N number of occurrences for which events A and B are defined, then $P[A \backslash B]$ represents the proportion of events in which A and B occurred jointly.

8. The coefficient of k in the estimated equation (3) of Table 9.7 is statistically significant at 10 percent level.

9. Although borrowers in our formal model were differentiated according to the size of their landholding, this type of classification poses estimation problems in our empirical study. Differences with respect to soil quality, topography, market accessibility, and agroclimatic factors among the sample borrower- households make standardization of effective landholdings difficult. At the same time, land markets in Philippine agriculture are undeveloped, which makes the prevailing land market prices a poor proxy for a land standardization index. For example, only 57 percent of the total alienable and disposable land area in the Philippines has been surveyed for classification, land valuation, or registration.

The land standardization problem is further complicated by the different degrees of control that farm households have over their land as reflected in the different tenurial arrangements. This compels us to use a second-best proxy for economic status of borrower-households, the household income level. The following statistical results are therefore predicated on the assumption that income levels largely determine the bargaining position of the borrower in the credit market. This suggests that any interhousehold differences that may arise with respect to income affect the terms and conditions of exchange in any market, including credit.

10. The former category represents loans to establish an agency relationship with a farmer to serve as an intermediary lender; the latter category includes a small number of cases of labor contracts. See Floro and Yotopoulos (1991).

11. Interest rate calculations are not available for loans linked to the transfer of land rights, since a one-period survey cannot provide the information to calculate the capitalized value of the stream of land returns that constitute the payment for the principal and/or interest. Given the special characteristics of such loans, however, namely, that they account for one-third of the total loan volume, they occur mostly in the marginal areas, and they are primarily contracted for meeting the consumption needs of the household, they seem to be geared primarily to the transfer of the usufruct rights of land rather than representing simply a financial transaction.

12. For instance, the minimum administration cost of government agricultural credit is estimated to be about 11 percent, and the minimum transaction cost of small borrowers is 25 percent of interest charges (ACPC 1989).

References

Adams, Dale W. 1983. "Mobilizing Household Savings through Rural Financial Markets." In *Rural Financial Markets in Developing Countries*, ed. J. D. Von Pischke et al. Baltimore: Johns Hopkins University Press.

Agricultural Credit Policy Council (ACPC). 1989. "A Three-Faceted Strategy Toward the Provision of Credit for Small Farmers and Fishermen." *Policy Brief* 2, no. 3 (April 3): 1–4.

Arrow, Kenneth. 1974. *The Limits to Organization*. New York: Norton.

Asian Development Bank (ADB). 1985. *Improving Domestic Resource Mobilization Through Financial Development*. Manila: Asian Development Bank.

Bell, Clive. 1988. "Credit Markets and Interlinked Transactions." In *Handbook of Development Economics*, Vol. 1, ed. H. B. Chenery and T. N. Srinivasan. Amsterdam: Elsevier.

Braverman, Avishay, and T. N. Srinivasan. 1980. *Interlinked Credit and Tenancy Markets in Rural Economies of Developing Countries*. World Bank Development Research Center. Washington, D.C.

Braverman, A., and J. E. Stiglitz. 1982. "Sharecropping and the Interlinking of Agrarian Markets." *American Economic Review* 72 (September): 695–715.

Burkner, Hans-Paul. 1980. "Savings Mobilization Through Financial Development: A Study of Savings in the Philippines." *Philippine Economic Journal* 19, nos. 3–4: 451–82.

Diaz-Alejandro, Carlos. 1985. "Goodbye Financial Repression, Hello Financial Crash." *Journal of Development Economics* 19, no. 2: 1–24.

Esguerra, Emmanuel. 1987. *On the Use of Informal Lenders as Conduits for Formal Credit: The Case of the National Agricultural Productivity Programs in the Philippines*. Economics and Sociology Occasional Paper no. 1351. Ohio State University.

Floro, Sagrario L., and Pan A. Yotopoulos. 1991. *Informal Credit Markets and the New Institutional Economics: The Case of Philippine Agriculture*. Boulder, Colo.: Westview.

Ghate, P. B. 1986. "Some Issues for the Regional Study on Informal Credit Markets." Background Discussion Paper for the Design Workshop, Asian Development Bank, Manila.

Greenwald, Bruce C., and Joseph E. Stiglitz. "Externalities in Economies with Imperfect Information and Incomplete Markets." *Quarterly Journal of Economics* 101 (May): 229–64.

Isaac, R. Marc, and Vernon L. Smith. 1985. "In Search of Predatory Pricing." *Journal of Political Economy* 93, no. 2 (April): 320–45.

Lamberte, Mario. 1985. *Financial Liberalization and the Internal Structure of Capital Markets: The Philippine Case*. Philippine Institute of Development Studies. Manila.

McKinnon, Ronald. 1973. *Money and Capital in Economic Development*. Washington, D.C.: Brookings Institution.

Salop, Steven, and Joseph E. Stiglitz. 1987. "Information, Welfare and Product Diversity." In *Arrow and the Foundations of the Theory of Economic Policy*, ed. George Feiwel. New York: New York University Press.

Scherer, Frederic. 1980. *Industrial Market Structure and Economic Performance*. Chicago: Rand McNally.

Serrano, S. 1983. "The Economics of Linking Credit to Other Markets in Camarines Sur, Bicol Region, Philippines." Master's thesis, University of the Philippines, Los Banos.
Stiglitz, Joseph E. 1979. "Equilibrium in Product Markets with Imperfect Information." *American Economic Review* 69, no. 2: 339–45.
Stiglitz, Joseph E., and Andrew Weiss. 1981. "Credit Rationing in Markets with Imperfect Information." *American Economic Review* 71, no. 3 (June): 393–410.
Technical Board of Agricultural Credit (TBAC). 1981. *A Study of Informal Rural Financial Markets in Three Selected Provinces in the Philippines.* Presidential Committee on Agricultural Credit. Manila.
———. 1985. *Agricultural Credit Study.* Presidential Committee on Agricultural Credit. Manila.
Von Pischke, J. D., and Dale Adams. 1983. "Fungibility and the Design and Evaluation of Agricultural Credit Markets." In *Rural Financial Markets in Developing Countries,* ed. J. D. Von Pischke et al. Baltimore: Johns Hopkins University Press.

Chapter 10:   Tyler S. Biggs, "Heterogeneous Firms and Efficient Financial Intermediation in Taiwan"

Notes

The preparation of this paper was supported by USAID under the Enterprise and Employment Policy Analysis Project. The author would like to thank the Chung Hua Institute for Economic Research, Taipei, Taiwan, for support during field work in Taiwan. The author also acknowledges with thanks helpful discussions with Ya-Hiew Yang of the Chung Hua Institute and Michael Roemer for detailed comments on an early draft of this paper.

1. A detailed analysis of Taiwan's concessional credit controls is set out in a companion paper (Biggs and Yang 1988).

2. For more detail on the structure and performance of Taiwanese industry, see Biggs and Lorsch (1989).

3. For more on this subject, see Biggs and Levy (1988) and Levy and Kuo (1987).

4. See Carter (1988) for a stylized representation of the production and information environment in LDC agriculture and for formal mathematical proofs of some of the relationships cited in this section.

5. It is assumed that two distinct technologies are in use, one adopted by large enterprises and one by small enterprises.

6. That these average characteristics in fact do exist in Taiwan is reported in Biggs and Lorsch (1989).

7. Carter (1988, 88) shows that, in the case of identical loan contract terms, expected bank profits are higher on loans to large firms given the different average characteristics of large and small firms. Note that we have said nothing about the higher transaction costs generally involved in making loans to small borrowers. Taking into account lender transaction costs would increase the

expected profitability differential between loans to large firms and loans to small firms. As a result, small firms would be offered even less favorable terms.

8. Stiglitz and Weiss (1981). See also Ordover and Weiss (1981); Jaffee and Russell (1976); and Stiglitz and Weiss (1983).

9. For more detail on Taiwan's financial system, see Biggs (1988).

10. It should be noted that the large gap between official loan rates and curb market rates is somewhat misleading as a measure of interest rate disequilibrium. Hidden are the added increments to official rates that derive from collateral requirements, requirements for compensating balances, and other side payments involved in getting loans. See Biggs (1988) for more details on interest rate policies.

11. Note that the figures in Table 10.2 are not normalized for the differences in asset levels in each industry. It would be better in each case to compare loan asset ratios. Unfortunately, such data were not available.

12. These figures are compiled from information on the top 500 largest corporations in the Republic of China, China Credit Information Service Limited, Taipei; and from *Survey of Financial Status of Public and Private Enterprises*, (Central Bank of China, ROC, Taipei).

13. See Marsden (1986). One has to be somewhat careful in ascribing the share of domestic credit to the private sector in Taiwan as *all* private. Government holds investments in some large, ostensibly private firms in some industries.

14. *Financial Statistics of Firms* (Economic Research Department, the Central Bank of China, ROC), various issues; and author interviews in Taiwan, fall 1987.

15. Total factor productivity (TFP) is an efficiency measure that relates factor inputs, here capital and labor, to measured firm output. The technical efficiency index is highest for firms producing the greatest output with the same set of given inputs. See Biggs and Lorsch (1989) for the TFP indexes in Taiwan.

16. De facto intermediation from large firms to small subcontractors and suppliers, using credit obtained from banks, was also prevalent in Japan. The following is a description of the Japanese financial system from Cole and Wellons (1988, 21):

> The smaller, riskier firms borrowed both from the large corporations and the banks at rates of interest that could discriminate among them on the basis of risk even though the government set interest rates on credit by banks. The big companies loaned on substantial bank-supplied funds to smaller businesses, especially their suppliers and customers. These loans were generally at much higher rates than the bank lending rates. Small businesses were willing to pay higher rates because the effective bank rates to them were well above the nominal bank rates. Banks required compensating balances from smaller and riskier borrowers. Their well-developed system of price discrimination pushed the effective rates for weaker borrowers up to high risk levels, which not only covered the greater risk and administrative cost of such loans but also assured that borrowers would use the funds for high-return investments in most cases. The higher effective lending rates of the banks and the conglomerates to the smaller businesses also pro-

vided a cut-off or reference rate for the conglomerates in evaluating their own direct investment opportunities. If new investment projects of the conglomerates were not expected to earn higher rates of return than could be obtained from lending to small businesses at the so-called "grey market" rates, then the projects were not likely to be undertaken.

17. For a discussion of the domestic LC, see Rhee (1985).

18. In spite of the ostensible usefulness of these credit instruments, however, interviews with Taiwanese bank officials revealed that domestic LCs never composed much more than 3 to 4 percent of domestic bank lending portfolios (interviews with five large commercial banks in Taiwan, November 1987). Conservative bank lending practices had much to do with the low use of the domestic LC. Taiwanese bankers argued that even with a foreign export LC in hand, there was still a good deal of loan risk involved. Local manufacturers or subcontractors could still default or the exporter might not ship the goods.

19. For a detailed discussion of the sources of private enterprise credit in Taiwan, see Biggs (1988, 15–16).

20. Interviews with Taiwanese authorities, November–December 1987.

21. Interviews with firms in Taipei, November–December 1987.

22. Interest was charged on the full amount of the loan, which, of course, meant that actual interest rates were higher than official rates.

23. Thanks are due to Martha Fitzpatrick for research assistance on Taiwan's urban curb markets.

24. As one author argues in his description of credit relationships in the Taiwanese business community, "The very first thing to say about the structure of [credit] relations in Lukang, Taiwan, is that one does not do business with people one does not know. No one deals with strangers. Business relations are always, to some degree, personal relations[;] they need not be close, but both participants in a [credit] relation should be acquainted, familiar, 'siek-sai' as the Taiwanese say" (quoted in Deglopper 1972).

25. The rates for postdated checks in Table 10.6 are compounded annual rates. If the bank loan rates listed included the cost of collateral plus the cost of compensating balances and other hidden costs, the differential would be smaller.

26. Taiwan's government-funded system of industrial estates also played a role in this type of financing. Land and buildings could be rented in these estates. For those firms that could qualify for bank financing, low-interest loans were also available for land and factories from the Land Bank of Taiwan or from Taiwan Development Corporation that could be repaid in installments over five to ten years.

27. The fungibility of financial resources and the curb market's role in keeping aggregate investment efficiency high has also been noted in the case of Korea and in the case of Japanese development. See Cole and Park (1983); Cole and Patrick (1986); and Scitovsky (1986).

28. See Biggs and Yang (1988). By comparison, Korea has given firms, particularly export and heavy industrial firms, large financial subsidies through such programs. Interest rate differentials in Korea (especially in real terms) between

official and curb markets have been enormous. Explicit financial subsidies have been anywhere from six to nine times higher in Korea than in Taiwan.

29. Alchian and Woodward (1986) distinguish two types of opportunism: moral hazard and holdup. Moral hazard deals with the problem of monitoring the behavior of parties to a contract, and holdup describes the problem of one party reneging on the contract after sunk costs are incurred.

30. The argument for linking transactions is often made the other way around—namely, production contracts enable financial contracts. Here I argue that the causal link runs in both directions.

31. Electronics, machine tools, motorcycle parts, furniture, and textiles and apparel were the industries I studied.

32. Interviews with businessmen, Taipei, November–December 1987; and Deglopper (1972, 46–48).

References

Alchian, A. A., and S. Woodward. 1986. "The Firm Is Dead; Long Live the Firm: A Review of O. E. Williamson's *The Economic Institutions of Capitalism.*" *Journal of Economic Literature* 26 (March).

Biggs, Tyler. 1989. "Financing the Emergence of Small and Medium Firms in Taiwan: Financial Mobilization and the Flow of Domestic Credit to the Private Sector." Employment and Enterprise Policy Analysis Discussion Paper no. 15. Harvard Institute for International Development, Cambridge, Mass.

Biggs, Tyler, and Brian Levy. 1988. "Strategic Interventions and the Political Economy of Industrial Policy in Developing Countries." Paper prepared for Harvard Institute for International Development Conference on Development Reforms, Marrakech, Morocco, October.

Biggs, Tyler, and K. Lorsch. 1989. "The Structure, Dynamics and Performance of Taiwan's Industry." Employment and Enterprise Policy Analysis Project Discussion Paper no. 21. Harvard Institute for International Development, Cambridge, Mass.

Biggs, Tyler, and Ya-Hiew Yang. 1988. "Concessional Credit Programs in Taiwan." Employment and Enterprise Policy Analysis Project Discussion Paper no. 17. Harvard Institute for International Development, Cambridge, Mass. August.

Carter, Michael. 1988. "Equilibrium Credit Rationing of Small Farm Agriculture." *Journal of Development Economics* 28: 83–103.

Cole, D., and Y. C. Park. 1983. Financial Development in Korea, 1945–1978. Cambridge, Mass.: Harvard University Press.

Cole, D., and H. Patrick. 1986. "Financial Developments in the Pacific Basin Market Economies." In *Pacific Growth and Financial Interdependence*, ed. A. Tan and B. Kapur. Boston: Allen and Unwin.

Cole, David, and Philip Wellons. 1988. "The Role of the Financial System in Economic Development." Harvard Institute for International Development, Cambridge, Mass. Mimeo.

Deglopper, D. R. 1972. "Doing Business in Lukang." In *Economic Organization in Chinese Society*, ed. W. E. Wilmott. Stanford, Calif.: Stanford University Press.

Gold, T. B. 1981. "Dependent Development in Taiwan." Ph.D. diss., Harvard University.

Jaffee, D., and R. Russell. 1976. "Imperfect Information, Uncertainty and Credit Rationing." *OJE* 90, no. 4 (November).

Levy, Brian, and Wen-jeng Kuo. 1987. "The Strategic Orientations of Firms and the Performance of Korea and Taiwan in Frontier Industries." Employment and Enterprise Policy Analysis Project Discussion Paper no. 12. Harvard Institute for International Development, Cambridge, Mass.

Liu, Tai-Ying, et al. 1984. "A Study on Ways and Means to Redirect the Underground Activities in Taiwan" (in Chinese). Taiwan Institute of Financial Research, Taipei.

Lunberg, Erik. 1979. "Fiscal and Monetary Policies." In *Economic Growth and Structural Change in Taiwan: The Postwar Experience*, ed. Walter Galenson. Ithaca, N.Y.: Cornell University Press.

Marsden, Keith. 1986. "Private Enterprise Boots Growth." *Journal of Economic Growth* 1.

Medium and Small Business Administration. 1987. *Development Merit: A Collection of Papers on Small Business Development in ROC*. Taipei: Ministry of Economic Affairs, August.

Ordover, J., and A. Weiss. 1981. "Information and the Law: Evaluating Legal Restrictions on Competitive Contracts." *AER* 71, no. 2.

Rhee, Y. W. 1985."Instruments for Export Policy and Administration: Lessons from the East Asian Experience." World Bank Staff Working Papers, no. 725. Washington, D.C.

Riegg, Nicholas H. 1979. "The Role of Fiscal and Monetary Policies in Taiwan's Economic Development." Ph.D. diss., University of Connecticut.

Scitovsky, Tibor. 1986. "Economic Development in Taiwan and South Korea, 1965–1981." In *Models of Development: A Comparative Study of Economic Growth in South Korea and Taiwan*, ed. L. J. Lau. San Francisco: ICS Press.

Shea, J. D., and P. S. Kuo. 1984. "An Analysis of the Allocative Efficiency of Bank Funds in Taiwan" (in Chinese). In proceedings of a conference on Financial Development in Taiwan, Taipei Institute of Economics, Academia Sinica, December.

Small and Medium Business Assistance Center. 1985. "Financial and Management Services to Small/Medium Business in Taiwan, the R.O.C." Annual report. Taipei.

Stiglitz, J. E., and A. Weiss. 1981. "Credit Rationing in Markets with Imperfect Information." *AER* 71, no. 3 (June).

———. 1983. "Incentive Effects of Terminations: Applications to the Credit and Labor Markets." *AER* 73, no. 5 (December).

———. 1988. "Banks as Social Accountants and Screening Devices for the Allocation of Credit." Working Paper no. 2710. National Bureau of Economic Research, Cambridge, Mass.

Taylor, Lance. 1985. *Structuralist Macroeconomics: Applicable Models for the Third World*. New York: Basic Books.

Timberg, T. A., and Aiyar, C. V. 1984. "Informal Credit Markets in India." *Economic Development and Cultural Change* 33, no. 1 (October).

van Wijnbergen, Sweder. 1983. "Credit Policy, Inflation and Growth in a Financially Repressed Economy." *Journal of Development Economics* 13, no. 2: 45–65.

Williamson, O. E. 1985. *The Economic Institutions of Capitalism: Firms, Markets, Relational Contracting.* London: The Free Press.

Chapter 11:   Omkar Goswami, Amal Sanyal, and Ira N. Gang, "Taxes, Corruption, and Bribes: A Model of Indian Public Finance"

Notes

We appreciate the comments made by Kaushik Basu, Tim Besley, Arindam Das-Gupta, Jim Davies, Jesús Valencia, John Whalley, and by many who participated in the HIID Workshop on Parallel Economies in November 1988, and in the Public Finance Workshop at the University of Western Ontario in May 1989. Most of all, we are grateful to Shubhashis Gangopadhyay and Dilip Mookherjee.

1. Two facts need to be borne in mind. First, the agricultural sector accounts for approximately 40 percent of the Indian GDP and, second, agricultural income is not taxable by law; therefore, the relevant proportions are not 4.23 and 8.59 percent, but 7.05 and 14.32 percent.

2. The Policy Group (1985, 16). The data base for this study was created by interviewing 120 certified public accountants across India, each of whom had prepared at least 150 personal income tax returns on behalf of clients.

3. Currently, only those who declare a taxable income of Rs200,000 or more per annum are compulsorily audited, and such taxpayers account for a negligible percentage of the total returns. For others, there is a random audit scheme, in which the overall probability of audit is well below 10 percent.

4. The growth in revenue in 1986 was later discovered to be a sleight of hand. Unassessed returns of previous years were hurriedly assessed and reported as taxes for 1986.

5. The three exceptions that we know of are Chu (1987), Lui (1986), and Virmani (1987).

6. If (d_1, d_2) represent the threat points of the taxpayer and the auditor, then the solution is to choose an outcome (u_1, u_2) such that it maximizes the value $(u_1 - d_1)(u_2 - d_2)$. See Nash (1950). The equilibrium is stated in the Appendix.

7. We have assumed that if expected income from cheating is the same as the net income from honesty, then the taxpayer will be honest.

8. It is, of course, possible to have more realistic interior solutions where some taxpayers cheat and others do not; but this involves various risk-aversion parameters, utility functions, and extremely complex as well as messy mathematics. In any case, our simple case of risk neutrality suffices to derive results that illustrate interesting problems of tax collection.

9. There is a disquieting aspect of this formulation. In our model, the policy implication is that government should set penalty rates as high as possible—in fact, at the limit, the fine rate should go to infinity! In reality, there are definite upper limits to these rates; and it would have been reassuring to have an opti-

mal fine rate, just as we have an optimal tax rate. That we do not have an optimal fine rate suggests a need to marginally modify the model, which is a part of our future research agenda.

10. For a recent work on the role of wage incentives, see Besley and McLaren (1990).

11. For an excellent theoretical discussion on delegation see Melumad and Mookherjee (1989).

References

Acharya, S., A. Kumar, A.V. L. Narayan, and S. P. Chaudhury. 1986. *Aspects of the Black Economy in India*. New Delhi: National Institute of Public Finance and Policy (NIPFP).

Besley, T., and J. McLaren. 1990. "Tax Compliance and Corruption Deterrence: The Role of Wage Incentives." Typescript.

Chu, C. Y. Cyrus. 1987. "Income Tax Evasion with Venal Tax Officials—The Case of Developing Countries." Discussion Paper no. 8704, The Institute of Economics, Academia Sinica, Taiwan.

Government of India, Minister of Finance. 1984. Union Budget Speech, February 28.

Graetz, M. J., J. R. Reinganum, and L. L. Wilde. 1986. "The Tax Compliance Game: Towards an Interactive Theory of Law Enforcement." *Journal of Law, Economics and Organization* 2: 1–32.

Lui, F. T. 1986. "A Dynamic Model of Corruption Deterrence." *Journal of Public Economics* 31, 215–36.

Melumad, N. D., and D. Mookherjee. 1989. "Delegation as Commitment: The Case of Income Tax Audits." *The Rand Journal of Economics* 20(no. 2), 139–63.

Nash, J. F. 1950. "The Bargaining Problem." *Econometrica* 18: 155–62.

The Policy Group. 1985. "Estimates of Tax Collection and Evasion in Response to the 1985–86 Budget." New Delhi. Mimeo.

Reinganum, J. R., and L. L. Wilde. 1985. "Income Tax Compliance in a Principal Agent Framework." *Journal of Public Economics* 26:1–18.

Virmani, A. 1987. "Tax Evasion, Corruption and Administration: Monitoring the People's Agents under Symmetric Dishonesty." Development Research Division Discussion (DRD) Discussion Paper no. 271, World Bank.

Michael Roemer is an institute fellow at the Harvard Institute for International Development. He has been an economic adviser in Kenya, Tanzania, and Ghana, as well as Indonesia, where he was resident coordinator of several projects for HIID. In collaboration with Christine Jones, he organized the HIID-sponsored workshop on parallel markets that led to this volume and to the special issue of *World Development* on parallel markets (December 1989). Roemer, who received his Ph.D. from the Massachusetts Institute of Technology, has published a number of books, including *Modernization of the Republic of Korea: Growth and Structural Transformation* (with Kim Kwang Suk) and *Economics of Development* (with Malcolm Gillis, Dwight Perkins, and Donald Snodgrass).

Christine Jones is an economist in the Central and West Africa Country Operations Division of the World Bank. She received her Ph.D. in economics from Harvard University. She has also been an institute associate at the Harvard Institute for International Development and has taught African economic development. Jones has lived and worked in Cameroon and Zaire and has served as a development adviser in The Gambia and Malawi. She has published papers on women's labor issues.

Jean-Paul Azam is a professor of economics at the University of Clermont-Ferrand, France. He holds advanced degrees in economics, sociology, and mathematics, including doctorates in economics from the London School of Economics and the University of Aix-en-Provence, France. He has worked in Bangladesh and in a number of developing countries in Africa and has acted as a consultant to the Organization for Economic Cooperation and Development, the United Nations, and the World Bank. Azam has published numerous papers on issues in econometrics and development economics and is the author of several books, among them *The Impact of Macroeconomic Policies on the Rural Poor.*

David Bevan is a lecturer in economics at Oxford University and a fellow of St. John's College. He has been a consultant to the World Bank, the International Labour Office, and the Organization for Economic Cooperation and Development. He is a member of the Unit for the Study of African Economies at the Institute of Economics at Oxford. Bevan has written, with Paul Collier and Jan Willem Gunning, *Peasants and Governments: An Economic Analysis* and *Controlled Open Economies: A Neoclassical Approach to Structuralism.*

Tyler S. Biggs is an economist at the Harvard Institute for International Development. He has conducted research on agricultural policy and on urban and rural development and is currently studying industrial organization in developing nations. He has served as West African representative for the Ford Foundation and as a consultant to the World Bank and to the U.S. Agency for International Development. He is the author of a forthcoming book, *The Evolution of Industrial Structure in Developing Countries.*

Paul Collier is a specialist in international development economics at Oxford University and a fellow of St. Antony's College. He has been a consultant to the World Bank, the International Labour Office, and the Organization for Economic Cooperation and Development. Collier founded the Unit for the Study of African Economies at the Institute of Economics at Oxford and has written, with David Bevan and Jan Willem Gunning, *Peasants and Governments: An Economic Analysis* and *Controlled Open Economies: A Neoclassical Approach to Structuralism.*

Sagrario L. Floro is an assistant professor of economics at the American University, Washington, D.C., and a research associate of the Philippine Resource Center in Berkeley, California. An adviser to the Agricultural Credit Policy Council of the Philippines, she is currently working on the market structure of financial systems in developing countries and on the effect of financial liberalization on the informal sector. Floro, who received her Ph.D. from Stanford University, has written, with Pan A. Yotopoulos, *Informal Rural Credit Markets: The New Institutional Economics Approach in the Philippines*.

Ira N. Gang is an assistant professor of economics at Rutgers University. He has also taught at the Claremont Colleges, California, and at Duke University. Gang received his Ph.D. from Cornell University. A frequent visitor to the Indian Statistical Institute, New Delhi, Gang has published extensively on theoretical models of labor markets in developing countries, on foreign aid, on multinationals, and on growth and development policy.

Omkar Goswami is an associate professor of Economics at the Indian Statistical Institute, New Delhi. He earned a doctorate from Oxford and has taught at the Delhi School of Economics and Jawaharlal Nehru University, New Delhi. Goswami has also been a Fulbright fellow in the United States, at Tufts and Harvard Universities, and was a visiting associate professor at Rutgers University for the 1989–90 academic year. His research focuses on economic history, industrial economics, and theoretical models of corruption.

Jan Willem Gunning is a professor of economics and the director of the Economic and Social Institute at the Free University, Amsterdam. He has been a staff member of the World Bank and a consultant to the International Labour Office and the United Nations and serves on the National Advisory Council of the Dutch minister of development cooperation. Like David Bevan and Paul Collier, Gunning is a member of the Unit for the Study of African Economies at the Institute of Economics at Oxford; with them he has written *Peasants and Governments: An Economic Analysis* and *Controlled Open Economies: A Neoclassical Approach to Structuralism*.

David L. Lindauer is an associate professor of economics at Wellesley College and a faculty associate with the Harvard Institute for International Development. He frequently serves as a consultant to the World Bank. Lindauer's research on labor market issues in developing economies has been carried out in Kenya, Malaysia, Malawi, Sierra Leone, Sudan, Zambia, and, most recently, Korea. His work has been published in journals of economics and development.

Trien T. Nguyen is an associate professor of economics at the University of Waterloo, Ontario. Nguyen holds a degree in chemical engineering from the University of California, Berkeley, and received an M.A. in mathematics and a Ph.D. in economics from the University of Western Ontario. His research interests lie in computable general equilibrium modeling of public policy, taxation, international trade, economic development, and economic history.

Detlev Puetz is a research analyst in the Food Consumption and Nutrition Program of the International Food Policy Research Institute. He received his master's degree from the University of Bonn, Federal Republic of Germany, where he is a Ph.D. candidate. Puetz has been a consultant to the World Bank on a recent project in The Gambia, and his published work includes *Irrigation Technology and Commercialization of Rice in The Gambia: Effects on Income and Nutrition* (with Joachim von Braun and Patrick Webb) and *Structural Adjustment, Agricultural Development Constraints, and Nutrition: Policy Options in The Gambia* (with Joachim von Braun, Sambou Kinteh, and Ken Johm).

Amal Sanyal is an associate professor of economics at the Jawaharlal Nehru University, New Delhi, where he also obtained his Ph.D. He has carried out research on macroeconomic theory, microeconomic foundations of macroeconomic theory, development policy, and monetary theory and has presented papers on these subjects to the Econometric Society and the International Economic Association. Sanyal has also been a visiting professor at the University of Papua New Guinea.

Parker Shipton is an institute associate at the Harvard Institute for International Development and a lecturer in anthropology at Harvard University. A graduate of Cornell University, Shipton holds an advanced degree from Oxford and a Ph.D. from Cambridge. He has recently been a residential research fellow at the Carter G. Woodson Institute for Afro-American and African Studies at the University of Virginia. Shipton has conducted extended field research in Kenya and The Gambia and has served as a consultant to the governments of those countries, as well as to the World Bank and the U.S. Agency for International Development. He is the author of *Bitter Money: Cultural Economy and Some African Meanings of Forbidden Commodities*.

Joachim von Braun is the director of the Food Consumption and Nutrition Policy Program of the International Food Policy Research Institute, where he has focused his research on food subsidy policies, the effects of the commercialization of subsistence agriculture, and the prevention of famines. Von Braun received his doctoral degree from the University of Göttingen, Federal Republic of Germany, and has served as a consultant to that country's Ministry of Foreign Cooperation, Agency for Technical Cooperation, and Ministry of Agriculture. Von Braun is the author of *An Economic Analysis of Policies for Food Security in Developing Countries: The Case of Egypt*.

Pan A. Yotopoulos is a professor of economics at the Food Research Institute at Stanford University. He has published in the fields of economic development, agricultural economics, international trade, production and consumption theory, and economic demography. He is currently conducting research on exchange rates, trade and industrial policies for economic development, and the experience of newly industrialized countries. Yotopoulos has been recognized by the American Agricultural Economics Association for professional excellence in published research.

Schacht, Joseph, 239nn39, 48
Schaffer, Matt, 236n12
Scherer, Frederic, 230n6
Scitovsky, Tibor, 189, 249n27
Segal, M., 229n3
Serrano, S., 146
Sharpley, J., 64
Shaw, Edward, 16
Shea, J. D., 176, 192
Sheikh, Munir, 16, 20
Shipton, Parker, 236nn12, 13, 16, 239n42
Shoven, J. B., 93, 98
Small and Medium Business Assistance Center, Taiwan, 182
Smith, S., 229n3, 230n8
Smuggling, 19–20
Sonstelie, Jon, 16, 20–22, 25, 26
Special Provisions for Redeeming Bad Checks, Taiwan, 182
Srinivasan, T. N., 16, 145
Standard Bank, 116
Stelcher, M., 229n3
Stiglitz, Joseph, 8, 171, 173–74, 245n5, 248n8
Suebsaeng, Parita, 229n2, 230nn8, 10
Sundrum, R. M., 16
Swindell, Kenneth, 237n24

Tanzanian Price Commission, 64
Tanzi, V., 90
Tapsoba, Edouard, 236n7
Tax evasion, India, 201–2
model to analyze, 202–6
model with changes in tax rate, 206–8
Tax evasion, United States, 90, 101, 106
Taylor, Lance, 196
Technical Board of Agricultural Credit (TBAC), Philippines, 143, 146
Third-party check, Taiwan, 184–86
Timberg, T. A., 16, 190
Todaro, M., 81, 90, 94
Traders, private, 122–23
Tuck, Laura, 236nn7, 14

UMOA. *See* West African Monetary Union (Union Monétaire Ouest-Africaine: UMOA)
Uncertainty, 18

van der Gaag, J., 229n3
van Wijnbergen, Sweder, 16, 196
Venti, S., 229n3, 230n8
Vijverberg, W., 229n3
Virmani, A., 252n5
Voluntary organizations, The Gambia, 117, 123
von Braun, Joachim, 16, 26, 33, 35, 131, 226n1, 227n2, 236n7, 240nn52, 53
Von Pischke, J. D., 163, 237nn19, 25

Walker, Patricia, 236n7
Webb, Patrick, 226n1
Webb, R., 229n1
Weil, Peter, 121, 236n12
Weiss, A., 8, 171, 173–74, 245n5, 248n8
Welfare effects
of parallel markets, 18, 19, 23–24
of smuggling, 18
Wellington, Martin, 237n25
Wellons, Philip, 248n16
Wenig, A., 90
West African Monetary Union (Union Monétaire Ouest-Africaine: UMOA), 47, 54
See also Central Bank of West African States (Banque Centrale des Etats de l'Afrique de l'Ouest: BCEAO)
Whalley, John, 16, 20, 23, 27, 90, 93, 98, 103, 232n1
Wilde, L. L., 202
Williams, M. W., 89, 101, 232n9
Williamson, Oliver, 193
Woodward, S., 250n29
World Bank, 75–76, 236n11

Yang, Ya-Hiew, 247n1, 249n28
Yotopoulos, Pan A., 143, 145, 245n10
Yusuf, Ahmed, 237n25

ICEG Academic Advisory Board